D1146389

SUNDAY TELEGRAPH
GARDENING
BOOK

FRED WHITSEY

SUNDAY TELEGRAPH

GARDENING
BOOK

Illustrated by B. S. BIRO

Collins
LONDON · GLASGOW
1966

Printed in Great Britain by Robert MacLehose and Co. Ltd
The University Press, Glasgow

3222.

CONTENTS

CONTENTS

[vi]

PREPOSSESSIONS

Patchwork . . . *pastiche* . . . *collage* . . . even a rhapsody of sorts . . . you might call this book by any such name. Since this is what most gardens are, the most skilfully made and ingeniously contrived among them, and since the subject is garden-making, personally I prefer to regard it as a patchwork, worked on a repeated underlying ground.

To think of it as a *pastiche* would imply a more sharply defined direction than it possesses, with highly sophisticated overtones, when in fact it has — at least I hope it does carry this — the sense of simplicity one seeks in gardens. To call it a *collage*, though it has been made with paste and scissors and with much scratching out and writing in, would make it sound too clever by half. This would suggest that one was trying so hard to be right up to date — without knowing just where self-conscious innovations would take one. The word rhapsody implies a certain wayward-ness, of lacking firm roots; and I hope that the primary principle of gardening that the roothold must be sound does not go by default in these pages.

And so I think patchwork is the word that must stand to describe it. Almost all of it has been culled from writings that have gone on over several years — inspired by the weather that gardeners watch ceaselessly and often in agony, by plants that on some day or other have appeared so winning that one must tell other gardeners about them, by remarks heard in horticultural conversation that have caused a flash of insight and by the daily progress of the seasons in my own garden.

If it has a motto theme, a kind of *leitmotif* that rises again and again, if I may borrow the language of music, this is the very simple one that gardening is an activity of joy, not hardship. I hope you will find here none of the hectoring spirit in which gardening advice has often been delivered. Long ago the trusteeship of horticultural skill passed from the professional to the amateur, but to listen to much of the instruction offered, you would think that gardening at its best level was still the province of those dour head-gardeners who kept the vinery locked and whose permission had to be sought before his lordship dare pluck one of his own roses. These fellows would have it done this way or that and no other.

In truth, subject to certain enduring factors, there are many ways about most gardening jobs, and one of the underlying assumptions of this book is that in the contemporary social context the quickest and easiest is the best. This is not to deny the importance of such constants as using light soil for cuttings, laying paths only on firm foundations and treading the soil firm about roots. All I affirm is that there is no point in going the tedious way round when the short route will get you there.

By means of techniques, devices and potions, but not less by the choice of plants themselves, one can clearly garden painlessly today on quite a broad scale and still have leisure and energy left for other pursuits. (Though I should warn you that gardening can sometimes amount to a thralldom from which there is no escape.) Some of the ways by which this is possible are suggested, I believe in the first section of this book, which I have headed 'Plain Speaking'.

It is in the second section, 'Special Pleading', a series of essays on garden plants which I feel deserve some attempt at advocacy, that the patchwork imagery becomes strongest. Resolve as I will to have nothing in my own garden that is either unrelated to its fellow plants or to its environment, or that cannot sustain an isolated position, inevitably one goes on collecting plants, won over by their individual appeal, and places have to be made for them, even if it does mean modifying the overall scheme.

The term 'garden-making', used repeatedly in this book, is perhaps a misleading one, however: was any garden ever *made,* like a picture that has had its final brushstroke, or a piece of sculpture sent at last for casting? Certainly no garden worth exploring again and again, through every season, every week of the year, was ever translated straight from drawing board to plot.

No, it is made like some beautiful piece of patchwork, worked with a multitude of rare fragments over many years, with the help of an imagination quickened by each one, so that a unity eventually springs from diversity. And then one is never sure that it could not be bettered.

None of my plants that claim to have particular distinction is rare or esoteric. Nor are they any more closely related than all those bits of fabric picked up here and there. Their kinship is simply that they are the ingredients of a garden that takes little effort to maintain and that will span the four seasons in its appeal. This is why such favourite flowers as sweet peas, dahlias, chrysanthemums and gladioli get no more than a passing word, if any at all, and are relegated to the kitchen garden where they can be grown in rows just for cutting. I do not see where they can be fitted into a permanent garden. But I do believe in nourishing them well so that their potential can be realised for adorning the house, in company with snippets of other plants from all over the garden.

No garden-lover can hope to discuss the subject without falling foul of those who execrate Latin names and who angrily demand 'why don't these people talk in language we can all understand? Anyway, they're always changing their damned unpronounceable names, aren't they?' It hardly calms the anger aroused by retorting that we use them for the very reason demanded — clear understanding.

Latin names are certainly changed, but again in the interest of clarity. By international agreement uneasily arrived at plant names are subject to a 'law of priority', which declares that the first name given a plant since 1753, when Linnaeus published his *Species Plantarum*, should be its true one. It is a sort of right of primogeniture, for however much better a plant may be known by one name it cannot escape succession. It is this that causes the confusion; when, for instance, plants we have grown up with must lose the musical name of andromeda, say, in favour of cassiope, leucothoe and oxydendrum.

Paradoxically, the confusion arises from the work of botanists to classify plants precisely. This has been going on since the Greeks, and though it may be hard to disturb long-established custom, some day botanists do have to admit that, for instance, whitebeams are sufficiently distinct from pears to deserve quite different Latin names when they once had the same; or that when you compare closely the leaves of cypresses they can be so unalike that they need separate generic titles; or what we commonly call a geranium was better separated from other kinds, as it was in 1787, though we are still catching up.

'Uniformity, accuracy . . . and to discourage procedures leading to confusion and error' — these are the primary aims of the International Code of Plant Nomenclature.

Why Latin still, though, when as a language it is fast losing the vestiges of its former standing? Why *angustifolia* when narrow leaves are implied by a botanical name, or *mollis* when they are simply soft? Precision again. And also because it is universal, or can be. Most of our garden plants are of foreign importation, a large proportion from Western China. How could we cope with their common names here? Anyway, common names are often local. The bluebells of Scotland are nothing like what we call a bluebell in the south. And what Chelsea flat-dweller growing sempervivums in a window-box would recognise them from 'come-home-husband-however-drunk-you-are', one of the country names of these plants?

So I have no compunction in using one long botanical name after another in this book, though a little hesitation in adding still further to the gardening books that threaten to rival the limitless numbers of offspring a single shepherd's purse weed can produce. I send it on its way as a non-gardener might blow at a dandelion clock, and hope that here and there a seed may fall and perhaps enrich the garden where it may find a patch of fallow ground.

Spadework

Tillage = fertility: the spade of stainless steel: compost: peat:
an igloo of clay: Sleeping Beauty's castle: the rotary grass-cutter:
the master plan: constructing the paths: the paved terrace

All gardening begins with the spade. There is no escaping it. In the eternal equation tillage equals fertility — the fertility without which plants, one of the raw materials of gardening, will not flourish while the promise offered by a new garden can shrivel into disappointment, even despair. But if you cannot escape the labour of spadework, you can make light of it, with the tool itself and by the way it is used.

Smoothed by the constant rub of the hands season by season, as well as by a little fine sandpaper and a coat of linseed oil once a year on a wet winter's day, garden tools attract an affection that often outlives their efficiency. But none of the tools that hang in our shed is more warmly held than the spade of stainless steel. Always so shiny that it might have been made specially for some official tree-planting ceremony, it contributes as much to the pleasure of digging as a fine autumn day, as well as to efficiency. With it I find digging less tiring and the area covered in a morning's work a good deal greater than with even a well-cared-for spade of ordinary steel. The cost? About four times as much, but an investment that has paid handsomely.

But one must learn to use it with skill. One must learn the technique of taking small spadefuls, of thrusting the blade vertically into the ground and using the shaft as a lever, of sliding the left hand right down to the blade as you lift it and so easing any strain on the back. Trifling though these points may seem when read in a page of type, they hold the essence of easy tillage.

Why tillage at all? To open the soil to the air plants need about the roots, to allow rain to enter, to drain the soil and to enhance its texture, to make what is known as a 'free root run' for plants. The principle applies whether the plants are herbaceous or whether they are shrubs or fruit trees, and to grass as well.

Ideally, as gardening advice so often repeats, ground being prepared for planting should be double-dug all over. Yet who these days has the time or surplus energy for such a burdensome exercise? Certainly this process — putting the topsoil to one side trench by trench, turning over the lower level and adding decayed refuse to it, and perhaps lime if it is clay — improves drainage and opens up a root run that plants will gladly explore, showing their pleasure in extra vigorous above-ground growth. The minimum digging depth should be the full length of the blade of the spade, however, each sod being inverted as it is thrown forward.

Opinions differ sharply about whether the compost made in the garden is better thrown into the bottom of each trench, formed as digging goes on across the plot, or whether it is better to spread it on the surface and mix it with the top soil with every stroke of the spade. I have never yet succeeded in making compost myself in which all the weed seeds get decomposed beyond doubt and I would rather put them well down where they are less likely to germinate.

Whether the soil on which one has to garden is light or heavy, sandy or composed of clay, or whether it is old and tired or being broken in for the first time, this magic stuff compost has a benign influence. Teeming with bacterial activity that grows more intense as the stack of organic refuse gets hotter as decay goes on, it opens the stiff soil with which it is mixed and imparts to it some of its own nature. The paradox is that it also holds moisture in gravelly ground in just the right degree for fertility and it also has an effect on land of helping to drain the upper soil levels.

However, compost can not only be made in an established garden, from refuse of an organic character, largely plant remains, but from kitchen refuse as well. Coarse peat has a similar effect and is a more practicable proposition in a new garden, though to use it on any general scale can be expensive.

Peat can be made into an even better soil conditioner by composting it than by using straight out of the bag. This simply implies stacking it, between layers of the soil it is later to improve, in cube heaps at least four feet high. The magical forces of nature play upon it and in a few months it becomes a bacteria-laden agent.

Where straw can be obtained, it can be used similarly and sawdust stacked between layers of soil is another alternative, and so are fallen leaves when one can get them. Indeed, I notice that today they are collected by garden owners in the same enthusiasm with which they used to encourage the milkman to stop his cart outside the gate in our childhood. Fortunately, however, the wheel is coming full circle now, for after years of being denied farmyard manure, gardeners can now buy it in processed odourless, dried form, neatly packed in polythene bags. Of course, all this service has to be paid for.

No aspect of spadework worries gardeners more than trying to refine clay, let alone plant in it. How can anyone find it an agreeable job making a garden on soil usually too stiff to dig, too dense for roots to penetrate, which lies wet most of the winter and turns to rock in drought?

The real answer lies in prolonged weathering. Frost and snow, rain and wind, the worst of the winter weather, will act on a soil thrown up roughly, refine it and bring it to a condition favourable to plants and capable of being worked down with cultivator and rake for seed-sowing. But the full effect of this can only be achieved if the turning over work, perhaps by mechanical cultivator, is done in autumn.

Adding certain materials to the clay will serve to break it down. Lime, preferably in the form of ground chalk, has some good effect, but working in sharp sand or grit, or even gravel, will in time open the texture of the clay. Household ashes are some use but not the dust-like residue from slow-burning stoves, which tends to make the soil even more sticky. The dust should always be sifted out and discarded.

Strangely, the very clay that proves so frustrating can be used to refine itself after it has been burned, though it is an ancient practice seldom followed nowadays. The method is to get a fierce bonfire going and then pile lumps of clay round it in igloo fashion, with one or two channels at the bottom to give a draught. Such a fire can be kept burning slowly for weeks. The clods turn reddish and crumble as they are removed, when they can be replaced by freshly dug cheese-like lumps of soil. Returned to the ground the burnt clay has an almost unbelievable effect on it when assimilated.

The mess and chaos with which the hopeful new garden owner is left when the builders have at last packed up their gear and gone could easily put him off gardening for good. Especially when it gradually but painfully dawns on him that beneath the heaps of rubble and rubbish is no fertile top soil but the upper layer of an endless depth of clay.

The soil will have to be nursed slowly through a period of rehabilitation, but at least the refuse can be capitalised at once. Raked up and added to as more comes to light during digging, the rubble will prove indispensable for the foundations of the stone or concrete slab paths essential to a garden in our climate. Stones in soil will help serve the same purpose. Though they can be excessively irritating in digging — a fork is better than a spade on stony ground — they contribute to fertility, by draining the soil and, lying on the surface, hampering loss of moisture through evaporation.

New gardeners often ask if it is wise to treat the whole new garden with sodium chlorate weed killer, which kills all plant growth. Personally, I could not recommend this. The incidental improvement of the soil by disturbing it during forking to remove the weed roots is lost. When a potato crop is used to clean newly broken soil in the traditional fashion, it is the cultivation more than the plants themselves which does the cleaning.

If the soil had been infested with rapacious weeds like the far-straying couch grass, buttercup and nettles, I hope I should have enough resolution not to put in herbaceous plants in the first season. Experience has taught me how their roots become interlaced with the weed roots in a way for which there is no remedy. Rather I would use annuals for the first season, buying the plants, hoeing regularly and forking through the ground again in the following autumn, and removing the perennial weeds which would have grown from the root fragments inevitably left behind. But in the first spring I would not hesitate to put in a few bushes of ornamental trees and roses, and certainly fruit trees if there were to be any. A whole season's growth on these would be too precious to miss.

Although planting time extends from autumn until the end of March, I would delay until the spring in a new garden; not only in order for the soil to be improved but also to ponder on the best places for them. I would even go so far as to make 'mock-ups' of ornamental trees from branches if they could be found to see what their effect would be on the site a few years hence. Need one add a word about the folly of cutting down any bush or tree which could possibly make a permanent feature also without long pondering? A hasty stroke of the axe can bring long regrets and damage neighbourly relations as severely as the felled tree.

Suppose you have a patch of ground that has never been a garden or, if it was, has been neglected so long that human hand might never have touched it. Suppose it now stands shoulder high with the relics of last year's wild herbage, with the leaning stems of tall nettles and cow parsley, all interlaced with the barbed, leafless branches of brambles. How would you set about taming it? How would you apply theory to it? These are the questions asked again and again by those beginning to make a new garden.

It is a picture common enough, a situation likely to daunt anyone, especially if he has either little time or inclination for gardening but cannot live in chaos. It might also represent the position of the person who has a retreat at which only occasional weekends can be snatched. Between them, for eight months of the year, everything will go on growing. Visits could sometimes be like arriving at the Sleeping Beauty's castle, the vegetation having to be parted to reach the door.

In my view winter would be the time to tackle it, while the spent undergrowth discloses the old oil drums and prams and motor-car wings that always seem to collect on neglected land. The general natural decay would give one a start and it would be important to take full advantage of this.

Through the absorbing small advertisements columns of the local Press, I would contact a nearby contractor who would run over the lot with a motor scythe or hire out one for me to use myself. Failing this I would buy one of those 'Turk' scythes with a straight shaft and a broad blade (not difficult or dangerous to use) and cut everything with this. The foreign objects would be buried, the herbage burned.

Left with a fairly clear site for the present I would plant nothing but a few trees and shrubs, spacing them widely in roughly a horseshoe shape to leave an open patch within view of the windows. This would be my garden — a miniature park, if you like, all the shrubs standing individually in turf, not in beds, with enough room to walk round each one.

There may be no turf yet, but I would not worry about that for the present. Where the wild vegetation had been cut away, with the spring something would grow. Weeds would arise again undeniably, but among them would be rudimentary tufts of grass.

Now it would be necessary to make the one other capital investment, apart from the cost of the plants, the 'garden' would demand. Thirty pounds, or perhaps forty to enter the luxury class, would have to be spent on a rotary grass-cutter. So far there would be little grass to cut, but the machine would gnaw through the weeds just as well. Cutting would have to start with the new growing season.

Gradually the broad-leaved weeds would weaken and give up, surrendering their place to the grass that would surely take over. It may not be of the fine grade of which neat suburban lawns are made, but this would be outside the terms of reference.

The grass would be natural to the site, appropriate to its style of development. Certainly it would be inclined to grow rampant, but even after a month's absence the rotary cutter would be able to reduce it to fairly trim-looking turf again in an hour. If insufficient grass to reassure one had appeared by the end of April, a coarse grade could be sown. It would only be necessary to scratch the surface with a rake, scatter the seed and cover it with peat.

Early in the autumn I would plant bulbs by the basketful — daffodils of all kinds and snowdrops under the trees, where the grass and inevitable weeds could be left until the bulb foliage had withered, crocuses on the apron of open 'turf' immediately in front of the house, which would more resemble a gracious lawn.

Birch, ornamental crabs and cherries, laburnum and coloured thorns would be the main trees I would plant. The shrubs would include anything that can put up a good fight for itself and need little pruning — the spiraeas, deutzias, viburnums, weigelas and shrub roses plentifully.

The only attention they would need would be for the first two seasons pulling out the inevitable weeds over their rooting area.

As time went on I should undoubtedly add some hardy perennial plants to the scheme. But beds would still not be made; they would be in clumps free-standing in turf. Such tough growers as peonies, day lilies, hostas or lupins, all with sufficient 'architectural' form for such treatment, can stand alone. With the rotary mower it is possible to cut round and close to them quite easily.

A scheme of this kind, I am sure, is the best style of gardening for the reluctant, the disabled and the occasional gardener, perhaps even for the retired. The garden would be perennially interesting and attractive but quite undemanding. Its character would be casual but not unkempt.

You might say that the structure of a garden is built up on its paths. Laying them is therefore one of the first stages in distilling some sort of order from the chaos. They will only give the garden that 'feel' of rightness if they are direct and functional, taking you straight to your destination and only being turned to one side to miss some tree or other immovable object. The path that curls without reason always makes a garden seem fussy and contrived. Why should it be ashamed to admit frankly that it is utilitarian?

Yet if it encircles the garden in sweeping arcs by which you can circulate the whole area dry-shod, a path can add to a sense of spaciousness. In this case it might lie between flower beds and lawn, when it would also allow you to tend the plants without damage to the turf, and comfortably in damp weather, while disposing of the need for edge-trimming. Otherwise, a path becomes part of the design only if it is focused on something, whether a gateway, an urn or figure, a seat or a tree which it might surround as it finishes. If there is room a width of four feet will allow two to walk abreast.

A utilitarian approach belongs equally well to its construction. Any path that is to withstand heavily-laden barrows wheeled over it, or even years of foot traffic, needs the firm foundation of at least four inches of rammed hardcore 'blinded' with finer grade material. The continuous concrete path, harsh and uncompromising, has no place in a garden made to please the eye. The best one can hope for is that it will soon 'craze' due to its lack of expansion joints. If concrete is to be poured, the result is much happier if it is run between a framework of battens set over the foundation layer. Brushing the surface before it is set will help simulate the texture of natural stone. This is the next best thing to laying paving.

Constructing paths, drives and terraces in this fashion has been made much easier — and more tempting — now that concrete is widely available ready mixed so that one has only to have it poured into the laid moulds.

When natural or reconstituted stone or concrete slabs are used to form the surface, again a firm base is essential. I am sure, too, that it is best to lay them on a weak mortar, composed of seven parts sand or ashes to one of cement, and tamp the slabs into position, checking frequently with a spirit-level.

To fill the cracks I favour brushing in a strong mix, leaving the weather to moisten and set it, rather than 'grout' them with a trowel, when inevitably some of the cement disfigures the surface.

This, admittedly, rules out the romantic possibility of filling the cracks with creeping plants and allowing others that form cushions to spill over the stones. Many people I know like them, but in my experience they can be a perennial nuisance. Not only do worms thrust up their casts over the stones, but your guests are frequently embarrassed by inadvertently treading on a plant, obliging you to tread on another to put them at their ease.

For preference I think it is better to keep the plants that will soften the stonework to the sides, out of harm's way. The glare of concrete paving in sunny weather can be subdued by tinting it with either a solution of cow dung — one of the 'mock Tudor' builder's methods of faking the appearance of age — or of iron sulphate. Of course the concentration has to be decided by experimenting with a pilot patch until the desired sandy tone is reached, remembering that it will pale with weathering.

Unless they have a special non-slip surface, brick paths and steps can be dangerous in damp weather if they get that desirable patina of lichen over them. For comfort and safety, garden steps must always be shallower and have wider treads than stairs indoors.

In our damp climate I am sure a paved terrace is even more an essential extension of the house than in a hot one. Only by having somewhere that dries quickly can one take full advantage of what fine weather we get, though a gardener may have little time to lounge there himself. In siting it, an attempt must be made to resolve the problem that the sunniest aspect usually catches the full prevailing wind from the south-west.

The same considerations that enter path-making apply to building a terrace. But here the scope for making patterns by introducing bricks or cobbles is greater. This is particularly valuable when concrete slabs are used, which lack the soft edges of natural stone and the multitude of tints that weathering reveals.

Functional though the terrace may be — and also a setting for tubs and urns of plants that need a little winter protection —for much of the year its surface must stand as a garden feature in itself. Made with artistry and a sense of scale it can please the eye when the garden is bereft of flowers and foliage.

Design

Order or chaos: point of focus: 'Avenue at Middelharnis': suite of outdoor rooms: surprise and enticement: value of trees and woodland: the courtyard garden: expanding upwards: 'the little tent of blue'

An axiom of garden-making is that the design with strong outlines is always the most successful, particularly if it is to sustain the mixed collection of plants we usually try to cram into our plots as the appetite for them grows with wider acquaintance. Perhaps winter puts the design to the severest test though. Does the fall of the leaf bring you desolation or revelation, chaos or order? Does it leave a scene best forgotten about until the spring? Or does it reveal the firm outlines of a picture to mock the cold days to come?

It is an equally sound principle of garden-making that each window that looks out on to the site should have a view of some sort that is independent of the colourful plants that may embellish it in spring and summer. Both aims can be realised in many ways.

[10]

Even if the window looks out on to an ugly blank wall in a backyard the ideal can be achieved with a *trompe d'oeil* carried out in trellis. In summer it may support roses and clematis, but when they are leafless in winter it can bring you up with a start by its deception, as its false perceptive gives the illusion of an endless series of arches.

At the other extreme, if your garden commands a view of rolling country nothing should be done to screen or diminish this, but rather it should be integrated into the garden scheme. Of course, best of all is a view with, say, a fine church tower or a romantic ruin in the distance.

What is always needed is a point of focus. This is what most helps to give a garden, however small, a strong design. And this in turn is what enables it to retain an interesting structure through the leafless months rather than to dissolve into an inconsequent mass in late autumn.

Sometimes the point of focus can be a tree beyond the garden, perhaps different from all the rest on account of its tall bearing or outline, or the fact that it may be an evergreen. To give it isolated importance it can be framed on either side by trees and bushes planted in the garden itself.

But if you are penned in by other houses, all just the same, as most gardens are? Though it must stand within the narrow boundaries a point of focus can still give unity and significance to the scheme. Indeed, it will lead the eye away from the environs which may be so distasteful when not concealed behind the foliage of trees. I suspect that the view from the french windows of most semi-detacheds ends at a dreary piece of fence. Inevitably the eye wanders beyond, when instead it might be caught by some object that remains arresting all the year.

At best it might be a fine piece of statuary or an urn planted afresh with the seasons. Or it can equally well, and more cheaply, be an evergreen tree chosen specially for its individual character.

Another point of cardinal importance in creating a garden is making the site seem bigger than it really is by artifice. The smaller the plot, the greater relevance of the principle, which relies on perspective. Perhaps I can illustrate this by a fragment of autobiography in which the principle was denied, only to be affirmed many years later. It also heavily underlines the folly of seeking swift results. Both points can be seen illustrated in the disposition of some of our conifers, now standing at comfortable maturity. The whole prospect from one set of windows was laid out — on the ground only, I fear now — to give an impression of distance with the help of straight receding lines. I suppose somewhere in our minds when it was done was that Hobbema picture, 'Avenue at Middelharnis', in the National Gallery, in which the alley made by those trees seems to go on for ever.

Twin *Cupressus arizonica,* still slim and pillar-like, stand at the far extremity of this part of the garden, and between are accent conifers placed (as we thought at the time) to enhance the illusion. They have proved the trouble.

Our folly was that we didn't allow sufficiently for their disparate speed of growth. What time has left us with is tall trees in the distance, shorter ones in between them and the point of vision. It wasn't like this once. They were graded in the opposite direction when they were small, so that those at the extreme end seemed much farther away than they were. The error has been revealed only after many years which one cannot go over again.

You will see from this that the illusion of space can result from one's plantings, if they are chosen wisely. If progressively slower growers are planted as the view recedes from the windows a false perspective is set up. The point of focus of the garden will seem farther off than it would without this device.

The effect can also be created more directly by tapering the outlines away from you, so that short though they may be in reality, some appearance of distance, as on that piece of canvas in the Hobbema picture, is contrived.

It can be done with colours too. Brilliant shades in the distance have a foreshortening effect on the garden. Misty tones out there, with brighter shades nearer at hand, can lengthen it.

Another way of creating an illusion of distance within narrow boundaries, and of mystery too in this case, is to turn the end of a vista to one side, as though it is slowly curling out of sight — even if it is only leading to the compost heap. If it is not quite so satisfying, and belongs to the informal style of garden, it can be intriguing, and always suggests that the garden has hidden charms.

Legerdemain though all this may seem, even bogus, it has a value of great importance when you are constructing for yourself a retreat in which you will be able to stay when it has become totally impossible to reach open spaces by road.

Neighbouring buildings seem to increase their dominance over the garden in winter and bring up the question of concealing them by plantings. A thorough-going screen of tall conifers is often quite out of the question. Anyway, the nearer the buildings are the taller the screen has to be and this can add problems of shading to the difficulty. It is often better to settle for a single standard tree or two. As soon as they are planted the offending eyesore seems to get smaller, and this is a result that increases with growth. And the nearer they are placed to your own windows, consistent with not cutting off light and interference with foundations, the more certainly they will have this most desirable influence.

In laying out a small garden many of the most exciting features of comfortably sized gardens can be adapted and scaled down. Closely limited areas and unpromising shapes can be a challenge. In fact the most intriguing garden I have ever seen measures seventeen feet by eleven.

A well tried method of treating a long, thin strip, a dull suburban plot, to make it a garden full of surprises is to divide it into a series of compartments each with its own colour scheme or character. Unity can be preserved by a broad path — of paving or turf — linking all. The perspective effect could be enhanced by a series of column-like trees.

The compartments — a suite of outdoor rooms, if you like, each differently decorated — would be separated by hedges just tall enough to excite curiosity and make you want to see beyond. A point of focus would be needed at the far end of the alley linking them, and I can think of nothing better in this case than a golden-leaved cypress, so that as you look along it even on dull winter days it would seem that a shaft of sunlight was catching the tree.

Making a garden is largely a response to an existing situation; more a sort of organic growth than imposing a shape on the raw material. When we were planning ours we found a strip left on our hands twenty feet by a hundred and fifty, the walk to the vegetable patch. This we decided, could be a garden in itself and we adopted the series of outdoor rooms treatment.

Low hedges of rosemary, lavender, santolina and lonicera divide them. This was to be a summer garden, though I have since added spring bulbs and coloured primroses, while for a formal winter effect some of the beds are fringed with box and others with the silvery dwarf euonymus.

In the first enclosure we have grouped pink, carmine and crimson flowers. Roses at first had the second to themselves but these have since been abandoned in favour of an extension of the first with silver-leaved plants added. Two steps down take you into an octagonal enclosure where all the flowers are blue and white. From this chilly area you at once step into the 'hot' colours of scarlet, orange and yellow in the next 'room'.

Then you come to a patch where mock orange, peonies and irises are grouped to flower after the pink trumpet daffodils massed there are over. In turn they are succeeded by physostegia allowed to run and come up wherever it likes, and the path here is edged with ribbons of that valuable *Campanula portenschlagiana major,* with a flowering season that matches the length of its name.

As pillars through which you pass at each entrance, preserving the unity by their repetition, I planted the silvery *Chamaecyparis lawsoniana fletcheri.* But now I wish I had not been so impatient and had used the slower growing, column-like Irish yew.

If I had another long thin strip to deal with I think I should make one enclosure, concealed from the first glance, based on a circular lawn, as an extra surprise.

Concealment, surprise, enticement, and illusion — these are surely some of the elements that go to the making of a garden, and I am persuaded that they can be introduced to any site that can otherwise be taken in at a glance.

Sometimes the site is dominated by a tree that has taken many generations to grow and which it would be unthinkable to fell. This need be no hindrance to garden making, but is a measureless asset. It at once suggests for the site a style conveniently but ineptly known as wild or natural gardening — for a garden is an artificial assembly of plants in which the wild forces must always be kept at bay.

Still, the term has some validity and gardening in this fashion offers an opportunity of growing many of the most desirable of plants with the minimum of effort and upkeep. For a surprising number of shrubs and herbaceous plants are only really happy under a high canopy of foliage.

For the most part brilliant colourings will have to be eschewed, but anyway how often are they appropriate to our grey skies?

As the fortunate trustees of a fragment of light woodland, we find this increasingly the most absorbing part of our garden. In fact, if I had a flat, treeless site to start with I should now contrive to turn part into a bosky patch with quick-growing trees like birch and mountain ash, the bird cherry and several kinds of maples.

Under the shade of a trio of oaks and some tall hedge maples, we find we can grow many plants that would otherwise be denied us. The soil is fortunately acid, which gives us the whole rhododendron family to range among. Lace-cap hydrangeas take over from them, lasting till well into autumn, and both give extra shade to the roots of lilies.

A lofty vaulting of bare branches in winter reduces the severity of frost, and so we find we can chance tender plants here which in full exposure would quickly succumb.

The shade also gives comfort to the gardener. Instead of chafing against the bad weather behind windows I find I can work agreeably there in rough winds and in rain, while at no time of the year is weeding anything but easy. For the soil is always moist but never too wet. Long accumulation of fallen leaves has brought it to a moisture-holding texture, and the deep striking roots help to carry away surplus.

Not that there is much weeding to be done. In a wild garden patch of this kind the starry stitchwort, wild sage, the bright campions and foxgloves can spread how they like. I have introduced the woodruff to make refreshingly scented carpets of emerald.

When I started I foolishly thought it was sufficient to plant shrubs here and there in holes made between the wild herbage, chopping into the tree roots where necessary, in the way that some authorities advocate. But I quickly learned that it was better to make beds between sweeping, grassy paths, cleaning the ground of undesirable weeds and brambles.

The direction of the paths was decided by treading from point to point as places were chosen for different shrubs, and this contributes to the 'naturalness' of the area. Now moss is welcome to creep over them and inhibit the grass. The edges are trimmed with a grass hook rather than shears.

As groundwork to the shrubs in the beds, daffodils and other bulbs have naturalised themselves, and so have the hardy cyclamen and primulas. I am always hoping that one day the blue Tibetan poppies will, too.

Apart from mowing or scything, this is becoming an area which can be left to itself for weeks at a stretch without looking too unkempt, for the whole atmosphere is one of informality.

Fear that introduced plants will not have a chance against the deeply entrenched roots of existing trees are unjustified. If you give each shrub a good four square feet of area to itself at the start and about eighteen inches free of other roots below, it will establish in plenty of peat, and learn to co-exist, eventually deriving advantages from the stronger partner. The other plants are woodlanders by nature and need little coaxing.

Of course some tough navvying with spade and mattock is needed at the outset to prepare places for the introduced plants. Of course the surface roots must be cut away; but this seems to cause little harm to the existing trees whose right of occupation is decided by long establishment.

Gardening in this fashion is not necessarily gardening in the grand manner. Again, it can be scaled down to the small site with its single tree, which, once felled in a moment of folly, could not be replaced in a lifetime.

The important thing is that gardening under trees, even if they do have to be lopped to let in light, offers opportunities of enjoying the subtleties of the craft. If only all this were more widely accepted, and mechanical cutters, so swift and easy to use, were stayed, new housing areas would be spared their bare look.

What about the really tiny site in which you feel you could almost touch both sides at once by standing with arms outstretched? With an area like this my garden would become no more than a courtyard, another room added to the house but out of doors. The first problem would be to shed one's gardening prepossessions, the accepted notions of what the ingredients of a garden should be. Only by first admitting the severe limitations would the full possibilities be revealed.

There would be no lawn, though perhaps a little turf would be used as a token in the pattern of paving and cobbles that would cover most of the site.

Unable to exploit more than a minute area, I should see what could be done to garden upwards. The house walls would be strung with wires or covered with panels of trellis to support every climbing plant to which they would give room. Next I would surround the plot with woven six-foot fencing to enclose it completely.

For the first thing I ask of a garden, unless the surroundings are exceptionally congenial, is privacy, that it should be an intimate retreat with its own individual character. After all, the great classical gardens had their *giardino segreto,* concealed from the common gaze and remote from their splendid vistas.

The enclosing fences — if only they could be walls! — would all be wired to take climbing plants too. If the sun reached any of them they would be garlanded with roses. The varieties that flower all through summer and autumn, and all over instead of just at the top, would have to be chosen.

The sunless fences would be relieved from any drabness by winter jasmine entwined with clematis such as the long-flowering Nelly Moser and Comtesse de Bouchard to succeed it and continue all through the summer; by the climbing hydrangea through which the 'superba' variety of *Clematis jackmanii* would scramble; by both the showy early and late flowering Dutch honeysuckle, ruthlessly cut back immediately after the scented blossom was done; and by ivy with gold or silver-splashed leaves.

There would be a few shrubs, each chosen for its distinction of outline, as well as either a long season in flower or berry. Some that are over early in the year would later become hosts to more clematis and some of the annual climbers one can buy in pots in May. The holly-leaved *Mahonia japonica* would come right at the very top of my list, though it would be jostled by the evergreen *Choisya ternata* whose white flowers go on and on. Another would be *Pyracantha rogersiana,* splendid in white blossom, orange-red berries and outline.

For colour effects in the summer I should rely mainly on annuals and those perennials grown afresh from cuttings each year, all bought as plants in late spring. Penstemons would come first and, like geraniums, they would be planted generously. Rather than make the enchanted jumble of a cottage garden, however, the overstated 'riot of colour', I would use them rather formally, in single blocks of one tone, or two to blend or contrast.

There would be bold dabs of white to emphasise them, but also to stand out in the evenings, when, as a commuter, I suppose I should see the garden most often.

[17]

For the very early spring there would be all the forms of *Crocus chrysanthus* I could get. Though close to the wildings, these have a style suited to a formal evironment. Likewise, the daffodils I would plant would be the most expensive I could afford, on the grounds that the higher you climb the social scale in the narcissus community the more elegant their individual quality becomes. And in this setting they would have to stand by this; there would be no scope for them to draw on one another for their effect as daffodils in massed plantings can.

The relationship of the site with the sky being so slight due to the confinement, I would enhance it by means of a pool to mirror 'that little tent of blue'.

In these days of plastic liners, construction would be no problem. The excavated top soil would be a valuable addition to the flower beds. These could be retained by low brick or stone walls which would contribute to the formal outline, particularly in winter. They could be softened by repeat flowering pinks.

If the site were pitched at all rather than reduce it to one level I should make two, each shelf, as it were, being given a different character. Though there would be tubs and urns with 'sculptural' plants like yuccas and Japanese maples, perhaps camellias and clipped box, I hope I should be restrained and not attempt a Mediterranean patio under our too-often cloudy skies. But I should search and save long for the right piece of statuary of which I should not soon grow tired.

A formal outline, arresting shapes, a continuing succession of flowers, bold slabs of colour, a stone pattern for the winter, and just as important, elusive but distinct scents . . . these would be the components of my miniature garden.

Seclusion

Screen for a private world: walls: fences: chain link fencing: covering plants: ivy: the high hedge: preparing the site: evergreen screening with conifers: berberis: the flowering hedge

For all the attempts of enlightened planners to make new housing estates with gardens open for all to enjoy, in the American fashion, conversations with aspiring gardeners and observations repeatedly persuade one that the prevailing British idea of a garden is that it should be enclosed. Always the plea is for something to act as a screen, for plants that will grow swiftly and help create a private world, shut off from its environment. At the pub, and on the beach, we must all be together, it seems, but in the garden concealed from the gaze of others.

Brick walls, so hospitable to plants, are usually out of the question. If paled fences are erected I am sure it is worth the expense of setting the panels between concrete pillars. Otherwise sooner or later the posts, even of stout oak, will have to be reinforced with concrete piers.

Fences of red cedar can be both long-lasting and an agreeable background for plants. Woven fencing surmounted by panels of trellis can look gracious and is enduring, but again, owing to wind resistance, the posts must at least be set in concrete.

In my experience the surprisingly cheap wattle hurdles will give ten years of effective screening. Though the wind can get through them as it does through a dry wall on the moors, lessening resistance, experience has also taught me the folly of using to support them anything but the stoutest ash or beech (or oak) posts, especially in soil that lies wet. Their life can be greatly lengthened by peeling the bark off the ends and treating them with one of the proprietary wood preservatives.

Obligingly or unfortunately, according to your tastes, builders often surround gardens with chain link fencing. What can be done to subdue it? I have seen the rampageous Russian vine, *Polygonum baldschuanicum* planted to turn it into a wall of greenery, foaming with white flowers in August. This can be kept trim with shears in early spring. But in winter you are left with the bare branches entwining the bare wire.

A better choice, to my mind is the benevolent evergreen honey-suckle *Lonicera japonica halliana,* which with its deep green growth will mask the wire for ever, and fill the air in summer with a perfume that really can be described as 'exotic'. The plants can be set out eight feet apart.

Consider another suggestion. Released from an inevitable association with crumbling walls and sickly trees it threatens to engulf if not destroy like some evil serpent, ivy has earned itself a new dignity as a house plant. It also deserves at least a reappraisal for the garden.

Stretches of garden fencing could be turned into completely peep-proof walls if ivy were allowed to wreath them. Here the ivy could be cut with shears like any other hedge. Little would be taken from the soil, for will not ivy flourish on the strictest slimming diet? The common ivy would do. I am very thankful for the wildings of this which swathe the trunk of an ash tree in the view of our windows, for in hard winters it provides food for the birds. When starving they sometimes feed on the berries weeks before they are ripe. Had nature not planted the familiar English ivy (with a Greek name sounding like the movement of a train, *Hedera helix*), it would have been the gold-splashed aureo-variegata form which I would have planted there myself, to gleam as it caught the pale winter sun.

Town gardens could be rescued from looking dismal and un-inviting in winter if this were also planted against their walls or fences. Thus, by artifice, patches of sunlight would be contrived within boundaries which, during the drab months, could not be climbed by what few rays of sunshine there are then.

When one weighs up the possibilities of enclosing the garden with a high hedge, the first thing one has to accept is that seclusion cannot be had from the start. Some nurserymen do carry stocks of tall, mature plants, but never recommend them since young plants take to their new environment much more readily than old ones. A two-foot hedging plant will often outstrip a five-foot one in three seasons, growing lustily from its first day of planting while the old one takes time to settle down again after being disturbed. It may even find the change too much.

Another factor must influence choice. Any plant that advances rapidly while young is hardly likely to change its nature and grow slowly after it has reached just the height we want it to. The price of quick results is regular clipping later. Thuja hedges I planted years ago would still exceed by three feet a year the desired seven feet if they were not clipped twice during the season.

The royal road to rapid establishment, though, is to prepare the strip of ground, three foot wide at least, and work in all the organic manure that can be found. Stable refuse is usually out of the question, and few new gardeners have a stack of compost on hand. Hop manure seems about the best substitute to help promote fibrous root growth as well as yield nutrients. Coarse bonemeal at 4 oz. per sq. yd. will offer an extra supply of phosphates for the roots over several seasons.

If the summer is a good one, spraying evergreens with water at the end of hot days will not only see them safely through dry spells, but encourage them to make progress in their first year. And the much desired mulch over the whole rooting area of lawn mowings a couple of inches deep, or an inch layer of peat, will keep the soil round the roots moist without the need for frequent watering. On stony soil the stones will serve the same end.

Most of the best evergreens for screening are found among the conifers. The quickest grower of all has the tongue-twisting name of *Cupressocyparis leylandii.* So rapid is its rate of growth that in as short a time as six years after I had planted them I could look up in to trees twenty feet tall. It would make an admirable tree to plant in an established garden now marred by some recently-erected eyesore. Fortunately it endures constant clipping as un-complainingly as the familiar *Thuja plicata,* which has the great advantage of breaking afresh readily from old wood whenever it has to be cut back really hard. Both can in fact be kept down to close hedges seven feet tall with two clippings a year, one in April, the other early in September.

Chamaecyparis (Cupressus) lawsoniana is easier to acquire and only a little less quick to grow. But this also has named forms which are fairly slow in growth but make dense compact hedges more to scale with the smaller garden and less demanding in clipping.

The varieties called *fraseri* and *allumii* are both bluish-grey and slender growing, making hedges very suitable for the small garden boundaries with little clipping. The silvery and feathery *fletcheri* might also be used. All three would make thinner hedges than the others, since their natural inclination is to turn their branches straight upwards. The outlay on these may be greater, since they would have to be put eighteen–twenty-four inches apart against the others' three feet and they would take longer to do their job; but in a closely limited area, ultimately the result would be better.

Rather smaller in stature, hedges of berberis can look spectacular in flower, berry and autumn leaf colour. Usually they have a pleasing, sometimes loose, informality about them, and thus they take up room with their breadth. *Berberis darwinii* is an exception, however. It can be 'tailored' closely with the shears and keeps the bright green of its highly polished leaves all the winter. I have seen hedges of this as little as four feet tall and as much as eight feet — which shows how adaptable it is. As the owner of a berberis hedge, though, I have cursed the thorns that make weeding close to it, especially in its early stages, so painful a job. You see, for the quick establishment of a hedge it is essential to keep down competing weed growth.

Pyracantha is also prickly, but the thorns do not get in the way so much. A plant which can also be 'tailored' quite easily, ever-green and attractive in flower and berry, it seems to me to have everything in its favour as a hedging plant — if you are prepared to wait four or five seasons for it to perform its screening function.

Hedges of an informal character are of course most suited to front gardens and for dividing up the main garden into compartments devoted to different purposes or colour schemes.

In recent years, the flowering hedge has gained currency, with that ebullient floribunda rose Queen Elizabeth easily the most popular plant for the purpose. Growing in an upright fashion five–six feet high and prodigal with its flowers, it seems the ideal hedging rose, especially as there are few weeks in the year when it is without leaves.

If you prefer something less polished and formal, the hybrid musk roses can be set about six feet apart and their branches arched sideways and tied to wires. In time they will become bastions of thorny branches massed in summer with refreshingly scented flowers and blooming again intermittently until the end of autumn. Of course, most of the blossom will appear on the sunnier side.

Turf

An English institution: cathedral close: preparation of the site: treading: seed versus turf: when to sow: upkeep: levelling the site: dealing with moss: selective weedkillers: the lawnmower: rotary versus cylinder

The trim lawn that gives a sense of peace and spaciousness to a garden is a peculiarly English institution, at its finest in cathedral close and college quadrangle. It deserves cherishing from the start.

Whether it is to be seed or turf from which the lawn in a new garden will be made, the site needs the same studied preparation: unless it is drained, moss will inevitably challenge the grass later: unless certain weeds are liquidated the hoped-for sweep of turf will be marred by an unevenness it will be a long struggle to cure.

Ideally, draining the site implies laying a system of conduits such as moles might drive for you, all leading not to a mole's 'castle' but to the lowest point where they can discharge the water they channel. But who has time for this kind of textbook exercise? The next best thing is to make sure storm water drains quickly from the surface.

This can be done by adding refuse when digging, during the winter, the best time for preparing the site. As the soil is pitched forward, rubble — or broken glass, tin cans, ash from domestic fires, or half-rotted kitchen waste — is thrown into the trench you have made. All will help to build up a drainage layer nine twelve inches down.

A spell of weathering will leave the turned-over soil in a state when it can be combed through with a fork and the weed roots picked out. Frankly I do not think it is worth the trouble to remove them all. Who has ever seen nettle or docks, ground elder or even bind-weed, on a lawn? Lacking the ability to adapt themselves for survival by lying flat against the ground, shoots which do appear from any root fragments of these left in, perish under the first mowings. No, the weed roots to eradicate are dandelion, couch and buttercup.

The act of forking will help refine the soil and soon it will be ready for the essential treading. I can think of nothing more likely to make you feel abashed under your neighbours' mystified gaze than to be seen systematically treading evenly every square foot of ground you have just dug, as though you were solemnly exercising in a prison yard. Stupid though you may feel, this is unquestionably the best way of pulverising the lumps and finding the weak, uneven places that would otherwise become hollows later. A roller cannot do it nearly so well. Not until you have done this and you have got the surface uniformly firm are you ready for the alternate rakings and rollings that will make the surface true and ready to receive the seed or turf. Levelling can be aided by pegs hammered in at three-foot intervals until they all stand at the same height, confirmed by a straight edge and spirit level.

All this can go on during the winter months in preparation for sowing in spring, though turfing can be done as soon as it is complete, between early October and the end of March, even the end of April if you are prepared for fairly intensive watering.

Peat raked into the final surface will hold the moisture the thread-like roots need as they extend. Scattering the soil with superphosphate of lime will encourage the roots to take hold of the new soil quickly, but is generally considered unwise to add lime itself to a lawn site on the grounds that it encourages worms, clover and coarse grasses. The finer grasses thrive on acid soil.

If you aim at a lawn of golf green standard you must use only the most expensive seed. Not any kind at that, but a mixture graded for your particular soil, according to whether it is light or heavy. Here you have to arrive at some sort of compromise with yourself. The higher your ideal the greater the maintenance the lawn will need. The finest turf can be kept in condition only by constant fussing over it with fertilisers and weedkillers. It will not stand up to the frolicking of children: it is to be seen and not used.

Against this, turf, which will give you a lawn from the first day, has qualified advantages. The finest quality can be bought only at fantastic expense. Most of what can be obtained locally, in my experience, is sheep-nibbled or mown-down meadow grass. If you buy it locally you get grasses endemic to the neighbourhood which are likely to suffer least in the extremes of weather. But often you get a fair sprinkling of weeds and spores of moss as well and you have to set about eradicating them.

When you lay a lawn of turf, bonding the turves like bricks so that not all the joints coincide, you work from the point nearest to the stack, wheeling over boards laid over the turf as it extends. A refinement that helps to avoid dislodging the turves when mowing begins is to lay them diagonally across the line to be taken by the mower.

Whether you should beat the turves into position or not is one of those gardening matters on which the experts so frequently disagree. I think it is worth using some sort of broad-based tool to firm them.

The use of turf means that one can begin mowing fairly soon after the turf has been laid. When the lawn has been sown, however, the first cutting should ideally be done with very sharp shears for fear of dislodging the tiny seedlings with the mower. If this seems too formidable a job, though, and the mower must be used, the blades should not be set lower than an inch, being lowered only gradually over successive mowings.

Even when lawn seed is sown conscientiously at the rate of an ounce and a half to the square yard, making sure that the whole area gets the same dose, and in soil that has been treated with a 'pre-sowing' fertiliser, the results can be a little discouraging for the first few weeks. Sowing in early September is perhaps the time to be favoured most, but failing this, hoping that it will live up to its reputation, the month of April is the best time.

When the seedlings are up an inch the garden roller has a part to play. Pulled briskly over the tender young grasses, it will encourage them to spread — 'braird', as gardeners say — and cover up the bare soil that appears, somewhat alarmingly, between them in the early stages. Not that one would ever recommend buying a garden roller. The mower, tipped so that the cutters do not do any cutting, will serve as well.

The roller, indeed, has no place today in garden practice. Once upon a time, before there were washing machines and refrigerators, a peak of suburban endeavour was to acquire (or borrow) a garden roller. It was a symbol of some kind but also a phantom in the garden. What the deluded who used it with such zeal were doing was the opposite of what they intended. For rolling a lawn compacts the bumps and makes sure that these are the patches that turn brown first in dry weather. The roots of grass need air as much as those of any other plant, and to allow it to reach them the soil must be opened, not the reverse.

There is a brisk sale today in the hollow-tined forks, which, thrust in at intervals of about eight inches, remove cores of soil as they are withdrawn again. Particularly in heavy land, using one of these in autumn is an important practical step towards achieving the 'close sward' of a dream garden.

If you have an uneven lawn the only way to iron out the undulations is to lift the turf over the offending spots and add to or remove the soil below. It is safe to top up slight hollows — say, up to about an inch or so deep — with fine soil pressed firm, certain that within a month the existing grass will have penetrated it and all will be as before, save that the depressions will have gone. Slight bumps are not so easily corrected. If it doesn't seem worth the effort of cutting into it and rolling back the turf, then reducing the soil underneath, I would be inclined to slice them off with a sharp spade and sow afresh. A little preparation will ensure that the patch will be assimilated in the least possible time, though only if a matching grade of seed is sown. Loosening the soil with a fork, pricking in moistened peat and a 'pre-sowing' fertiliser, then treading it fairly solid is worth all the bother.

The same method can be used to refurbish turf worn away by games or reclining repeatedly in one favourite spot during the summer. It is also particularly applicable to those distressing bare patches from which weeds have been sent packing by selective weedkillers.

What you might call general debility of turf can be corrected by spreading over the whole area one of the proprietary 'autumn dressings', sold for lawns and presented as though it might be a cosmetic. Here again I think the preference might fall on one with a peat base, the peat taking the place of the mixture of sifted old manure and soil which was once the sovereign aphrodisiac for failing turf. The peat itself exerts a beneficial influence on the turf, whether the soil is light or heavy, while providing a little deeper medium for the grasses to make fresh roots as growth advances.

Autumn is not the only time to fertilise turf. Indeed, doing it then is uncongenial to some lawns. Most of the lawn fertilisers on the market do most good if put on during spring and early summer. Their main function is to stimulate growth. Thus they have the most effect if they are put on during showery weather, on the principle that plants assimilate their nutrients only in solution. Always the fertiliser should be watered in if no rain seems likely during the next twenty-four hours. Otherwise these substances can cause distressing discoloration that may last a fortnight. Any stimulus to the weeds also is only temporary, for the ultimate action of lawn fertilisers is to make the soil less hospitable to them as it becomes more acid, a condition which the finer grasses relish but which weeds generally dislike. For this reason it is rarely advisable to apply any lime to a lawn.

Spring is also the time for dealing with the moss that can creep through turf, often on damp land, disfiguring it and inhibiting growth. Where formerly gardeners would remove what moss they could with a rake, today it is realised that this simply scatters the spores to found new colonies. Nevertheless, rake we must, to dislodge from round the grasses the dead material whose presence will have an inhibiting effect on them when they need all their resources to restore themselves. A springy wire-toothed rake is the traditional tool for this, but also on the market is a giant rubber comb on a long handle, which is less tiring to use. For large lawns it is worth buying a wheeled scarifier.

The moss spores may get dispersed, but in any case the turf will need treating with the liquid moss-killer most hardware stores sell. A sort of spray-bar which can be fitted to the spout of a watering-can instead of the rose, makes distribution of lawn potions much easier and by making them go further saves frequent returns to the tap.

Not until everything is in full, lusty growth again, at the earliest towards the end of May, is it worth putting on one of the selective weedkillers sold for eliminating lawn weeds. They act through the leaves and the broader the spread of foliage the weeds open to them the greater harm they will suffer.

There is a case, however, for using lawn sand in April, which some gardeners on heavy land prefer to peat-based fertiliser. Some contain mercury in safe quantity and form which destroys moss. All make the soil more acid, strengthen growth of the grass and burn off the tops of weeds, thus debilitating them.

You can go into any local garden shop also and buy a bottle of selective weedkiller that has a special spite against clover. And the chemical manufacturers are responsible, or self-interested enough, to make it so that it will harm neither your pets nor the birds whose song is indispensable to a garden with the least enchantment.

What the companies' clever scientists cannot do is offer you a weedkiller that can tell between what broad-leaved plants you want to keep and those you want to destroy. So that if you fear any spray may have drifted on to cultivated plants you must rush for a can of water and wash it off quickly, before the hemlock has time to enter and slowly creep through the tissues.

The type of machine that is used for cutting the lawn is a matter for some detailed consideration, as a glance at the rows of them in the average garden store heavily underlines.

On the Continent and in America, to judge by the advertisements in the gardening papers published there, mowing is one of the tasks done by the junior miss of the household. Always, it seems, she makes the lightest work of it, clad in apparel which suggests she is just filling in time before keeping a date. She seems Martha and Mary in one trim figure.

What is really surprising to the hidebound gardener here is that the machine, which seems to move at the touch from her delicate hand, is always a rotary one, of the kind which we think of here as designed mainly for cutting long grass. But where we usually favour a cylinder machine for mowing our lawns, abroad the rotary is in fact in general use.

The difference arises from varying conceptions of what a lawn should look like. While here it must be closely shaven if it is not to be looked on with disdain by the neighbours, elsewhere it is still a lawn if it is cut no closer than an inch or so. This in turn arises from local conditions. We may be able to maintain lush green turf shorn almost to its roots every few days, but in places where they really do get what one could call a summer all would quickly get burned up. Leaving the blades of the grass to grow a little shades the roots and there is more chance of retaining a green sward.

If we were to do this in our maritime climate, you might reasonably argue, coarse grasses would be given their heads and soon they would supplant the fine ones. My own experience denies this. For many seasons now, I have used a rotary machine on turf in what we like to call, rather pretentiously, our 'grassy glades' and I find that it is the fine species which are prospering at the expense of the coarse. The fast spinning motion of the horizontal blade of the machine has the effect of drawing up to it any prostrate growth. Turf brought in from carved up meadow soon loses its pastoral look under this treatment and takes on the look of a sedate vicarage lawn.

Until we had this machine, mowing was something that dogged our lives. You have doubtless noticed how often weather that has been fine from Monday to Friday declines in time for the weekend, when the wretched commuter goes forth to mow. When we did get a fine weekend we could never close the door behind us and leave it all behind. Always there was the lurking thought of the problem that the unshorn grass on our heavy soil would present even the motor mower after a spell of neglect.

Several times I have had to rise early day after day when the dew softened the stems, and scythe the lawn before we could use the mower again, simply because of a succession of missed weekends. Now it can grow as luxuriantly as it likes. The rotary machine will always be able to cope and quickly restore it. I find that I can use it even when the grass is wet and the cylinder machine would graze the surface or clog up and refuse to budge.

[30]

A third point in the rotary's favour is that one can cut close to trees standing isolated in turf without fear of chafing the bark. Also, I find one can gently push the machine under the over-hanging branches of shrubs, where formerly I had to do this with the scythe and then rake up the swathes and barrow them away. The rotary machine minces up everything it cuts finely enough to leave it, unless you have been cutting down the two-foot high grass round withered bulb leaves.

If you do not want to leave the clippings several machines on the market of this type are fitted with boxes to collect them. They can be adjusted to cut almost as close as the conventional mower, but the wheels can be raised a couple of inches, when it will quickly gnaw through vegetation waist high. Another advantage of this machine is that it can be used to collect the fallen leaves in autumn.

I have not laid aside the scythe altogether, nor honourably retired the cylinder mower. I should not like to lose a skill acquired with the one, and convention too deeply rooted to discard decrees that turf near the house should be extra close and bear the parallel lines that denote a garden tended with devoted care, and only the machine with the cylinder can accomplish this.

Seed Sowing

*The greatest sense of triumph: sober-sided restraint: sowing in
the greenhouse: polythene and fibre pots: pricking out: plastic
pots: peat in the drills: the meringue-like crust*

No matter how long he has been at the craft, any seasoned
gardener will tell you that his greatest sense of triumph
always comes from raising a plant from a tiny seed. The larger
and larger scale of the sale of ready-grown summer-flowering
plants cannot succeed in diminishing the magic of this. A mild,
still day, a break in the clouds for an hour or two, giving the idea
that the winter is past, and you are filled with an urge to go out
and scatter seeds in the garden with whole-hearted vernal abandon.
But standing in the background, wearing his usual reproving
look, is the sober-sided gardener of long experience urging
restraint. 'Not just yet,' runs his solemn counsel. 'Not until the
soil has warmed up and you can knock it down fine.'

If you have a greenhouse it is different. The time for sowing
the summer's bedding plants is before spring begins, in February

and March. This will give you plants already advanced enough to be setting out on their flowering career by the time planting out is due in May. Another factor in achieving this is, of course, pricking out the seedlings into the compressed fibre pots which are set in the ground to decompose, thus avoiding the check to growth otherwise inevitable.

Apart from this advantage of hastening development in raising your own plants from seed, how else can you be sure of having varieties which exactly fit your colour scheming? Or be able to grow the new varieties heavily starred in seedsmen's flamboyantly-coloured catalogues? You might think that in our day of hurry, gimmickry and kinkiness, breeding new flowers that can only be grown by the slow process of raising plants from seed would be in the decline. In truth, it is a facet of horticulture that is gathering momentum.

Polythene, the fibre pots and the so-called no-soil composts have all helped to make seedling-raising a much less troublesome and time-consuming business than is commonly believed. Seed germination under a polythene covering is certain, quick and anxiety-relieving. Use of the fibre pots makes 'potting on', as gardeners call transferring small plants to larger pots, quick and easy.

Composts in which the main ingredients are peat and sand of carefully selected grades, activated by special fertilisers, are clean to handle, can be stored at home and carry neither disease spores nor weed seeds. Personally, I find them preferable, all in all, to the celebrated John Innes composts. You cannot satisfactorily mix them yourself, but they are easily come by, and make greenhouse work lighter and more agreeable. It certainly aids swift germination if the compost is pre-warmed by storing it under glass a week or two before sowing.

Electric heating equipment that adjusts itself according to the weather, and even ventilators that operate with uncanny foresight, have almost brought anxiety-less seedling raising in greenhouses within the scope of those away from home all day. Plastics can do the rest.

An unexpected burst of sunshine when such seeds are germinating under glass can be disastrous. This is why growers have always covered the containers with panes of glass and then sheets of paper, and anxiously watched them every day so that the minute springing seedlings get the light as soon as they need it. Polythene without the paper and instead of the glass is better. You simply slip a polythene bag over the sown pot or box and have no need to fear that the seedlings will get drawn if they come through and lack attention. Indeed, the polythene covering can be left on during that danger period when the seedlings are still tiny and liable to shrivel if the crust of soil below which their roots scarcely penetrate gets dry through someone not being at hand with a syringe.

When it is time for pricking out, the plastic seed box has a distinct advantage over the familiar wooden type, assuming that one does still prick out into boxes. There is actually a very good case for transferring the seedlings individually into small compressed-fibre pots, even sowing direct into them when the seeds are big enough to take hold of with tweezers. Drop one or two in each as you would when sowing marrow seed.

Or if the merest pinch of seed is sown in every fibre pot, all but one of the resulting seedlings can be discarded. With the whole potful of soil to itself and no close competition, the lucky chosen one will be bigger by planting out time than box-raised seedlings and suffer no check whatever when it is planted. This course can both advance the too-brief time of summer flowering by several weeks and yield a much greater bounty of flowers the whole while.

More room is needed, of course, but it is easy to improvise frames for the rising families of plants by covering four boards nailed together with wire-reinforced plastic sheeting. The same equipment will serve for raising pot plants for transferring to the home as they come into bloom. This seems to me one of the chief justifications of running a greenhouse, which, even on a tiny plot, can so widely extend the range of plants which can be enjoyed.

Plastic pots are weightless, hardly breakable and relieve one of both the tedium of watering in rooms perhaps a little over-heated for plants, and those anxieties about plants drying out while they are left to themselves. Yet the plants in them do not suffer from the equal danger to their health of having too much water about the roots if enough fragments of smashed clay pots come to an honourable end as crocks at the bottom of their plastic successors.

Cyclamen, salpiglossis with ornate trumpet-shaped flowers, butterfly-like schizanthus, velvety gloxinias, primulas that flower for months at a stretch, and freesias that fill the winter days with fragrance — all these are within the amateur gardener's compass.

If the temperature of about 55 degrees F. required for germination cannot quite be attained reliably in the greenhouse, this is usually possible in a position just above the household hot tank. Here the pot of soil in which the seeds are sown must certainly be enclosed in a polythene bag to hold the moisture as necessary to germination as the warmth. Otherwise, things may be good neither for the seedlings nor domestic harmony.

Peat also has an important use in sowing out of doors, whether the seed is of vegetables or flowers. The so-called 'drills' — I am never quite sure why, when they are shallow trenches — are made with a stick or the corner of a 'draw' or swan-necked hoe, and lined with damp peat, into which the seed is sown. Germination is usually quick and certain in this, and the seedlings progress in the speedy way most who garden (without having been long at it) demand. What one must never do is water a seed-bed after sowing; the surface takes on a *meringue-like* crust that neither rain nor air can enter easily and the seedlings come up fitfully or with their energies spent, it seems, by the effort.

Planting

Quick results: care of the roots: moisture: mulching: puddling
in an evergreen: polythene screens: fertilisers: liquid manure

All who start to make gardens have one area of common ground, so to speak: they always want rapid results from their plantings. How can one make sure that the tree or bush or even tiny rock plant put in takes to its new environment at once and begins quickly to show what it is worth? We may have all manner of new equipment to make garden work lighter — if less relaxing — but planting methods can change little. I should say that the most potent factor in ensuring quick establishment is the practice of tucking something round the roots that will encourage them to make new fibres, through which the plants feed, plentifully and swiftly.

Everyone knows that plants like the soil pressed firmly home round their roots but that wet soil firmed is liable to 'cake' round them and hinder the exchange of oxygen and carbon dioxide, to the plants' discomfort. A supply of dry soil mixed with moist peat and worked round the roots before any excavated soil is returned will allow the firming to be done without such dangers. Here is a valuable end for the once-used John Innes seed or potting compost, quite dearly bought.

Personally, I find that a mixture of moist peat or leaf mould and sand serves admirably, both promoting quick root growth and holding the moisture to see the plant safely through the difficult days of spring drought that we always seem to get just when our new plants and sowings need the rain. I have found that it pays good dividends to use this mixture round whatever I plant — even bulbs on the clay on which I garden.

Where I diverge from long-established technique is on the question of double digging. Who, as I have said, does have the inclination to put the top soil to one side and fork over the subsoil, often heavy uncompromising clay? Come to that, what fruit farmer laying out a new orchard does more than plough and add farmyard manure to the soil? Yet since his pocket is deeply involved he must have a special interest in quick returns.

For most of us it must be sufficient to put compost, hop manure or even old turves at the bottom of the single-spit hole after scattering some lime on the clay subsoil beneath, and this I have found gives adequate results. Anyway, I have noticed that on heavy soil where I have made holes for fruit trees two spits deep in the time-honoured way, these have become sumps into which the water has drained.

A soil that lies wet in winter is of course slower to warm up in spring than a well-drained one, with a consequent later start of new growth. Certainly, then, some form of drainage must be contrived and a well-tried method of planting on heavy land is to set the bush fairly high in the ground and pile soil over the roots.

As always, the roots must be spread out to their full stretch. This is an indispensable fragment of technique. Failure to observe it and allowing a root to remain curled up can easily be responsible for a plant's tardy progress.

Firming the soil round the roots is of equal importance, using the heel on trees and bushes, the handle of the trowel for anything small. To go ramming and stomping ground you have just patiently dug and loosened, making it hard again round the apparently fragile roots of new plants, seems the height of folly.

Yet the roots do need the intimate contact with the soil resulting from firming. Where I have lost plants due to dryness in summer, I have found that in almost every case it has been where planting had been done hastily on a wet day. The soil had been left fairly loose for fear of causing it to 'cake' and I had neglected to go back another day when it was drier and press it well home with the heel of the gumboot.

Of course, anything 'planted high' needs to be tied to a stake firmly driven into the ground. But so does every tree or bush likely to put up any wind resistance and rock. For if it does, as fast as the vital new root fibres are made some will snap, and establishment will be hampered.

When planting is finished, to insulate the roots against the drying effects of wind and sun from the spring onwards, the soil over them must be covered with a mulch, that magic gardening aid applied in spring that keeps the roots cool and moist in summer, suppresses weeds, saves you the trouble of watering and has such a remarkable influence in speeding growth.

For my own part, I prefer a two-inch layer of last season's leaves in the belief that they slowly deliver up nutrients on which the plants will feed. Peat or hop manure will serve too, even the lawn mowings, provided they are not put on more than two inches thick and so get too hot while decomposition goes on. I never use compost as a mulch, for one can never be quite sure that any weed seeds it may contain have been totally destroyed.

Experience has taught me the wisdom of puddling in any evergreen. Once I moved a batch of evergreen azaleas on Whit Monday when they were in full flower. Had I had any idea of the dry weather that was to follow that season I hope I should not have been so foolhardy. As it happened the bushes, some three feet across, did not suffer in the least. They were not even watered again, only sprayed over in the evenings occasionally. But as they were replanted, plenty of wet peat was added to the ground and more washed round the roots by flooding them afterwards. A couple of days later all was trodden home firmly.

I am sure this is the technique to apply to conifers and other evergreens being planted or moved about on account of second thoughts.

Harm to recently planted evergreens that results from the cold winds we often get early in the year — when that old wind gets round in the east and stays there, in the anthropomorphic parlance of gardeners — can be avoided by screens of polythene. You have only to push four canes in round the plant, lap the film round these and secure it with strings, and the plant will stand there snug and unconscious of what the weather is like outside. The same covering will also keep those plants inclined to be delicate safe from considerable frost.

Similarly, allowing weeds or grass to get a hold immediately round newly planted shrubs can also hinder their early development by draining off the nitrogen the cultivated plants would otherwise use. The whole rooting area must be kept quite clear of them for the first couple of seasons. Indeed, areas of ground planted with fruit trees are frequently 'grassed down' for the express purpose of damping down their growth and sponsoring fruiting; which shows the influence grass or weeds can exert.

There remains the question of fertilisers. Bonemeal, a ready source of the phosphates that help promote root development, can be added plentifully to the top soil for permanent plantings, and the coarser it is the longer it will remain effective in the soil.

While some authorities are horror-stricken at the idea of feeding hedges and shrubs in summer with quick-acting fertilisers, as you would pot plants or, say, dahlias and chrysanthemums, I am told that the famous hedges at the Hidcote National Trust Garden that look as though they had been there for centuries, were fed every week in summer with liquid manure in the years after they were planted, actually within the present century. And if the term 'green fingers' has any validity, I am sure it derives from an understanding, innate or acquired, of the importance of unromantic acts like all these.

Propagating

*Gift beds: plant division: layering: tip layers: popping in a few
cuttings: the use of polythene: cuttings — the shoots to use:
sand as an aid: jam-jars in the rose bed*

Never have I met the garden-lover who wasn't anxious to
share the pleasures of his garden with others. You never
visit the true gardener without before long seeing him down on
hands and knees, digging up for you a plant of something you
have admired. Some I know even maintain gift beds tucked away
in the kitchen garden, where plants for the parting guest are
diligently hoed and nourished.

At the simplest level, plant propagation is just lifting a plant,
pulling it to pieces and replanting the younger portions, the
method which applies almost universally to herbaceous plants,
the job generally being done in autumn or spring.

To keep the supply of new shrubs going, however, there is no
easier way of raising them than the practice of 'layering'. It has

the advantage over propagating them by cuttings or seed in that pegging down a branch into the soil is all that has to be done. No spraying, no watering, no pricking out or potting. If it is done in spring, by the autumn you have a good-sized plant in most cases at least a season in advance of any rooted cutting.

Anyone who has planted shrubs in a new garden but still finds it disappointingly sparsely furnished can increase them by layering if a couple of low-growing branches can be spared. A clump which becomes a thicket is nearly always more effective (as a self-maintaining weed-smotherer as well as visually) than a lonely, single specimen.

During the late spring, when many of the jobs that could not wait are behind me, I try to spend a couple of hours going round the garden layering as many as possible of our shrubs with young branches near enough to the ground. For preference I use two-year-old wood but if possible last season's shoots of such slow growing hard-wooded plants as maples, witch hazel and magnolias.

The only equipment needed is a spade, some pieces of wire bent in hairpin fashion, a batch of two-foot canes and a barrowload of a mixture of sand, peat and soil. I take out half a spadeful of soil just where the branch will meet the soil and replace it with the compost. Then I scratch the bark with the thumb nail at this point, or twist it if it is tough, and peg it down with wire into the soil.

Beside each layer a cane is used to hold the branch upright, partly because it produces a balanced plant, but also because it helps divert the sap flow to the wounded, pegged-down point, from which roots will be produced.

While the general run of shrubs, including shrub roses, propagated in this trouble-free manner, do produce new plants by the following autumn, layers from the hard-wooded types and rhododendrons are rarely safe to move for another year.

So popular is that blessed thing, the loganberry without thorns, that I can never raise enough to pass on. But like all its kind, the blackberries and hybrids from them, it can be increased from so-called tip layers.

This means that you do not need to use a whole branch. You simply peg down the tips of the branches, and each will become a new plant in six to eight weeks. Not only can you get a new plant from each of the old branches, while arching it in a fashion that will make picking easier, but you can even use the new season's growths also when they are sufficiently well developed.

The same technique can be adopted for increasing rambler roses, and some climbers respond, though not all, I have found. The clematis a friend has admired can also be propagated successfully by layering, though in this case into a pot of sandy soil set in the ground.

Rooting cuttings of many kinds of plants on an everyday home scale has become much less a hit or miss process with the use of polythene covering instead of glass. You simply put the cuttings in a pot of moist light soil, insert three or four stakes, then draw a polythene bag over the lot and secure with an elastic band round the pot, and then stand it in a light position; there is little more to it than that.

The broad principle behind this elemental piece of horticultural practice is that you must keep the leaves charged with moisture until roots have formed and begin to replace the natural loss. To this end, cuttings standing in closed glass frames are sprayed over several times a day. Under polythene, provided air is not admitted, spraying is unnecessary. The cuttings remain turgid in the close atmosphere induced.

Cuttings of shrubs of most kinds can be rooted in this very simple way, some roses too; all are worth trying. It is certainly important annually to strike cuttings of shrubs that have a limited span anyway, like cistus and ceanothus, or which eventually grow too ungainly to be allowed to live out their natural days in the garden and are better replaced by their younger scions.

The shoots used for cuttings must be of the current season's growth; neither soft nor ripened yet into a hard condition. They are preferably pulled off this parent growth to come away with what gardeners call a 'heel', which must be trimmed of its tag of loose bark. Otherwise if this would make them too long, they are actually cut off, making the cut with a razor blade just below a leaf joint; the lower leaves are stripped off and sometimes the tip, if the cutting is inclined to be whippy. Dipping the ends in hormone powder sold for the purpose makes rooting more certain.

The soil mixture to use must be open, as gardeners call it, three parts of sharp sand being mixed with one of loam and two of peat. But fertiliser-treated rooting media — hardly more expensive and cleaner to use — are now on sale. If these are used in

[42]

small fibre pots impregnated with fertiliser, producing new plants from cuttings becomes a quick and sure process involving the least possible trouble.

Even so, it is still important to use the age-old process of spreading a layer of coarse sand over the surface of the rooting medium. Then, as each hole is made in the compost a little falls to the bottom, and the base of the cutting from which the roots are formed rests on this.

In this case one cutting goes to each tiny fibre pot, and these are stood under an improvised propagating case made by removing the bottom from a wooden box and replacing it with a sheet of polythene. Whatever the method used, when new growth at the tip shows that rooting has taken place, each new little plant is transferred to another polythene covered frame to which air is admitted. When roots show through the fibre they are transferred bodily to clay pots of heavier compost, and like others so potted on will be kept safe in an airy frame for the winter. By April they will be strong enough plants to set out in their permanent positions.

By the same method tender plants such as geraniums, penstemons, heliotrope, verbenas and gazanias can be rooted in late summer and large plants raised to give a good show from the start in the following season, though of course they will have to be kept in a frost-proof place for the winter.

In my experience polythene gives sufficient shade and the polythene-enclosed pots or the propagating case can be stood in full sunlight. But at any sign of wilting the bags or case would have to be opened and the cuttings sprayed and closed again. Then they must be stood out of the sun.

During late summer it is possible to root plants easily from riper shoots out of doors. You merely prick sand into a patch of soil and spread some on the top and insert the cuttings in this, covering them with the polythene-topped box. In three to six weeks a high proportion root and are ready for potting.

The equipment I use is simply this. The wooden boxes, six-eight inches deep, in which plants arrive during the winter are saved, and the bottoms and tops, if any, are knocked out to leave them as bare frames. A double thickness sheet of polythene is tacked over each — I say double, because this avoids any need for shading, and cuttings root quickest in full light.

However, I have found that really broad-leaved plants, from which moisture loss is greatest, are better rooted under frames made from the deeper apple boxes, whose sides cast some shade during the day.

The boxes are first placed on the prepared soil to mark an imprint of their outline on it and the cuttings are pushed in within the lines made. They are watered and the polythene-topped boxes placed over them. Then one could go off for a long holiday confident that they would need no more attention and that a sufficient proportion would have rooted by the autumn. In fact, here all except the most tender could stay until the spring.

The impression must not be given, though, that any soil will do. First I fork it over and add peat and sharp sand or grit plentifully, then tread it firm again. To receive the cuttings, little furrows are made and lined with either sand or the vermiculite sold for gardening purposes. Both hold sufficient moisture in their texture yet discard a surplus. Cuttings that stand firmly on either have the best possible chance of quickly turning into plants.

Growing new plants from old by this simple technique one can build up a stock of shrubs and other plants already growing in the garden or with gift cuttings from friends. These, by the way, can be carried home in sealed polythene bags without loss of the vital moisture from the leaves.

Peeping over a garden fence one day for a closer look at the rare treasures it obviously contained, I was invited in by the owner, an elderly woman who told me she had grown most of her shrubs and trees from cuttings. How had they been rooted? Under jam jars in the rose bed, she told me.

All the rudiments of successful vegetative propagation lay here: the rose roots drained the soil, the leaves cast dappled shade and diffused the sunshine, and the neck of the jar resting roundly on the soil ensured the close atmosphere in which the cuttings would not wilt. It was not green-fingered magic, just common sense and an understanding of nature's ways.

When a seasoned gardener loads the boot of your car with plants, there is no need to feel embarrassed, if you are a newcomer to the craft, because you have nothing to offer in exchange. There is a continuous one-way traffic in plants among amateurs, and your donor is probably the lucky recipient of plants from someone even more experienced.

Borders

The inroads of shrub planting: an English compromise: a burst
of colour: herbaceous plants: shade and sunny patches: blending:
the plant bank: partners: marriage broker: the love-match: host
plants for climbers: garden transformation scenes: the series of
distinct effects: 'fifty springs are little room'

The herbaceous border is held in such warm affection as a
national gardening institution that one would hardly think
it might sometimes be challenged or even regarded as *passé*. Yet
the inroads made on it by the cult of shrub planting are so deep
that the case for hardy plants does need loudly restating occasionally.

My own dalliance with shrubs went on too long, and I was at
last forced to admit that for all the appeal of their outline in
winter and their labour-saving merits, quite apart from the beauty
of their flowers, you lose a great deal if you completely forsake
hardy plants for them. You lose the opportunity of bold and
sweeping colour effects and the plastic and subtle medium they

[45]

offer for colour schemes. You lose the distinction of foliage that many possess. Above all, you lose time. In the years shrubs spend settling down before they flower on any scale, you could already have enjoyed the best of hardy plants several times over.

Not that I am disenchanted with shrubs, but I do advocate the typically English compromise of what are inaptly known as 'mixed' borders. Here the two, shrubs and herbaceous plants, complement one another. Perhaps bulbs can be added as a third tier, to show themselves in spring and then retire.

If I were making a new border now, the shrubs I would choose would flower more or less together in spring and early summer, on the inviolable gardening principle that a sudden burst of colour is more satisfying than an intermittent spotty effect. Their season done, they would be succeeded by the hardy plants in a rich outpouring of summer colour, for which the shrubs would form a leafy background.

The hardy plants chosen for the scheme would need particular qualifications. They would not need to be dug up and pulled to pieces every second or third year to rejuvenate them. They would have to be content to be left to themselves for three or four times this period, so that the bulbs between them need not be disturbed.

True to our principle of making the least possible work, they would need no propping up with twigs and canes. Some would have to make their flowers in spires to contrast in form with the rounded shape of most shrubs. For preference they would spread themselves to cover the ground and deny weeds a chance to establish themselves. And some would have to endure a little shade.

Fortunately there are many herbaceous plants which meet all these demands. All the big campanula family meet them, from the dumpy *Campanula glomerata* to the *Campanula lactiflora*, of noble bearing. With them I link the balloon flower, platycodon, whose obese buds burst to form bell-flowers. You have only to add peat or leaf mould to the soil to make the moisture-loving astilbes flourish and send up their pink or red spires above equally attractive reddish foliage, and they last for many weeks. Similar soil suits the aromatic-leaved monarda. There are many others suitable for this purpose.

The herbaceous polygonums hardy plant growers stock have none of the rampageous ways of the climber of this name of such ill-repute. Sanguisorba, also known as poterium, is one of those plants that bear their flowers in bottle-brush fashion, and in this case they are bright rose. A little-grown spire-like plant of considerable grace is cimicifuga, unhappily called 'bugbane' but none the less distinguished for that, as it has airy plumes of ivory flowers.

The Japanese anemones come within our terms of reference, like the day lilies, or hemerocallis, now offered in a huge range of colourings since it became a 'hobby flower' in America. Our favourite old 'Jerusalem cross', *Lychnis chalcedonica,* qualifies too, for it is as intrepid as the crusaders who are said to have named it.

If all these will thrive where the soil is shaded for part of the day, there is an equal choice for the really sunny patches. Red-hot pokers and *Coreopsis verticillata,* never without its golden stars all summer; eryngiums, echinops and eremurus; sedums, achilleas, artemisias and the new brightly coloured forms of heuchera; all will go on from year to year, asking for nothing more than an occasional tidy up.

But there is more still to making borders than gaining a widening circle of plant acquaintances and setting them in the garden as you find them. They must be paired and blended to bring out the best in each other.

One could not deny oneself this thrill of allowing rein to the acquisitiveness that is in all gardeners. But it is better to give the latest acquisition a pot, and put it in the 'plant bank' — plunged in a bed of ash — perhaps even to propagate from it until it can be made to merge rather than intrude.

Otherwise the garden is liable to become like one of those country museums, where fossils and ostrich eggs, bits of meteorite and stuffed birds, are all jumbled up among faded labels, instead of resembling the Victoria and Albert Museum or the Louvre, where as you enter the heart leaps at the sense of harmony derived from the inspired arrangement.

When we set about planting our garden we could hardly have avoided having intimations of this. But that acquisitiveness gradually led us into the folly of gathering as large a collection of shrubs as possible, collecting rather than selecting. We thought it would be enough to contrast them in outline, on the principle that they are longer out of it than in flower. But the result was still something of a rag-bag.

Experience has taught me to accept that it is better to restrict the number of species and plant several of one kind rather than one of each of many that are different. You see this principle in practice in quite small gardens on the Continent. As a result they look as though they had been designed, instead of being a fumbling effort to reproduce the colourful sweet disorder of a cottage garden, an ideal unattainable and rarely appropriate.

Planting that is going to prove satisfying every year also entails matching up plants in the way that one does furnishings in the home. It involves putting together plants that flower simultaneously — playing 'happy families' with them, if you like. Indeed I regard match-making with plants as one of the most important aspects of garden-making. Nothing one can put in is not either enriched or torn apart, encouraged or deflated, by its partnering plants. In the most successful gardens, though one may not be aware of just why from a glance, it is always through their relationships with one another that plants make their strongest effects.

Gild the lily, then, adorn the rose? Yes! Both will shine all the brighter in sympathetic, convivial society. The lily made shy by its lankiness needs some rotund company, the rubicund rose something spire-like and graceful nearby.

To take an example of a plant found in many gardens, the winter-flowering daphne has a captivating scent when you are close to it, but the flowers hardly show up from a distance and lose their sweetness on the chilly air if you can enjoy them only from the windows. Surround it with a carpet, though, of the white *Erica carnea* Springwood and at once its stems of rosy mauve are thrown into relief. Or notice how dull red winter heathers can look by themselves against their peaty soil, when their colour could be made to glow by setting some white or pale pink varieties just behind them. Similarly, the beautiful red Lenten roses can look lost from a distance without a fair sprinkling of the white ones among them.

No carpet of even turf or neatly forked ground can compare with a sheet of grape hyacinths spread beneath flowering cherries. Their pale blossom seems even more delectable as a result of the richness of the blue below. Grape hyacinths, indeed, are specially valuable bulbs for partnering the spring trees and shrubs that flower in pale colourings, especially as they multiply perhaps more generously than any other kind. Scillas might come a close second, sowing their own seed carelessly but never where it could be unwanted.

By itself, the busy little *Magnolia stellata* can look ragged and inconsequent, a waif of a shrub. But give it a ground cover of the blue *Anemone appenina,* which flowers simultaneously, and it no longer has to stand or fall on its individual merit but becomes a component of a garden vignette.

To flatter and promote the proud golden forsythia, in danger of losing caste by being so common, one can plant a groundwork of, say, the red lungwort, *Pulmonaria rubra,* which spreads with such willingness. The upright-growing habit of the forsythia alternatively lends itself for complementing with a companion planting of the spreading japonica, in its variety of red tones. The same contrast of both colouring and shape might be achieved by setting the shrubby potentillas with lemon-coloured flowers among the more gaunt ruby or blue-flowered hibiscus.

To partner camellias nothing less stylish than a foreground of alpine auriculas will do, their dull pewter leaves making those of the camellias seem all the glossier, and once lilacs have flowered they are better seen no more for the year — unless the very dullness of their foliage is used as a background for, say, the handsomely carved leaves of peonies, which the lilacs accompany in flower.

We find all the silver-leaved plants congenial companions for the shrub roses, and can afford to be generous with them in our plantings as they are all so easy to raise from cuttings. The common kitchen sage is used along with lavenders of all the varieties we can find and that easy-going *Senecio laxifolius,* which you can hack back mercilessly in spring always sure that it will quickly renew itself. All root well enough from shoots pulled off and simply pushed into the ground.

The close planting of the silvery blue Atlas cedars with red-leaved maples at the Westonbirt Arboretum is well known, and on a miniature scale which we could all adapt, one might achieve a similar effect by setting the blue-grey leaves of the common rue against the burnished copper of a dwarf cryptomeria, to the benefit of both.

In the role of plant marriage broker I find myself always looking for new partners to join, and whenever I acquire a fresh plant try to place it in company in which it will flourish in all respects. Sometimes, though a pure love-match occurs, like the yellow Montpelier broom that has sprung up beside our plant of ruby Californian gooseberry and the crimson Tuscany roses that have suckered all round a mock orange, and flower together.

Another kind of partnership, which cannot be ignored in the smallest garden — where, in fact, it is of the greatest significance — is using trees and shrubs as host plants for climbers, as I have mentioned in the section on clematis, some of which are the most decorous of plant guests. Doesn't the tree or bush suffer, you may ask? Not unless you plant it with twiners like honeysuckle or wisteria, which can strangle the branches. Plants which simply hang on are safer, and foremost among these, for trees, are roses.

When this is practised you usually see the climbers planted on the perimeter of the tree's branches, being led into the head on poles. This is undoubtedly the best method when you are garnishing a mature tree. When you are dealing with a mere stripling it is sufficient to plant the climber in a box of soil about half the size of an orange-box, and set this in the ground close to the trunk on the side that gets the most rain. By the time the wood of the box has disintegrated the rose will be able to fend for itself. Or if you are planting from scratch, both climber and tree can go in the same hole.

The favourite rose among the *cognoscenti* for growing in this way is the Kiftsgate form of *Rosa filipes,* an incredibly exuberant rose, climbing to the heights of tall trees and flinging out showers of heavily scented white flowers like an exploding firework. I am tempted to recommend the vigorous Albertine for tree planting, but the pruning it needs can be so difficult that the choice should really fall on varieties that need none. So it must be the new race of perpetual-flowering climbers. In small gardens these can be happily planted to garland the stems of standard trees of flowering cherries, crabs and laburnums to wring a second and much more prolonged season of flowers from them.

Since the roses don't grow much above eight feet they are not likely to become difficult to manage. Their other great virtue is that, extending slowly and making plenty of short side branches, they flower from top to toe — or almost! Each year the rose catalogues, contain more of them, and growing them on trees enables one to admit an increasing collection to the garden.

Golden Showers, and the scarlet Danse du Feu and Coral Dawn are already well known. Less familiar is the pink-scented Aloha. Both Köln am Rhein and Ritter von Barmstede are a deeper shade, while you get varying tones of red in Sweet Sultan, Wilhelm Hansmann, Hamburger Phoenix and Parkdirektor Riggers. Meg stands alone, being an apricot shade.

The idea of using quite small shrubs as hosts of the more slender-growing clematis came to me on one occasion when I was pulling out bindweed trying to adorn our bush of *Viburnum tomentosum mariesii*. This, of course, makes its branches in horizontal tiers, the flowers perching on top of them in May. Until its leaves take on their *vin rosé* tints in autumn there is nothing to admire about it but its shape all the summer. But if the bindweed would clamber over it, why not a clematis?

The variety I chose for this role is Abundance, one of the viticella group. Choice fell on this because of its rather slight bearing and suitable 'wilding' look. Each small purple flower will face upright on the flat top of the viburnum bush, but this is not smothered, for this clematis is one that has to be cut back hard every February.

Another flat-growing bush I have used in the same way is the favourite *Cotoneaster horizontalis,* often planted to flank a flight of steps. While undoubtedly it is handsome both when in flower in May and thronged with bees, and again in autumn when the crimson of the leaves matches the red berries, in summer only its form distinguishes it. The gap can be filled in by contriving a summer liaison with the clematis.

A different type of plant relationship, in which another kind takes up the relay as one ceases, can be contrived in what I have called — rather extravagantly, I fear — 'garden transformation scenes' as though the garden were a stage. This unwieldy term connotes a series of successional effects, different with each act, all produced on the same patch of soil. I can perhaps best explain it by recounting how one was planted in our garden.

One Sunday morning I found myself clearing a patch of ground under some trees, trying to get something useful done while sheltering from the inevitable weekend rain. Hardy cyclamen like the shade, I reflected, and the frost protection offered to camellias by an overhanging canopy of branches is proved. So some tubers of *Cyclamen neapolitanum* I had on hand were planted close to some Japanese azaleas on the site already. The cyclamen would give an autumn effect lasting a couple of months. Gradually they would seed and multiply. Between them and here and there over the whole area I tucked in a couple of hundred snowdrop bulbs for February flowering. Just as these were going over the camellias, which I put behind the azaleas, would begin to flower, and as these finished their season the azaleas would take over in May.

Now would come a pause, but not for long. By early August lacecap hydrangeas could be showing colour. These I alternated with the camellias and they would go on well into the autumn, when it would be cyclamen time again. Even then their day would not be done, for in the autumn one can snip off some of the hydrangea flower sprays and put them in a vase without water. Here the elegance they take on in the fullness of their season becomes petrified, as it were, and one can have a reminder of summer all through the winter.

Standing back to survey all this and with the imagination leaping across several seasons, I decided some sort of ground cover was needed. A collection of coloured primroses due for dividing offered just the touch to add. Now they accompany the snowdrops in flower. The early summer hiatus worried me, though. Yes, of course, lilies! Squander on them! Drop them in between the camellias and the hydrangeas and the azaleas lavishly! Cover everything with a layer of bonemeal to release its goodness slowly, and then another of old leaves to keep in the moisture and add still more food!

This is the kind of planning scheme I really prefer most of all. I aim at a series of distinct effects each made with the same kind of plant, one succeeding another as the year unfolds.

Here is another example of what I mean. The site was a crescent-like border at the far end of a strip of lawn. At the back we put an arc of pyracantha to give white flowers in May, scarlet berries much of the winter. In front was placed an arc of the white *Hydrangea paniculata grandiflora* which in turn makes a background for a sweep of blue veronica Autumn Glory alternated in clumps with the spiky cream *Sisyrinchium striatum,* all of which are out together in summer. The veronica, though, begins in June, and the hydrangea goes on well into the autumn.

Before these plants have anything to show for themselves we

get a drift of white daffodils, for which the evergreen foliage of the pyracantha makes an increasingly flattering background. The daffodils are followed by the blue of the common bugle, which covers the ground with its evergreen foliage and flowers until the veronica is beginning.

Another idea for a plant grouping that would yield three distinct bursts of flower from one patch of ground in the sun while becoming a self-maintaining area uses only two plants.

Due to their character and preferences, brooms will co-exist peacefully with heathers, which can be planted effectively as a groundwork for them. The stems of the broom, set with only very small leaves are too sparse to cast any shade the heathers might dislike.

For the first four months of the year the winter-flowering heathers, varieties of *Erica carnea,* in white, pink and several shades of red, could take the stage. Then would come the brooms in early summer. It would not be long before it would be the turn of more heathers to take over, this time patches of *Erica tetralix* and *Calluna vulgaris* in their many colour forms, having been planted alternately with the carneas.

Though the others have no such inhibitions, the last two plants are admittedly intolerant of lime in the soil, and on chalky ground their place could be taken by, say, the blue *Ceratostigma plumbaginoides,* or *Polygonum affine,* pink, both turning their leaves russet in the autumn while waiting for the winter heathers to appear again.

You might think that all this sort of thing involves spending lavishly to plant on the scale needed to bring off an effect — well, no maxim has brought me more reward or comfort in my gardening than the Wilde-like epigram that 'the only extravagances you regret are those you don't make.' It is a watchword to engrave on your heart with masochistic glee, to steady you when studying the plant catalogues.

As a gardening spendthrift — you can justify the most imprudent squandering to yourself if you don't smoke! — I find I always have on hand a fair selection of plants in pots plunged in my bed of ashes. They are bought when the fancy takes me and out of the shameless acquisitiveness gardeners develop. They now go into the plant bank I keep, until places can be found for them or I get some inspiration. They sit waiting side by side in their pots together with the surplus of common plants such as London Pride.

Match-making also involves moving plants around. Some plants move easily and are often better for it. They include all the peat lovers and hydrangeas. Some will not suffer it at all, though. Notable among these are the big pea family, and brooms in particular. Others outside the two categories can often be moved up to the age of, say, ten, given some care.

The method I have used successfully — usually in early spring — is to cut round the plant a couple of feet from the stem on a day when the soil is wet enough to hold together, work underneath the root mass with the spade, then insert a large shovel, on which I find I can drag it to its new and more favourable position. The time-honoured method is to wrap sacking round the roots to prevent soil falling away. Polythene is better, though, and more readily to hand.

Of course, it takes seasons of observations, or constantly making changes, to achieve plant relationships of the kind I have attempted to outline and sometimes one is inclined to think with Housman that '... to look at things in bloom fifty springs are little room ...' But the skill and taste of the flower showman can help, and we can poach from other gardens.

The most important equipment to summon to one's aid is a critical eye, exercised all through the year, and a notebook and pencil with which to record projected changes. With these one can gradually weave order from the disarrayed aftermath of all the seductions of the nurseryman's catalogue, and one can snatch at the chance of pairing off a couple whenever you notice them apart, solitary and lonely. Then you can send them off beaming from your horticultural marriage bureau.

Bulbs

'Instant gardening': daffodils in parkland: planting: 10,000
varieties: deportment: tulips: interplanting for prolonged effect:
miniature bulbs: planting snowdrops: the dog's-tooth violet and
the trout lily: bluebells: autumn bulbs: the source of saffron:
lilies: indoor bulbs: using the greenhouse

No greater possibilities exist of gardening successfully and
producing the full results quickly at the cost of little
trouble than by exploiting bulbs. They offer the best means of
'instant gardening'. They rarely take more than six months from
planting to flowering, often less, and the only point you really
need to know about growing them is to give them a soil covering
that is roughly twice their own depth. But there are considerations
involved.

The ideal of a spring garden bright with daffodils nonchalantly
rising from green turf is one of those gardening prepossessions
that need questioning when planting bulbs at that moment in the
gardening year when the shadow of winter falls across the dregs

of summer and when there is a modulation to the minor key all around. No one would try to go better than nature in this and deny that grassland is the happiest setting for drifts of daffodils; but how far is what is known as naturalising practicable in the owner-maintained garden? It is necessary to discuss this at some length because where the bulbs are planted is something of paramount importance; or so I have found.

If you have rolling acres as your canvas, or a mature orchard, you can plant lavishly in grass without having to meet the problems that often follow flowering in a small area. When the grassland is lawn of sorts, second thoughts may save a lot of trouble. Starting with a bit of field from which to make our present garden, I thought that planting daffodils Wordsworth-like in rough grass was the thing. Only by the hard way did I learn that before it was time to cut them down in early summer the natural herbage would have grown up round them in an indescribable mess, scattering weed seeds everywhere.

For as everyone knows, unless you leave the daffodil foliage until it has almost withered before cutting it, the bulbs will deteriorate and perhaps not flower again. By this time it may be late June and, especially in a damp season, the growth round them will have become as tall as the flower stems were and you will have to scythe it, by hand or motor, then cart away great barrow-loads of hay to the compost heap.

Beneath will be white patches that will soon turn brown but not green again for a couple of months. In the meantime coarse grasses will have a chance to prosper. The exception, of course, is where the land is sandy and only fine grasses flourish naturally.

For practical reasons, then, but also on grounds of economising in space and wringing several shows of flowers from the same area, I favour planting in beds, between shrubs and permanent plantings of herbaceous plants, where their dying foliage will be masked by the spread of the foliage of the summer flowers. Here, though, the ground would have to be mulched every year, perhaps with old leaves rather than forked, with weeding done only by hand or very lightly with the hoe.

So resilient are daffodil bulbs, so thrifty is their way of storing their own nourishment and making their flowers and leaves in embryo a season in advance, that you can hardly fail with them. Certain essential points should not go by default, however. For instance, the base of the bulb must lie squarely on the soil, not stand suspended in a hole made not quite big enough. This can be as much a cause of failure as delaying planting till late autumn.

The 'blindness' often complained of in established daffodil plantations can also be insured against when laying them down. So often, just when the bulbs are gathering resources in late spring for another season's flowering, before taking their summer rest, we get a dry spell. Their industry is hampered and they are unable to garner enough to complete their development, and the result is a flowerless season next year.

This means that in making a daffodil plantation that is to be a permanent one, compost or hop manure, or at least coarse peat (not fresh farmyard or stable manure) should be added to the soil. Just as it does on any vegetable plot or rose bed, it will help to provide the bulbs with a moisture reservoir on which they can draw as they need to, while by the texture it induces it will ensure that the roots will not lie in soggy ground. That is something the bulbs loathe. The need of daffodils for moisture in some degree, however, is one good reason for planting the bulbs in light shade. Here the flowers are also likely to last in bloom longer than in full sun.

In a place from which the sun is veiled but where the shade is not deep, their ripening off at the end of the spring, another essential factor, is still possible. This can be aided by the extra nourishment given the bulbs. While they certainly respond to bonemeal being added to the soil at planting time in the conventional way and to more added annually, their performance in successive seasons is also improved by putting round them some of the bonfire ash commonly allocated to the roses and fruit trees.

Another factor causing blindness can be overcome by a little insecticidal treatment in spring. As the soil shrinks away from the stems in dry spells the winging narcissus fly spots the fissure and sees it as a safe crèche for her young. Down into it she goes, lays her eggs and her life's work is done. Soon the grubs that will continue the race will begin to feed on the bulbs, choosing the hearts and destroying the embryos of next year's flowers.

All this can be thwarted by dusting D.D.T. round them at the same time as you snap off the spent flowers to spare the plants the strain of seeding, a practice which is essential in ensuring a good flowering in the following year.

When it comes to weaving one's way through the multitude of varieties of daffodils, practical considerations disappear. One is left in the shadowy, uncertain realm of taste. More than 10,000 different varieties have their names lying honourably inscribed in the international register which those who have the time for such dedicated research keep. If you saw the flowers all together you might reasonably decide that there was so little to choose between a great many of them that it was hardly worth the bother of thinking up the names. In fact, more, many more, are added to the roll every year.

Why? Because daffodil breeding is a pursuit in the hands of fanciers who have their ideal of perfection. From most of us who garden all the crossing and selecting and showing that goes on is remote. Yet it is to this activity that we owe the immense range of varieties in which the distinctions are readily and fortunately apparent, apart from the maintenance of the daffodil's resilience.

From a first visit to the show devoted exclusively to daffodils held every spring in London you might come away bewildered, but as your acquaintance with daffodils grows you would find that two varieties which before seemed identical are distinguished by something I can only describe as 'poise'. This is the quality that breeders are getting in their new creations, I believe. But you have to pay more for it.

Is it worth it? The smaller your garden, I would say, the more important it is to restrict your choice to plants with the most pronounced personality. Here you get on close terms with them and look more searchingly into them than you would in a park. Some reveal all at a glance. Others, usually costing more, have qualities revealed only by deepening acquaintance.

Now I would not decry the favourite Fortune and King Alfred, Actaea and Golden Harvest with which we have grown up, but I am sure that if I were planting a small garden and could grow only a handful I should go partly by price, spring the extra few shillings and invest in, say, the lemon-yellow Peking, tangerine-and-gold Krakatoa, orange-and-white Kilworth and the faultless Ice Follies, curiously described in one list as 'serene'. Cost, I fear, is a rough index of that elegant deportment that daffodil fanciers so much applaud. To my idea the softer colourings among them belong to informal schemes, the vivid, orange-cupped varieties to more stylised sites.

You will see from this, by the way, that I do not distinguish between daffodils and narcissi. They are one and the same, but grouped in divisions in catalogues according to the length of the trumpet or cup. And who, if the two terms are to be used, would care to say, with this arbitrary distinction in mind, when a narcissus becomes a daffodil?

In bulb catalogues you frequently see 'good for naturalising' in the bewilderingly enthusiastic descriptions of the varieties. I have never yet planted a daffodil that has proved otherwise. Invariably they seem to flourish and multiply naturally.

Usually I have bought them in dozens and planted all twelve in one patch together, adding to the collection every year, the idea being to get the maximum variety over the longest possible season, while avoiding a spotty effect. Occasionally I buy a hundred of one sort for a big woodland bed, but what I will have none of in the place is the mixed lot. I like to see a bold drift all out together, one patch taking over as another ceases.

Sometimes, however, I am told by gardeners that they don't want those 'blown-up' big flowers but something nearer to the wild daffodil. Can one buy them? One season we planted a hundred bulbs of the little Tenby daffodil, found in the lists as *Narcissus obvallaris*. We were pleased to find them out before all the others and standing there bravely upright when other varieties were beaten down by rain and wind for the slugs to nibble.

Another alternative is the group known as the cyclamineus hybrids now being distributed fairly widely. A good way removed from their parent, which stars the hillsides in Spain and Portugal in early spring and which is seen on rock gardens very correctly labelled as *Narcissus cyclamineus,* they grow about a foot tall but still keep something of that engaging way of turning back their perianth segments like puppy's ears.

Their merit is that they increase specially freely, start flowering early and go on for nearly two months if planted in light shade. February Gold, March Sunshine, Peeping Tom and Wanda are the names of the most easily-obtained varieties.

Most of the little daffodil species, I find, however, need a sunny spot and well-drained soil, and perhaps they are never better grown or more enjoyed than in raised troughs where, nearer to eye level, their exquisite charms are revealed.

This also goes for the jonquils which have now made a return to favour with gardeners and which are small enough to please the more fastidious of them. The blooms show a scent strong enough to overpower that hoary canard that 'flowers don't smell like they once did'.

For the artist in the gardener, no flower that blooms in the spring offers a richer palette than the tulip. Every colour you can expect of a flower, even black and blue and green, is to be found among them, offering scope for colour scheming that could go on without repetition for a whole gardening lifetime.

Unlike most plants grown for the colour effects they make in garden décor, they give their full bounty in a few months. You visualise your picture, plant in autumn and come what may it will be fully realised in the following spring. For tulips do indeed 'bloom as they are told', in Britain as well as anywhere else where Rupert Brooke may have observed them. They are almost like those Japanese toys that you drop into a glass of water and watch expand into paper flowers before your eyes.

Only the brevity of their spell of glory, that magic three weeks from bud burst to petal fall, tells against them. Yet this can be overcome by the practice of interplanting. The tulip's finest hour lasts from early April till the end of May, the different types following in succession. By mixing them in the patch the whole period can be covered.

One might vary the colour schemes during this time, a different one rising as the former fades — rather like the colour patterns of the Versailles parterres being changed by an army of gardeners while the court was indoors for lunch. Thus you will see that I favour planting these in rather formal beds of their own, though I also grow them between roses.

If garden budgeting will allow only one display, I would plump for the single early type. Not only do the plants remain stocky, but they are over in good time for an early start for the summer-flowering plants that will succeed them in the formal flower beds.

I prefer the simplicity of the singles myself to the multi-petalled complexity of the doubles. But one must own that the latter, some looking like peonies before their time, do have the longer season in flower.

In an interplanted scheme the Triumph tulips would form the next relay after the earlies, continuing until it was the turn of the tall Darwins, which surpass all others in their colouring.

If you prefer flowers of individual character, the bulb catalogues contain many varieties that might be plucked from a
Dutch old master's still-life. The varieties of which a single bloom
can inspire a whole floral decoration are collectively called
'broken' tulips, some appropriately subdivided as 'Rembrandts'.
Their flowers feathered with contrasting colourings, they are
afflicted by disease that only enhances them.

In character the 'parrots' are very close. Shaggy and fringed,
they have a romantic opulence, fit not for the garden but for
indoor decoration. In contrast the lily-flowered tulips appear cool
and refreshing in their slim elegance, and more suited to the
sparse décor of a modern house. But all three types are now being
challenged in the flower arranger's esteem by the rise of the
descendants of the green tulip, *Tulipa viridiflora*. The first was
called Artist, in which terra cotta was mingled with the green,
and this has been followed by a yellow and green in Cherie, and
carmine and green in Pimpernel, the colours always subtly
interwoven.

The tulip as we know it is part of a noble line that extends back
over four centuries. Inevitably, the breeders had reached a point
when they turned again to the wild species to start afresh. The
result is new races still.

Everyone who gardens now knows that vivid scarlet tulip
named both as Red Emperor and Mme. Lefebre. So dazzling
is it, that it is hard to think that anything so artificial-looking
could grow wild, even in the remoteness of Bokhara. Personally, I find the only position where I can make it merge is in a
tub.

I have rather similar reservations about the stumpy Kaufmanni-
anas, called the Water Lily tulips, which fling back their petals to
display all their scarlet, yellow, carmine or crimson colouring,
often bronze or black at the base.

A further attribute has been added to the tulip family in the
maroon or brownish markings on the leaves of the greigii
hybrids. Growing less than a foot tall, both might well be enjoyed
in a window-box, where the plants have to withstand the closest
scrutiny.

But in our concern with making striking garden effects we
must not appear to treat those loosely lumped together in lists as
'miniature bulbs' with any suggestion of disdain. Indeed, these

should really get first attention. It is hard to turn the page before summer has run its full course, but these tiny bulbs demand that we should rise from our well-rounded swing hammocks and plant them while the ground is still warm.

Unless they are planted before September is out they cannot be relied on to show how bravely they can defy the declining days of winter and paint the first touches of spring on the vacant garden canvas.

They have the winning charm of all tiny things. One may hesitate to pay sixpence or more for a bulb little bigger than a pea, but few of the miniature bulbs remain single. Most of them are eager colonisers, multiplying themselves prolifically. Crocuses in February coming up in sheets in every unlikely crevice where a seed can fall, even on the dormant crowns of herbaceous plants, are nothing but welcome.

Horticultural literature is apt to recommend you to 'plant them in the alpine garden', as though everyone has one, or ought to have. Undoubtedly, if you raise them somewhere, such as in an old sink abandoned to miniature plants, or on the top of a bank of soil, you get the best from them. Here you can admire the depth of their colour, the wonder of their markings, perhaps sniff their fugitive scent, and watch the crocuses turn back their segments in delight as the pale winter sun strikes them to reveal vivid orange parts within.

Personally, I am content to enjoy them in a less intimate way and plant them in the foreground of shrubs where they can spread as generously as they like. Of course, no hoeing or forking must threaten them, but then you must never use a tool near plantings of miniature bulbs for fear of mistaking the little seedlings by which they spread for blades of grass. Most of them, of course, need sun to ripen their bulbs for another year, for do they not belong to the Latin countries and to those farther east?

The most willing crocus you can plant to people your garden in February is *Crocus tomasinianus,* whose slender lavender flowers have the silvery sheen of a moth's wings. In some gardens of long establishment you see it appearing wherever there is an inch of soil. Grateful for its fertile increase, I also like to have a patch of its deeper-coloured form, Whitwell Purple.

These flowers are quickly followed by the mauve *Crocus sieberi* and soon it is the turn of the *Crocus chrysanthus* varieties.

The bulb catalogues now list many of these, until recently found only in the gardens of those who regard themselves as connoisseurs. Now you can get blue, ivory, bronze and mauve varieties freely. Often they have contrasting 'featherings' on them. All are characterised by a slender outline. In their well-bred elegance they make the bold Dutch crocuses which follow them look a bit brash.

The easiest of these to obtain are Snow Bunting, whose cream flowers are lightly touched with purple: E. P. Bowles, deep yellow, marked with still deeper colours: and Zwanenburg, in which the orange is overlaid with a purplish tone. Look farther and you will find Cream Beauty, Moonlight, Blue Bird, and the irresistible Lady Killer, deep blue edged with white.

I cannot think why *Chionodoxa luciliae* should bear the common name Glory of the Snow. In our part we should be vexed if we got snow as late as when this clear blue-eyed treasure is about, especially as it is one of the keenest self-seeders. In fact, it rivals the prolific *Scilla sibirica,* which, far from home, encroaches almost irresponsibly.

Its kinsman, *Puschkinia libanotica,* deserves the closest scrutiny. The ice-blue flowers are intriguingly striped. Equally, the chequered *Fritillaria meleagris* is a flower of individual fascination, each flower marked with chocolate overlying maroon.

The minute irises, in my experience, will have nothing but the warmest places in light soil. Here, if no slugs get them, *Iris histrioides* will flower in a mild spell in January, and *Iris reticulata* with a little red in the blue, follows in February.

It is easy to cut down in a hasty moment the foliage of triteleia, correctly, but less familarly known as ipheion, for it looks much like coarse grass. This, if left to thrive, will give you carpets of blue stars.

All these treasures are not the exclusive province of garden owners. Flat-dwellers can grow them successfully in pots left in window-boxes for the winter and transferred to the indoor window-sill when the buds show colour.

Those whose gardens get a fair degree of shade need not eschew 'miniatures'. If you plant snowdrops, for instance, in a sunny place you are likely to find their seedlings appear only in some spot where they can get a little shade, as though to let you know what their real inclinations are.

I know few more tedious gardening tasks than planting snow-drops, but in the following February one is mightily satisfied at having spent so much time putting in, one by one, these tiny bulbs between other shade-loving plants whose day comes later.

In our bit of woodland we are content with the common wild snowdrop, *Galanthus nivalis*. If we had a little town plot or a trough garden, where each plant must suffer individual inspection, we would be more selective and plant some of the forms which are of such quality as to deserve pet names.

Once we planted a batch of winter aconites in an open place with the idea of seeing them dappling the turf with flecks of gold from the windows on an otherwise dreary day. They announced their dislike of such exposure by never flowering. Now we put them under trees, where even though the soil may be rather dry, they express their content by multiplying.

We ourselves are quite happy that they are the common kind, *Eranthis hyemalis*. The Grecian species. *Eranthis cilicica,* we have not been able to please, but the hybrid between the two, *Eranthis tubergenii,* spreads vegetatively, and demonstrates that it can out-shine both by remaining in flower longer, due to being a mule, condemned to work hard at its flowering but never seed.

Borrowing zoological terminology for a different reason, the dog's-tooth violet similarly prefers the shade. You would hardly expect to find a plant in the sun whose spotted leaves have earned it the other common name of 'trout lily'. I have not had a chance of verifying how apt is another one still — 'adder's tongue' — nor would one particularly wish to. In outline, the nodding flowers have a touch about them of an oriental roof in the way the segments curve and roll back just a little. The easiest species to buy is *Erythronium dens-canis,* so named on account of the resem-blance of the corms to a dog's fangs.

What is particularly curious about these plants is that there is also a whole group which grow wild along the Pacific coast of America yet are perfectly hardy here. Whereas the European *dens-canis* has flowers varying from the colour of a plum through pinks down to white, the Californian *tuolumnense* is a gleaming yellow and, as you would expect, is twice as big all round. The rosy tinted *revolutum* also has big flowers, dangling them from shorter stems without looking squat. Each offers foliage for a spell in spring which one can admire for itself.

[64]

The Spanish bluebell similarly adapts itself to our damp, chilly climate. After long being known as *Scilla campanulata,* under which it remains in catalogues, it has now been endowed with the elegant name of *Endymion hispanica.* It is like a large edition of our own bluebell. Having enough of the latter growing wild, I find the pink and white forms of the Spaniard well worth adding to shady parts of the garden, where it seems grateful for relief from the sun it presumably knew at home.

It is equally surprising to find that both the Greek and Italian anemones like to take refuge in a shady copse here. *Anemone appenina* is a low growing plant with stars of sky-blue and fern-like leaves. The flowers of *Anemone blanda* are a little bigger and range through many shades of pink and blue from deep mauve to white.

But these must not be allowed to obscure the charms of our own wild anemone. A form we grow in company with the ordinary white *Anemone nemorosa,* called *allenii,* has lilac flowers. Like all these other bulbous plants, it is a gracefully delivered reproach to those who would chop down trees where new gardens are being made.

Spring is not the only time when bulb flowers, nor autumn the one stage in the gardener's year when they are planted.

Consider the strange behaviour of the belladonna lily. When all other late flowers are already getting themselves up to take part in the autumn pageant, this plant, certainly a member of the cast, is nowhere to be seen. Lying where you might expect it to be is a heap of withered, cast-off foliage.

At least this means that it is still around somewhere, and one morning soon you will see a stem rising naked from the ground with reassuring haste. For *Amaryllis belladonna* does things in her own time and way.

When her clusters of pink trumpets are over in autumn, she at once produces her leaves. These remain all the winter and die down in late summer, a little before the exceedingly handsome flowers appear. Now this means that the only possible planting time is the latter part of the summer.

You cannot expect flowers in a week or two, nor even perhaps next season. But in time, if you plant the bulbs in the lee of a south- or west-facing wall your rewards will come abundantly, especially if you modify time-honoured advice to plant six inches deep and instead divide this by half. Then the bulbs will get the ripening they need to flower well. But you will also have to anchor some polythene over them during the worst of the winter as frost protection.

The ways of another group of bulbous plants, the autumn-flowering crocuses, planted also in late summer, are equally curious.

The harsh words said about the grotesque untimeliness of chrysanthemums in March and the daffodils thrust upon us in November are withheld from these engaging crocuses. It is natural for them to bloom in autumn, and in the right setting they are neither unwelcome nor wear an out-of-season look.

Once you have seen them on a damp early autumn morning, stretching out in a dense colony across some Swiss meadow with the Alps beyond, your heart is lost to them by their winning surprise. Had you passed that way a couple of days before, you might not have suspected their existence. They will have appeared there like mushrooms in the night.

It is the same in the garden. You plant the bulbs in August and think no more of them until one morning the ground there is speckled with pale lilac buds well above the surface.

If you are one of those people who look for quick returns from everything you plant, you would not have long to wait in this case. They are just about the speediest bulbs I know in showing what they can do. Hardly a month after they are planted they are in flower.

In character they resemble the slender crocus species that flower before the winter is over. They are as anxious to reproduce themselves and provide you with more, too, spreading both by seed and by making new little corms. In fact, once they are established in the garden you are unlikely ever to eliminate them, unless you have an unusually hungry strain of mice about.

The place to plant them — if you have no rock garden, or even rockery, that could do with enlivening in autumn — is again in the forefront of shrub borders, even though the ground may be covered with creeping plants. Provided the mat is not so thick that the corms do not get ripened, the buds will pierce this.

The ground-covering foliage will then provide a groundwork for the crocuses, whose leaves are not produced until the spring. Some of the less rampant dwarf campanulas would be just the right over-planting for them, as these would not come into flower until the crocuses' foliage had died away.

First of the season to flower is *Crocus zonatus,* with flowers of pinkish lavender marked with bands of bright orange at the throat, from which the specific name derives. The other most easily obtained one is *Crocus speciosus,* which differs in being quite a strong blue for a crocus, lightly touched with pink. Several named forms, in which the blue tone is more pronounced, are offered. When you look closely at the flowers you find all have a characteristic prominent veining.

Like *Crocus zonatus,* all are some of the cheapest bulbs to buy, which makes it possible to plant in the prodigal fashion in which they are most effective in the garden.

The source of saffron, *Crocus sativus,* belongs to this group, but it is inclined to be a disappointing plant in our climate, flowering only fitfully. Indeed it gives support to those who say our summers are getting worse all the time. For apparently there was a flourishing saffron-growing industry in Essex a couple of hundred years ago. What it needs to prod it into producing its flowers, in which the saffron-bearing stigmata are so showy, is the warmest spot the garden can offer and frequent lifting and division. This apparently makes the corms think they had better get on with the business of reproducing their kind in case they expire themselves.

Now, confusing though it can be, all these must be distinguished from the meadow saffrons, or colchicums. Though similar when in flower, these are not crocuses at all but lilies, botanically. They produce true bulbs the size of pears which steadily fatten, not like crocuses that make corms, which are swollen stem bases and perish after handing over to successors.

These are planted in late summer too, but less haphazardly than the true crocuses, for their foliage is coarse and even unsightly from spring until early July, lacking the freshness of the bold lilac or white flowers that mock the sobriety of the autumn days.

In their time of flowering, lilies are different again, but these you have to plant whenever you can get the bulbs in autumn or late winter. Now an aura hangs about lilies, of *hauteur,* of Chelsea Show-wonder, of pre-Raphaelite immaculateness, and of great horticultural difficulty. The bulbs are expensive to buy and they are rarely seen growing on any scale anywhere but in the gardens of expensive people.

The prices are part of the trouble. They cause demand to be slack; the bulbs hang about in the shops while the roots and the outer scales shrivel and toughen, imperilling their future in the ground. When they are bought and planted by someone — feeling a bit venturesome I dare say, at the idea of paying five bob for a single bulb — there is no more than a chance that any more will be seen of them.

Thus the 'not-for-me' reputation attaches to the family as a whole — or almost, since one must always except the irrepressible *Lilium regale,* which would settle down in a slum.

So you must start with sound bulbs stored away from the drying air by the supplier. But even then I fear you must treat them as deferentially as you might your exacting managing director. Indeed, in their fads, lilies have a close affinity to clematis.

They will have their moisture at the roots but also free drainage of any surplus to what they want. While they like to have their heads in the sun, it must not be allowed to shine hot upon the soil where their roots lie. You see, then, you have to behave towards them like a fluttering companion arranging the rugs round a spoilt millionairess.

When you get them to thrive and they flower, you feel like a millionaire yourself. Every year when our clumps of *Lilium henryi* flower in increasing abundance, I feel like a self-made Midas. Looking at them standing there in great sheaves five feet tall and swinging bells of finely wrought gold with self-conscious nonchalance, one is well satisfied with the compound gains of ten years.

They are growing in a sort of copse — a 'shaw' my neighbour calls it with countryman's erudition. And I suppose this offers just the situation that suits them — you might say down to the ground. The roots of the trees and the shrubs that we have added drain it. The fall of the leaf over centuries has made the soil nourishing, spongy in texture and of moisture-retaining capacity.

As companions for shrubs in gardens where the soil lacks lime lilies are very well suited — and so is their owner then. The lilies benefit from the shade cast and the draining effects, while they flower in July and August, when most shrubs are over and when areas devoted to them have become dull.

But lily-growing is not the exclusive province of people with mature plantations of shrubs. It is worth planting them in such borders still in their early stages and as ingredients of beds of hardy herbaceous plants. The moist soil they like can be arranged by mulching the ground with peat or, better still, leaf mould.

Nor need lily growing be denied those who garden in paved courtyards. Lilies make highly satisfactory tub and pot plants. In fact, to my taste, the massive, richly-scented *Lilium auratum* only looks right grown in this 'artificial' way. It hardly accords with informal schemes.

The containers are half-filled with peaty soil after being well crocked for good drainage, and the bulbs are set on this layer and only just covered at this stage. The space at the top is left for adding more soil as the stems extend. Most lilies root from the stems as well as from the base of the bulbs, and this is to be encouraged.

To this end, with the exception of *Lilium candidum* and *Lilium martagon* which like to be close to the surface, the general run of lilies on sale now from bulb dealers need a soil covering of five to six inches in the garden.

Most of these lilies offered in garden shops today are hybrids bred on the western seaboard of the United States. This does not mean that they are not hardy here but they need efficient drainage. Often the flowers are of rich or brilliant colours, but there are many soft shades too, notably pink tones and some fascinating ones in which a greenish tint suffuses the white of their miraculously-formed trumpets.

For all the possibilities of open-ground gardening with bulbs, however, one must not forget the adaptability of some kinds to indoor gardening, to flowering when the weather is vile outside. A few more practical details are involved. If the bowls in which they are grown have no drainage holes hyacinth and daffodil bulbs must be planted in inert fibre. (They have all the resources they need within their brown tunics!) And the fibre must be soaked beforehand, then wrung out to rid it of a surplus.

Some of the bigger bits of charcoal it contains must be picked out and put in the bowls first. At the bottom they will save any water collecting there from becoming foetid. The first layer of fibre must not be pressed firm or it will become a launching pad for the thrusting roots, which will try to eject the bulbs.

How much of the bulb is left showing above the surface is immaterial. The higher it stands the more room below for those white coiling roots on which the plant depends for its moisture intake. And a frequent drink is all that is needed by a bulb leading an artificial sedentary life on a window-sill indoors.

Now the delicate business of gestation. All indoor bulbs must go through it, except that redoubtable trio of narcissi Paper White, Soleil d'Or and Cragford. Pistol, Bardolph and Nym would be better names, for they go through anything and turn up smiling and wheedling their way into your hearts. You can even stick them in bowls of pebbles, pour water over them and leave them on your window-sill from their first to last day. That is, if you can stand the scruffy sight of them before they bud.

Just as it has altered so much else in our lives, polythene enters here. There is no longer any need to worry about finding dark cupboards in which to house the planted bowls during the two or three months that the bulbs are busy interlacing the fibre with their roots. You simply wrap them in black polythene, and keep them anywhere cool, even out of doors. Inside this, glazed bowls will be safe and the bulbs in complete darkness.

Equally important, they will not be in danger of suffering from lack of moisture if you forget about them. Such neglect is often a cause of failure or, at least, delayed flowering. Root development gets halted by a spell of dryness. This seems to me so much more practical also when the bulbs are planted in pots of soil than covering them with peat or ashes, the latter a commodity now growing scarce. Who has soil space to devote to this, anyway? The rain to which they are then exposed must drain through them and away somewhere. Wrapped in black polythene the pots can stand anywhere out of the way, perhaps along hedge bottoms.

Now that so many greenhouses stand in small gardens as well as large, but often left empty until seed sowing time, there are widespread possibilities of extra early daffodils and tulips being grown in them specially for cut flowers. There is no need to turn on the heat, either. After a couple of months out in the cold and dark, the bulbs will show their appreciation of being brought into the cosy shelter of even an unheated house by coming into flower long before their fellows left behind outside.

Those expensive plastic seed trays, otherwise out of use in winter, will serve to hold them, and reduce the need for watering to a minimum. Kipper boxes, discarded but still redolent, are the traditional receptacles used by professionals, but in fact the bulbs seem to do just as well in containers no deeper than traditional bulb bowls, and sensitive growers are not offended.

One immense advantage of growing your own daffodils, narcissi and tulips specially for cutting is that you can let the fancy roam as you leaf through the bulb catalogues in the early autumn and turn it into reality, instead of having to put up with flowers of the handful of varieties, scarcely subtle or distinguished, that you can buy in early spring.

Similarly, among the hyacinths to be planted in bowls you can get colourings the like of which you will not find in every green-grocer's shop window once we have got Christmas out of the way. Of course, if you want to make the holly and the cyclamen and the winter cherry look a bit dowdy then you will plant 'prepared' hyacinths in September (following closely the instructions given in the leaflet supplied with them). Or you may prefer to be less extravagant and plant the airy Roman Hyacinths. Personally, I am content with them in January, but to be sure of them even then, one must not delay planting long after the summer holidays.

Fruit

Growing your own fruit: a worthwhile occupation: apples:
pyramids and espaliers: pears: gages against a wall: soft fruits:
training raspberries and blackberries: grid-iron cordons: pests:
pruning, how and wherefore: wounding the bark: dehorning

The reflective pleasures of gardening are never more piquant
than when you are enjoying the fruit you have grown yourself. None can taste better! But do they always justify all the care
and garden space they demand? Is home fruit-growing on a very
small scale worthwhile? It can be — provided you adjust your
choice to the limitations.

In the main I would say that apples of keeping varieties are the
most rewarding, so long as the varieties planted are known also
to crop regularly. This rules out the excellent Laxton's Superb
and Newton Wonder, both determined biennial bearers.

From a twelve-year-old Cox's Orange Pippin tree, a closely
pruned bush less than eight feet across, we have picked a crop of
a bushel and a half of fruit, or about sixty pounds. Cox, I admit,

is not reliable on not-too-well-drained soil. My choice of dessert varieties for any garden to yield a succession of fruit would therefore be James Grieve to last till mid-November, Egremont Russet to follow, with Sunset next and Orleans Reinette to finish the season. I can also recommend Tydeman's Late Orange for New Year eating. Three cooking apples I can recommend are Rival, to use up till the end of the year, Lane's Prince Albert and Monarch to see you through till the end of April.

All are prolific varieties that respond to close spur-pruning, which I have satisfied myself is the only practical method of treating fruit trees in the small garden, whether they are bushes or so-called 'trained' trees.

If I were planting again, I should buy pyramids. These are really cone-shaped trees with rising tiers of branches radiating from a central trunk, each closely set with fruit spurs encouraged by hard pruning at the end of July. These can safely be planted as closely as three feet apart in rows with five to six feet between them.

There is a case for planting standard trees on clear six-foot stems here and there in place of the ornamental trees we are so keen on having in our gardens, none of which can surely outrival apple or pear blossom in spring.

I am less enthusiastic towards pears, but only because they have fewer keeping qualities, and a glut of anything can be an embarrassment. Again I would plant pyramids in a new garden and perhaps espaliers, too, to line a path.

From the utilitarian standpoint the choice of pears would have to be Conference and Joséphine de Malines. Only its shyness and susceptibility to scab disease would exclude that queen of pears, Doyenne du Comice.

From the smallest garden I fear one must also exclude plums. Unlike apples and pears, which are always sold grafted on to a stock which keeps them compact in growth, plums have no such restraining influence. The trees just grow and grow, producing so heavily in seasons when frost and cold winds allow the blossom to become fertilised that you cannot give them away.

Here, though, there is a case for growing one of the delectable gages, such as Denniston's, of a quality you can never buy, trained in fan fashion against a sunny wall, confining the roots within barriers of corrugated iron to restrict growth.

Of the soft fruits, raspberries and blackcurrants seem to me both the most profitable and the least trouble. Again, economy in space can be achieved by planting raspberries beside a path. Malling Jewel is a good-flavoured variety with the least inclination to sucker in the prolific manner of most raspberries.

The easiest way of training raspberries seems simply to run several strands of stout galvanised wire from post to post and back again, to form a narrow pen in which the canes can grow up and be prevented from flopping to either side. No more support than this is necessary. When the time comes to cut them out and allow the new to take their place, pruning is easy and there are no strings to release and tax the patience. Like the simple pruning blackcurrants need also, you just cut out the fruited growth when the crop has been gathered.

The other cane fruits made admirable screens to divide the garden, conceal the compost heap, or break the force of the wind, especially if they are supported by the rigid panels of plastic-covered or galvanised six-inch mesh wire you can buy these days, and which have only to be fixed to stout posts.

There is no escaping tying in blackberries and loganberries, unfortunately. The difficulty here is how to control the new canes, which can be eight feet long before the crop is gathered and it is time to cut away the canes that have borne it. The tangle produced can be vexing enough to make you give up growing them. This can be avoided by each year training all of one season's canes to one side of the rootstock, instead of in the conventional fan shape. Neither picking nor pruning is any trouble then. You have the growth classified into two types, the old on the left, say, and the new on the right. The following season their positions will be reversed. This, of course, presupposes sufficient room and is a suitable method to adopt when the plant is grown against a fence or wall. Where it is trained on a short trellis with both sides accessible a different system can be adopted. All old fruit canes are tied to one face of the trellis, and as the new canes develop these are pushed through to the other and tied in. Again you have one season's growth all in one plane and the positions are reversed the following year. Picking and pruning are no longer jobs for which you need to wear a suit of armour!

Growing redcurrants and gooseberries the most economical way is as 'grid-iron' cordons, each plant composed of several upright stems with side shoots pruned hard. They are trained against a fence or wall of the shed from which it would be easy to drop down some netting to protect them at times when the buds are attracting the birds. This, indeed, is a hazard you must be prepared to face if you set about growing your own fruit of any sort. The only full insurance cover is to enclose all the bushes in some kind of netting.

And what about insect pests? Is it necessary to spray as often as the text-books advise? A tar oil spray every other winter, and occasional shower of insecticide left over when the roses are 'de-greenflied', serve well enough. Certainly, these little difficulties are forgotten when you are enjoying the delectable fruits of your own growing, perhaps on a mid-winter's evening.

Forgetting about the pests that afflict them for the moment, though, the trouble with garden fruit trees is that they don't know when to stop. You look on with dismay that increases in proportion to the rate at which growth goes on soaring — until you have learned to gain the mastery over them.

'I've cut them back, but they seem to grow all the more', runs the familiar complaint. This is usually because the pruning has been done at what is commonly regarded as 'the proper time' — in winter when the trees are at rest. But cut them when they are wide awake and you really can succeed in subduing apples and pears.

Pruning in winter, when all the leaves are off and the trees have time to think up their response while gathering their reserves, is a stimulus rather than a check. But by pruning in summer, on the other hand, you get the better of them and they allow themselves to be trained in the way you think they should go.

By depriving them of a proportion of their leaves, which help to nourish them and forward their progress, you damp down their ardour. Look how pest or disease attack, by hampering the activity that goes on through the leaves, stunts the plant, or how it never gets a good start if sun or wind dehydrate its leaves.

This simple fact of life can be exploited. It is the principle underlying the tailoring of apple and pear trees into the formal and fanciful shapes seen in the business quarters of French gardens. The heavy crops of high quality fruit borne by severely pruned trees surely commend them for small present-day gardens.

In essence, the method is simply cutting back — indubitably

in late July and early August — every new side shoot made in the current season. If the shoot arises from a main stem, cut the shoot back to the third leaf above the cluster at its base. If the shoot has grown from an old one which has been cut back previously, prune it harder, to one leaf above the basal cluster of leaves.

Summer pruning, as this is called, has formerly been confusing because gardeners were taught to cut so far in summer, a bit farther in winter. This is no longer considered necessary, unless a wet late summer causes much secondary growth, which does have to be trimmed back in autumn — to one leaf from the point of origin.

Trees trained as bushes by the nurseryman can certainly be kept within garden size by applying the 'three and one' principle. In time they come to resemble multi-stemmed cordons if they have open centres, pyramids if they have a central leader.

Of course, single cordons, or what are known as 'horizontal-trained' trees or less descriptively as 'espaliers', have to be pruned in this way to preserve their shape. The end of the leader, by the way, is not cut off until May, a time when such pruning is least likely to cause a tuft of new unwanted shoots to arise just below the cut.

Those masters of pruning techniques, the French, are not content to train their fruit trees to look like palisades or five-bar gates. Even in commercial orchards you see them trained to wires and pruned with systems of branches in herring-bone fashion or grid-irons with four and five cordon-like stems. When free-standing they are trained as baskets.

To the best of my knowledge one cannot buy trees ready trained in this highly decorative manner in this country. One has to start with maiden trees — single-stemmed saplings — and train them oneself. This is done by pruning at first in winter (usually by half) to promote the development of the main or framework branches and tying these in the direction they are to go, and by 'notching', or making little cuts, just beyond buds required to develop to subsidiary branches.

It could be fascinating work to apply to a tiny garden with horticultural opportunities limited by area but widened by such resourcefulness. The ultimate triumph would be to train a tree as a vase or goblet, or perhaps to fashion an arbour in fruit trees, certainly to have the flower beds edged with horizontal-stemmed trees resembling the low rails that go with 'keep of the grass' notices in public parks. These could yield crops without taking up any room at all.

But what about the mature apple or pear tree that obstinately refuses to bear a blossom but bounds away with more and still more lusty growth? Spring is the moment to make one move and cry 'Check!'

Nothing more than a slender strip of bark — a thin sliver of tissue — can stand between you and the prize of basketfuls of fruit that have eluded you. Indeed, if the tree is young, you may have only to run a sharp knife round the trunk, cutting into the bark like a mischievous youngster with time on his hands and a new Scout knife, to bring the tree into bearing. The principle is that by injuring the bark and diverting the sap flow, not only upwards but back again from the leaves, you allow it to coagulate in the twigs and occupy itself by forming flowering spurs instead of its energies being squandered on racing growth.

To this end, better than a simple knife cut is the removal of a girdle of bark only an eighth of an inch across right round the trunk just below the point from which the lowest branches radiate. Some people cannot be made to believe that this will not harm the tree irreparably. Its simplicity is suspect. Very well then; they may be less discomfited, and the tree as certainly doctored, by two half circles being removed, not entirely meeting. These are in fact each made on opposite sides of the tree and prevented from encircling it by being spaced an inch apart.

Shakespeare, of course, knew all about it, just as he seems to have known about everything else. That gardener in Richard II instructed his assistant:

> *We at time of year*
> *Do wound the bark, the skin of our fruit trees,*
> *Lest, being over-proud in sap and blood,*
> *With too much riches it confound itself.*

Whether the wound is wide or narrow, it must be covered with an antiseptic seal of insulating tape or one of the substances sold in tins for dressing tree wounds. I cannot promise you that all will be well by the following spring, but the year after that the tree will show a response to being bridled in this way.

The appropriate treatment for refurbishing a hopelessly overgrown, neglected apple or pear tree, is known to gardeners as 'dehorning'. The tree is almost entirely stripped of its proud head of branches and encouraged to make another, giving it a fresh start.

Each main branch is sawn away, cut back to a couple of feet from its origin, so that the tree is left with only a trunk and a few stumpy branches like a giant's fingers. Ruthless though this method may seem, it is not haphazard, for each cut is made just above a slender, outward-striking shoot, which is spared. These will be the growths from which the new framework of branches will spring.

First a cut must be made on the underside of the branch and then another made on top so that the two meet. Then the branch will not fall and tear a long strip of bark from what little old wood is being retained if it is removed in this way.

You might find that an entire branch or two will have to be removed from the middle of the tree, in this case right back to the crotch, this in the interests of promoting a new tree that is open at the centre, the head of branches eventually taking on the shape of an inverted vase.

The tree's response to all this may be a little too exuberant, and more new shoots may be produced than adequately furnish the tree. Accordingly you have to watch it in the first season and rub out the surplus shoots while they are still small.

Any tree being rescued from the effects of neglect needs a restorative. Bonemeal pricked into the soil round it over an area equivalent to the spread of the branches, followed by a layer of compost or hop manure, proves to be the elixir required.

Cabbage Patch

Are vegetables worthwhile: flavour: broad beans: lettuce:
spinach: the onion tribe: the 'unusual' vegetables: asparagus, a
class by itself: the layer of sawdust: globe artichokes: marriage
of flowers and vegetables: a monarch's mistress: the herb garden:
painted sage: borage for a summer drink

A giant, challenging question-mark stands beside the problem of
whether vegetables are worth growing in the home garden
nowadays. With deep inroads already made on kitchen garden
space for flowers for cutting, under the inspiration of the floral
art movement, the thought of the work involved might tip the
balance against growing any vegetables at all.

Is it worth all the effort? Especially now that you can buy
almost all the staple vegetables frozen-fresh and apparently straight
from the garden, on any day of the year.

Of course, flavour is always subjective, and just as with your
own apples and pears nothing you could ever buy would ever
taste as good as anything you have grown yourself.

The old magic of the first dish of peas of the season has gone, however, and with the birds to reckon with I know few who do not rely on the deep freeze in the shop for these. Yet there are possibilities of growing vegetables without great effort, sometimes of kinds that can never be bought. The frozen food trade, for instance, has not yet realised how delicious broad beans can be *mangé tout,* eaten pods and all when young, and broad beans are absolutely no trouble to grow. The seed can be sown in March in soil that you hardly need to knock down.

Perhaps salad crops, however, can be the most profitable. It is not really all that bother to make a fresh sowing of lettuce seed every fortnight from mid-March till mid-August, perhaps about a ten-foot stretch at a time. The seedlings can be thinned with the hoe in the way that farmers 'single' turnips. Carrots for grating are no trouble to grow from spring sowings, while beet seems to grow anywhere and be immune to all maladies. Both will give good returns, for no more than thinning and weekly hoeing. And with the stainless steel hoe tedious labour has almost been removed from both jobs.

Spinach is a special case. Though the frozen crops may be free of grit, to my taste they lack the characteristic tang in the flavour. By growing the 'perpetual' type, sowing in spring, religiously thinning the plants to eight inches apart and mulching with the lawn clippings, you can be sure of successive crops until the following spring, without fear of 'bolting' bringing the plants to a premature end.

Crops that will give a succession of pickings are so much more appropriate to shrinking kitchen gardens than cabbages and cauliflowers, each plant of which may take up several square feet for most of the year for one dish. Sprouting broccoli, white, green and purple: the various types of kale, including the delicious asparagus kind: and of course brussels sprouts themselves in the compact growing varieties, will give a continuing yield over many weeks. And when the last are apparently spent they can be pulled up, heeled in on a patch of ground already dug and left to produce a crop of deliciously succulent secondary shoots that have some of the quality of asparagus.

All are raised by sowing in April in a seed bed prepared by raking and firming and sprinkling the soil with superphosphate of lime, the seedlings being transplanted when they are big enough and the weather showery; that is when they 'take' best and relieve you of the tedium of watering.

The onion tribe seem to ask for so little attention on soil reasonably well replenished with compost and, in that absurd but meaningful phrase of gardeners, 'in good heart'. From sets — immature bulbs from the previous season's sowings, sold by every seedsman — you can grow fine keeping onions that go three to the pound with no more effort than planting them five inches apart in a trench two inches deep and the weekly hoeing to keep down weeds.

Leeks are similarly undemanding. What could be easier than just making a hole with a dibber, dropping in the plant you have bought or raised from seed, watering it and leaving the weather to fill up the hole as the plant grows and the stem gets blanched? Less trouble almost than ringing up the shop, and the crop can be dug over several months.

Does anyone still pickle shallots, or use them to flavour the salad bowl? Again they are grown without trouble or foe.

The 'unusual' vegetables need to be approached with more caution than enthusiasm. Our experience is that, paradoxically, while you can go on eating the duller, mundane kinds very frequently, you rapidly tire of the more exciting vegetables that are highly flavoured when they reach the table.

Asparagus is in a class by itself, an undoubted permanency that many who once used ground for a succession of crops now devote quite a large area to and leave it at that.

Since asparagus is a plant that must have a very well drained site to avoid its fleshy roots rotting, the ground on this occasion really does have to be double dug unless the subsoil is gravel. Asparagus beds on heavy soil are usually raised, anyway, so that the plants' roots stand well above the level where water is inclined to lodge in prolonged spells of bad weather.

But the bed system, by which strips four feet wide were prepared, for three rows of plants fifteen inches apart, is being supplanted by the simple method of growing single rows four feet apart. Rather in the manner of celery growing, a trench eighteen inches wide is dug over. After thorough clearing of perennial weed roots, planting is done on ridges in spring, draping the roots over the sides and covering the tops of the crowns with about four inches of soil.

Every succeeding spring, a dressing of general fertiliser is added, and throughout the season hoeing has to be done to keep down competing weeds. Special care has to be taken, for asparagus is a member of the lily family and demands the respect due to its noble lineage. No crop can be taken until the second or third season.

Crowns one or two years old can be bought for spring planting, but the advantage of raising them at home from seed sown in spring is that you can sex them. Controlled tests have shown that in asparagus the male is certainly superior to its counterpart, giving more and better shoots than the female, which bears berries in late summer and thus squanders energy in the process of seeding, while leaving unproductive foundlings about the place.

Asparagus would lose some of its special appeal if we had it all the year, but there were formerly early and late cropping strains bred for the French asparagus industry around Argenteuil. These, however, seem to be extinct in this country today. In any case, by the end of June cutting must come to an end. For after all, the part we eat is the young shoots, and if none were allowed to develop and help build up the plants they would expire through exhaustion. It would be like constantly hoeing the weed that at last gives up.

Seakale, another perennial vegetable, though not lasting so many years, almost went out with the decline of the big well-kept private garden. It is wistfully recalled at auction sales by an occasional item at the end of the catalogue with the scarcely saleable impedimenta as 'a quantity of seakale pots'. It was not grown in pots, but only covered with them to blanch the first stems in spring. As an open ground crop, it can have a longer season than asparagus. Again it must have clean, well-drained soil, for it is a seashore plant, and in fact was once gathered for market where it grew wild, being blanched by piling up the pebbles round it.

The plants are bought in spring — they are raised from root cuttings — and planted twelve inches apart in double rows divided by about fifteen inches. Some growers earth them up like celery in January, but a better method is to treat them like early rhubarb for the first crop and cover them with boxes or pots, surrounding these in turn with leaves or compost to provide warmth and induce early etiolated growth. If the crowns are treated in this way successively, the crop can extend over several months.

The salsify which I notice appears increasingly in published recipes is a no-trouble root crop which, most conveniently, you can leave in the ground all the winter and dig only when you feel like some. The seed is sown in spring like turnips or parsnips, and the seedlings later thinned to five six inches apart.

The simplest way of growing courgettes and zucchini, whose appeal is also pressed on home cooks, is to choose some patch of ground where the soil keeps pretty moist, fork in some compost, tread firm, push a couple of seeds in and cover the spot with a jam jar. If both seedlings are spared by slugs one can later be sacrificed. Allowing the vines to clamber over a strong hazel bough thrust into the ground, or a trellis or arch, seems better than letting them find their way over the ground and then offering the fruits to the slugs as they ripen. The same method, in all its details, can be used for the ornamental gourds grown for varnishing for winter decoration. But as all are very swift growers, early May is early enough for sowing them.

If home vegetable growing is done on a lesser scale to save labour, surely, you will say, weeding has still to be done, even if flowers and permanent crops are taking the place of vegetables that are changed with the seasons?

One answer, if the constant use of the hoe between the rows sounds too formidable a task, is to cover the whole area with a layer of peat or sawdust. While many weeds will never appear through this, most of those that do come through can easily be pulled out by hand. Any with determined deep-striking roots can be despatched with a puff from the same selective weedkiller used on lawns and applied in this case from discarded 'squeezy' detergent containers.

Globe artichokes are enjoying a great vogue now, largely because flower arrangers have drawn attention to their splendid silvery leaves. Like asparagus, the plants need light soil but are vastly different in that they are good only for three seasons. After that their crop potential declines to the point when they are no longer worth the space they require, a patch three feet square for each plant. Then their place must be taken by new plants pro-duced from offsets from the old ones. The handsome appearance of these plants brings up the whole question of the prevailing ugliness of cabbage patches, often put forward as reason for not growing vegetables in small gardens.

But why does the vegetable area of so many suburban gardens that one sees from a train window have to be cut off from the rest, foreshortening already limited areas? Does a kitchen garden need to look so ugly that it must be entirely screened from view? Why, indeed, does the garden shed have to remain a dingy hut serving no more than its mean utilitarian purpose? Why should its sides not be strung with wires and embellished, where it catches the sun, with a loganberry, or morning glory, roses or even nasturtiums?

The flowers we grow for cutting, can beautify a kitchen garden to some degree. Those divisions of herbaceous plants like heleniums, rudbeckias and Michaelmas daisies, which must be pulled apart often and become embarrassing in their increase, can be given a home here. This is also the only garden setting for gladioli which we find agreeable.

The French, inevitably occupied with gastronomic matters at the aesthetic level — they even have a *rose de feuilles laitues* — have a different outlook altogether on the matter from us, which we might borrow from. Even in the best-bred French gardens you can never always be sure which is flower and which is vegetable, even, I found, in the garden of a monarch's mistress. The areas given to vegetables and fruit are usually conceived in the same plan which is decorative throughout.

Visiting the garden of the exquisite little *pavillon* Louis XV built for Madame de Pompadour beyond the walls of Fontainebleau, I noticed that some of the main vistas struck right through beds of lettuce and chervil, carrots and seakale, to the figures and ornaments on which they were focused. Pears and roses adorned the walls cheek by jowl. All were edged with flowering plants or clipped box.

Could we not tear away bits of those hedges that keep our vegetable patches decently covered, and extend our lawns to the limits of the site as grassy paths running between trained fruit trees or a pair of rows of raspberries and leading to, say, some tree or urn?

Receding parallel lines as I have argued in an earlier chapter, always appear to lengthen a garden, and there is often no reason why kitchen garden paths should not aid the illusion. The torn-up rows of potatoes or yellowing Brussels sprouts can still be hidden from the house by the espalier of apples or the neatly tied-in raspberries, which never offend the eye.

The forlorn look which a vegetable patch must inevitably wear at some seasons can be reduced by trim edgings to the paths, perhaps of pinks for cutting which can also contribute to the lengthening deception.

As part of our reorganising work one season — what garden isn't always in process of improvement? — we lined one kitchen garden path with hybrid tea roses just for blooms for cutting. Later, finding an embarrassing superfluity of irises on my hands after lifting and dividing them, I added these between roses and path. While taking up little room, they have certainly had an embellishing effect with their leaves alone.

Of course, other vegetables have their own decorative quality, besides the majestic globe artichokes, which can be exploited to offset the plainness of humbler kinds. On a smaller scale, there are cabbages and kales whose ornamental leaves do not detract from their kitchen value, and who with eyes to see could not admit the pretty effect made by the interplay of the vinous leaves of beet and the fern-like soft green foliage of carrots? One gardener of my acquaintance plants lettuces between his roses.

Perhaps we needed the adventuring flower arrangement movement to open our eyes to the beauty to be found in vegetables, and pressure on space can heal the schism between flower garden and vegetable and fruit patch and so make little gardens seem bigger.

What self-respecting young housewife today, with a husband's business friends to entertain (or her own contemporaries to withstand) can afford not to put rosemary in the lamb, borage in the summer drinks, basil in the casserole (never stew!) or not to make the broiler poultry 'interesting' with tarragon?

Herbs are back. No longer do they represent 'folkiness', like the little posies of herbs hard-faced judges are said to carry on special occasions to shield their fastidious noses from receiving offence. Herbs are part of contemporary horticulture. Even window-boxes sprout them.

You certainly don't need a herb garden devoted to them, planted perhaps like a cartwheel as in those neat little drawings you see but which are impossible to keep so orderly. Many herbs, as well as having aromatic leaves, are so decorative that they are worthy of being planted in mixed borders in company with shrubs, bulbs and hardy flowers. All they ask is a place in the sun and soil that does not lie wet for long.

Even the common sage becomes a beautiful plant once it is removed from purely utilitarian associations. The leaves seem poised to make a flattering setting for the spires of flowers that sometimes verge on being violet. One form we grow even has elegance, having silvery green slender leaves and white flowers. Near it stands the misnamed 'red sage'. Its leaves are purple, covered with a bloom like a fresh-picked ripe plum. Unhappily, ours does not flower, but I have seen examples with purple blossom too. The more aptly called 'painted sage' has tints of purple, carmine and cream in its parti-coloured leaves. Both are good companions to plant with, say, old-fashioned roses to help offset their lankiness. This is a purpose for which the variegated mint is recommended, the silvery markings on the leaves giving a lightness to the grouping. Here, too, it can be allowed to wander where it likes, covering the ground against the invasion of weeds.

Similarly, the common wild marjoram makes an effective ground cover, which is attractive in flower; but better and more dense is the golden-leaved type, a little tender perhaps, though safe on soil that drains readily, in time making large flat cushions.

By contrast, the lemon balm used in salads grows up to two feet. Tenacious, denying roothold to any other plants that might fancy the same spot, this is a good plant, which will endure shade, to set behind a seat which you may have sited under a tree. The tree's roots will keep it from excess moisture and you will still sense the refreshing tang of the leaves on the air as you sit there.

Thymes seem to me good wall border plants, if lowly ones. The lemon-scented type, the variegated Silver Queen, the golden-leaved form, even the common one, all make pleasing little bushes less than a foot tall, to grow at the feet of other plants that need sheltered positions. Having broad patches of the pink, red and white creeping thymes I now lift bits and replant them in any sunny places where the ground needs covering with a close carpet, even at the base of small conifers.

After the savagery with which the 1963 winter treated rosemary plants everywhere, one will always be inclined to plant it again in the lee of a south or west wall — unless you fear the petticoat government that is supposed to ensue wherever rosemary flourishes. In defiance of this danger, I have replanted the richly coloured Tuscan Blue variety and the narrow-leaved gorse-like Corsican type. There was no need to replace the prim Miss Jessop's Upright, for as propriety should, this curiously named one survived, even as a low hedge, for which it is well suited.

Certain herbs are worth growing for their appearances alone even though they no longer have any practical use, except in pot pourri. I doubt if anyone today would need to strew the floor with tansy to keep fleas away, but this is a strikingly handsome border plant. The leaf is most beautiful and the yellow flower clusters last as long as dahlias are in bloom.

Does anyone bother to candy their own angelica? A tall, statuesque plant, this is winning a place in the schemes of modern-minded garden designers, who use it to contrast with such dome-shaped plants as skimmia. I have noticed they use fennel in the same way, particularly the purple form which has lately been transformed to 'with-it' status from being a plant curiosity. This, of course, does have a value in sauces for fish dishes, and both kinds can be used; the colour makes no difference.

While these pass with the autumn, the shrubby rue, also in current fashion, loses little of its charm in the winter. The most striking form is called Jackman's Blue — the leaves are almost the colour of those of the blue Atlas cedar — but equally cherished is the variegated form, whose leaves, the characteristic intricate shape and giving off a sharp, refreshing odour when crushed, are pencilled with silver.

Most of all, though, we cherish the borage, that seeds wherever we let it. The leaves are slightly hairy and the flowers are as blue as the summer sky ought to be. On a hot day it has its uses, too — as a refreshing addition to cooling drinks.

Shade

*Problem or opportunity: character of shade-loving plants:
hostas: lenten roses: campanulas: meadow rues: aquilegias: the
yellow loosestrife: japanese anemone: the bleeding heart: silver
for relief: shrubs for the shade: the butcher's broom: the berberis
family: evergreens: a Victorian survivor: other candidates*

Problem or opportunity? Do you look on shady areas of the
garden where the soil is always damp as just wasted bits of
ground to be filled up? Or do you see in them scope for growing
some of the most interesting of plants whose favours would be
denied you if the garden were entirely in the sun?

The fact is that there are many herbaceous plants that not only
put up with being planted in these areas but actually thrive in
them, and these frequently give a longer season of flower than
sun-loving plants. A quick glance through this book will show
that I am biased in favour of many of them.

Though many of the plants that like shade may have little of
the flamboyance of those that flourish in sunshine, they can

nevertheless compensate in character, for they often have foliage that in itself would deserve garden space.

For this merit alone the hosta, or plantain lily, is one of the most fashionable plants of the day. In the most sophisticated modern gardens, laid out for easy maintenance and where the form of plants as well as colour is emphasised, you see bold plantings of it in the shade of shrubs, made for the sake of its leaves as much as its spires of lavender lily flowers in summer.

For a pleasing contrast I grow hostas interspersed with patches of *Iris sibirica,* from among whose grassy foliage rise exquisitely poised flowers of clear blue in the Heavenly Blue variety, violet in Caesar, white in Snow Queen.

The Lenten roses, *Helleborus orientalis,* growing in dense shade, delight us annually with their rose, palest pink and white flowers, all spotted with crimson within, and again they have foliage which is attractive in its own right. But the most 'architectural' of the hellebores is *Helleborus argutifolia,* which stands nearly three feet high with leaves that would embellish any baroque monument, and great clusters of yellow-green bell-like flowers which open in the spring.

Although not flowering until high summer, the hemerocallis, or day lilies also make an early start. Soon their bright green grass-like foliage casts a shade too deep for any normal weed to endure, and from early July to September they give a succession of trumpet flowers in gold, orange, copper, bronze, or mahogany according to the varieties chosen from the abundance now found in all hardy plant growers' lists.

Even when tidying up shaded patches in early spring, one gets whiffs of the fragrance of the first leaves of the monarda, a three-foot plant that makes a tightly-woven mat of roots as it spreads. The curious flowers, like circlets of honeysuckle, are best known in gardens in scarlet and pink forms.

A shady patch is certainly the place for most of the taller-growing campanula group. I know no more handsome member than *Campanula lactiflora,* particularly in its violet Pritchard's variety and the pale pink Loddon Anna. The flowers appear in huge plumes on four-foot stems stout enough to need no staking. Violet-blue is also the shade of the vigorous Highcliffe form of *Campanula latiloba* and the Brantwood variety of *Campanula macrantha.* Some of the most desirable varieties of *Campanula persicifolia* are white, notably Fleur de Neige and Snowdrift, though if you plant these, or such blue varieties as Beechwood or Wedgewood, in a few years they usually get submerged by the self-sown seedlings that surround them — some inferior in their flowers, others well worth preserving.

The plants found in catalogues as aconitum are very different from the aconites planted in autumn to flower with the snow-drops. An aconitum may reach four feet, with helmet-shaped flowers of light blue, violet or indigo. Varieties I have found specially desirable are Barker's and Spark's.

The cultivated meadow rues, to judge by their name and origins, might seem to need open places, but I find them in-different to shade — and bolder in leaf there. Their fluffy flowers may have little attraction, but the foliage is always in demand for cutting in our household and is described by the specific names of the two kinds we grow, *Thalictrum aquilegifolium* and *Thalictrum adiantifolium,* which, of course, resembles the maidenhair fern.

Aquilegias themselves do not mind some shade, and if most strains are of pale shades and need to make their effect mainly with the intricacy of their spurred flowers, what are sold as Sutton's Red Shades, which can be flowered from seed very hand-somely in two seasons, do give some very intense colourings. Unfortunately they have to be treated as biennials for the best results, when other shade-tolerant plants I have recommended endure for many seasons; though aquilegias do seed themselves, even if the strain deteriorates gradually when this is allowed.

Perhaps the yellow loosestrife, *Lysimachia punctata,* has some of the invasiveness of its lowly relative, the old Creeping Jenny, but it is most valuable where it can be allowed to spread. *Lysimachia clethroides,* however, is more graceful, making spikes of ivory flowers. Cimicifuga is a little-known plant with four-foot spires of white flowers that flourish admirably in shade.

The ways of the Japanese anemone, one of the best of plants, now apparently called *Anemone hupehensis* correctly, are very curious. Divisions of old plants that put up with shade, and so rampant as to embarrass their owner, sulk for a season, often two, after planting. Then they revert to their former habits and settle down to compensate for lost time, producing armfuls of white or pink flowers every autumn for half a generation without further prompting.

Contrast in shape again is provided by liatris, a plant valuable for bringing the brighter colour tones of sunny places to the shade. Its common name of 'blazing stars' describes, perhaps a little ineptly, the very striking mauve flowers that cluster along the two-foot spikes, unaccountably opening from the top downwards unlike most other spire-like plants.

Equally curious in their formation, the flowers of *Dicentra spectabilis* hang like Victorian lockets on the stems and have won for this plant the sorrowful name of 'bleeding heart'. The leaves are fern-like and it makes a good companion for Solomon's Seal, *Polygonatum multiflorum,* from whose arching stems dangle white flowers made all the more conspicuous by the bright green of the foliage.

In any border scheme, silvery leaves are needed for relief, especially in a shady site where the richness of foliage can be heavy. *Sedum spectabile,* preferably in its Brilliant variety, succeeds here: and so does *Phlomis samia,* whose yellow flowers are arranged in tiers on stiff stems that rise from clusters of broad, greyish leaves. I have also had success with anaphalis of several species, and these are valuable ground-cover plants.

Have you forgotten the old London Pride or even the dauntless Lily-of-the-Valley, best in the Fortin's Giant form? Or the whole range of hardy ferns? None should be despised for as shady ground plants they would be as highly valued as the blue willow gentian, another to grow in shade, if only they were less common.

Of the shrubs that do not shun the shady parts of a garden and tolerate 'ordinary' soil, one must give precedence to skimmia, an old plant which is in the ascendant for the sealing-wax red berries have no appeal to the birds and so remain on the bushes all the winter. Two plants are needed of the common *Skimmia japonica,* male and female to secure pollination, but *Skimmia foremanii* is a hermaphrodite berrying freely in celibacy.

The butcher's broom, *Ruscus aculeatus,* got its common name because butchers are said at one time to have used the stiff stems to clean their blocks with. Again plants of the two sexes are needed to produce a crop of scarlet berries, but the bushes remain small enough for the average garden.

The suckering habit of *Mahonia aquifolium* need not tell against it. Its yellow flowers, its blue-black berries in winter and its holly-like foliage — all help to make up a remarkably attractive shrub, which looks all the better when mixed with its purple-leaved form, atropurpurea.

Other members of the berberis family coming well within the terms of reference are the hybrids bred from the popular stenophylla. Their gracefully-arching branches carry many flowers ranging from yellow to scarlet. On the principal that as the garden grows only the best forms of new plants can be added to it, my choice of berberis would be the evergreen *Berberis linearifolia* Orange King, *Berberis stenophylla* Brilliant, and *Berberis lologensis* Highdown variety, all brilliant in flower, and the deciduous Buccaneer, Barbarossa and Pirate King, each of which can be startling when hung with translucent berries in autumn. A special word of caution, though; never plant them in anything but really clean soil that thereafter can be hoed, for hand-weeding round the prickly berberis is the most irksome gardening chore I know.

In shade, too, one can grow both *Osmanthus delavayi* and its hybrid with another genus, *Osmarea burkwoodii*. The first is low-growing and spreading, while the latter is bolder and more vigorous. Both are well worth planting for the delicious scent of their superabundance of tiny white flowers, which are made to seem all the whiter by the rich olive-green of the evergreen foliage. Here also one can pick the sweet-scented sprays of sarcococca, a valuable ground-covering little evergreen, in winter.

Perhaps the noblest in leaf for this purpose is that Victorian relic *Fatsia japonica,* so often miscalled the castor oil plant. In recent years it has won a new recognition on account of its marriage with an ivy to produce that good-tempered room plant *fatshedera*. But it is striking and handsome itself, the five-fingered leaves, not unlike a fig's, always highly polished.

Although it is a native of Mexico, *Choisya ternata* is shade-tolerant and it has the same glossy quality in its leaves, which are also refreshingly aromatic if you crush them, while in flower it has one of the longest seasons of any shrub I know. Like many other white flowers, the blossom is sweetly scented.

Another Victorian survivor which has won a new dignity, *Viburnum tinus* is not only evergreen, too, but has the merit of bearing its pinkish-white flower clusters in late winter. I have also had a fair degree of success in the shade with the other winter-flowering guelder roses, *Viburnum fragrans* and the even finer *Viburnum bodnantense,* both of which have a heady perfume.

Perhaps the best viburnum scent comes from the broad white flower clusters of *Viburnum carlesii* sending their heady perfume on the air in May. The foliage is covered with a whitish down which can be emphasised by planting it close to one of the Japanese maples, preferably *Acer palmatum dissectum atropurpureum*, an unwieldy name describing foliage like delicate lace of ox-blood colouring. All the 'japonicas' catalogued as chaenomeles or cydonia, are suitable and according to personal taste one can have the flowers in orange or blood-red, pink or scarlet, or even white. Since it is spreading in growth, it can be grown very happily with the upright double kerria, set with chrome yellow ball-like flowers in spring. Incidentally the bright green stems of this one are of special garden interest in winter.

The large cotoneaster family can similarly accommodate themselves to being put in the shade whether they are those ground-hugging kinds *Cotoneaster dammeri* and *adpressa* which make close carpets studded with scarlet berries, or such tall growers as *cornubia* and *lactea*, whose massive clusters of berries arch the branches in autumn.

The spiraeas are another large group which will serve admirably here. The bright carmine-crimson Anthony Waterer loses none of its merit by its familiarity, for it has a very long flower spell and can be cut back hard every March; by summer it will have renewed itself. Of the graceful white-flowered kinds that blossom in late spring none surpasses *Spiraea vanhouttei*, especially as the leaves turn to hectic shades in the autumn.

A characteristic of some of the hypericums which specially appeals to me is the pineapple scent of the leaves. Perhaps the selected forms of *Hypericum patulum* are the most rewarding of these and the Hidcote hypericum has an enthusiastic following among those who grow it. The St. John's Wort flowers are of exquisite shape and a shining gold, bringing a suggestion of sunshine to the dullest corner.

But this does not exhaust the shrubs that will give a good account of themselves in shade. Those common but none the less beautiful kinds, the deutzias, hydrangeas, weigelas and mock orange, will all flower reasonably well in sites that get little if any sun. The important thing is to observe and experiment and certainly never to write off such places.

Walls

The south wall: the most precious garden asset: treatment for the favoured plants: a selection of climbers: the first rose of summer: the north wall: plants for the shade: honeysuckle for quick results: shrubs: training climbers: cutting back: the capricious Mermaid

Next to a fertile top soil the most precious attribute a garden can offer to anyone who likes to adventure in the limitless world of plants is shelter from the north and east, provided by a south-facing wall. Here, in the place which gets all the sun going, one can try, and often succeed with, the most challenging of plants which wouldn't stand a chance elsewhere in the garden.

When preparing what gardeners call 'wall borders' for plants it is usual to remove patiently the refuse left by builders if the house is new, or at least add some fortifying manure if the ground has supported plants before. For south wall plants — and I think the site is worth reserving for the most delicate of them — this is not necessary, indeed unwise. Keep such plants a bit hungry and with only enough moisture to maintain them and they will grow wiry and stand a better chance of coming through cold winters unharmed than if they are well-nourished.

Of course, though, I give them a bit of bonemeal to encourage them to make strong root growth. And I spread the bonfire ash round them, even scattering a little sulphate of potash sometimes, in the belief that it toughens growth. But no nitrogen-predominant fertiliser would I allow them.

In choosing plants for this highly favoured site I eschew almost all those whose season of beauty is brief and which can be persuaded to thrive elsewhere, reserving the south wall for those plants which will have nothing else but shelter and the reflected heat from the sun.

At the head of any selection of climbers for a south-facing wall I put the solanums, the potato vines. Their flowers are exactly like those of the potato, which we never have time or inclination to admire, except that they appear in huge clusters.

A plant of *Solanum jasminoides album* I put in one spring as a six-inch rooted cutting had grown twelve feet by early August and gave an exquisite showing of its clear white flowers in its first season. Fortunately, frost cut it back almost to the ground in the succeeding winter without killing it. It sprang up again the following spring and flowered through the summer just the same. This cycle has been repeated year by year.

Rather tougher and not quite so exuberant, but a climber that also shows what it can do pretty soon, *Solanum crispum autumnale* produces clusters of blue flowers all through the summer. It is one of the most appealing plants I know.

Equally fast and often recommended for this site are the scarlet trumpet vines, found in catalogues variously as bignonia, tecoma and campsis. I have tried both species offered and the hybrid from them but never a flower did we see on them. They need, I believe, more heat than we might get. The superb summer we might get once in five years is sometimes a notable occasion for bignonias flowering, but who wants to wait in hope for such a season?

The evergreen banksian rose, the first rose of summer, is highly pleasing on a south wall, and to compensate for its brief flowering season, during which it produces charming white or buff 'St. Valentine's day card' blossom, one can plant morning glories to use it as a host and scramble through it. In my experience the only place where the common jasmine will justify the space allowed it by flowering abundantly is a south wall. Few people, by the way, seem to know the pink jasmine, *Jasminum stephanense*.

While all these can support themselves by clinging on to their supports, other tall growing shrubs need to be tied in and relieved of their surplus shoots. From this group I exclude the early flowering ceanothus on the ground of brevity, but two which comes into bloom later *Ceanothus burkwoodii* and Autumnal Blue, are acceptable, carrying on for weeks at a stretch. So does the pomegranate, *Punica granatum,* a superb south wall shrub.

If the soil is suitably poor a passion flower will keep up an incredible succession of its strange symbolic blooms. In addition to the familiar mauve kind sold in little pots as a house plant, *Passiflora coerulea,* there is a white form that shows up better, called Constance Elliott.

Even if it never flowered it would be worth growing a myrtle bush for the refreshing aroma of the foliage, but the plants blossom regularly in late summer, producing fluffy white flowers also filled with scent. The only place where you can rely on getting flowers from a winter sweet, *Chimonanthus praecox,* is in the lee of a south wall, though I fear that even here one has to wait several seasons before they do appear. And then, how richly scented they are!

Supreme in its big family is *Veronica hulkeana,* whose elegant plumes of lavender flowers often stand a foot high. But then almost any shrubby veronica will really show what it can do if it is given the advantage of this supreme garden position. Starting with the roses, the flowers are often still there when the chrysanthemums are going over.

Going from one pole to the other, if you have north facing walls or fences the main problem obviously enough is to find plants that will flourish in the shade and thus help to conceal their drabness.

The primrose stars that shower from the winter jasmine in countless town gardens which the sun hardly reaches, demonstrate that this can be done.

Not that the winter jasmine, called botanically *Jasminum nudiflorum* because the flowers appear from the leafless stems, is a natural climber. In open ground sites it makes a fountain-like bush, and this arching manner of growth makes it very attractive as a wall-shrub. Here the main growths can be tied to some support, the side shoots — trimmed back every year once flowering is over — being allowed to pour forth from the wall.

The ornamental-leaved forms of ivy, particularly those blotched with gold, can give the illusion of bringing the sun to dull walls or fences quite impressively. My own preference is one burdened by the name of *Hedera colchica dentata variegata,* for its leaves are the boldest and keep their primrose splashes well. But there are several others, and personally I would give an outdoor trial to any of the forms of ivy sold as house plants.

The mess made by the fallen leaves of the scarlet 'Virginia Creeper', *Vitis inconstans,* is a poor end to its autumn hour of glory, but few neater climbers recover more swiftly from severe annual pruning. Its less rampant relative, *Vitis henrya,* is distinguished by the ivory and purple markings that decorate the leaves in shaded sites.

Even some roses will not disdain a north wall, though admittedly they are not so generous with their flowers here as in the sun.

Still, I have seen very good results from the palest blush Mme. Alfred Carrière, scarlet Allen Chandler and the yellow Mermaid. It is said that the pillar-forming kordesii type of rose will flower well here and doubtless there is room for experiment.

A north or east facing wall is the only one really suitable for growing twining honeysuckles against. Given more comfort, they fall prey to both mildew and aphis, and succumb so readily that it is well nigh impossible to control either plague once it has gripped them. They avoid both troubles on a more chilly site.

If you have a big ugly wall that seldom gets the sun and which simply must be concealed quickly, the honeysuckle to use is *Lonicera japonica halliana.* Only in the worst of winters does this lose its foliage. Once it has taken a comfortable roothold, it romps away, making great rope-like main branches that tightly entwine whatever support they are offered. In late summer the scent of the pale yellow flowers is ravishing.

This determined way of taking hold means that a honeysuckle is no fit plant to try to mix with any other in the way that you can pair off, say, climbing roses and clematis. It will always get the upper hand and relentlessly strangle its companion. Always it must be given the place to itself, unless the host is an old tree that you can afford to have weakened or written off in time.

Perhaps it is the degree of protection given by the north wall that accounts for this stoical indifference to weather of our plant of *Lonicera brownii fuchsioides.* But it is not for this that I also recommend this strange honeysuckle. It is one of the most brilliant in flower in summer and is seldom recognised as a honeysuckle by those meeting it for the first time.

Another exotic-looking variety that contemporary architecture could support happily, when it may look rather brash against weathered bricks, is *Lonicera tellmanniana,* a hybrid of Hungarian origin and one of the few garden plants, I believe, ever to come from that country. In this case the flowers are of the familiar wild woodbine shape but much bigger and bright yellow tipped with scarlet. One must pay for such splendour, however: like *brownii fuchsioides,* it lacks scent.

The climbing *Hydrangea petiolaris* has all the grace of the lace-cap members of its family and proves as long-flowering in summer. The forsythia I like best of all is *Forsythia suspensa atrocaulis,* for the flowers are primrose, contrasting sharply with the blackish-purple stems. Both flourish in this position.

Some shrubs which do not need the sun will submit to being trained against a north or east facing wall. The favourite 'japonica' found in plant catalogues under chaenomeles, lasts much longer in flower here, and perhaps the birds are less likely to take the berries of cotoneasters which are trained close to human habitation.

The best I have seen in this position has been the evergreen *Cotoneaster salicifolia,* though the fishbone-like *horizontalis* can be decorative whether in leaf and berry or not. This is more suitable for limited sites, where one might also grow the variegated *Euonymus radicans* Silver Queen.

Sometimes the large-flowered clematis, notably the purple *Clematis jackmanii,* are seen in flower here; in other cases it only 'goes to leaf'. *Montana* is more reliable, though.

I am sure that the most satisfactory way of training climbers to walls is not on wires strained between bolts set in the mortar, but on panels of wooden trellis or stout wide-meshed wire netting. If the walls are of a kind likely to need attention, the panels can be made in such a way, by being hung on hooks, that they can be unfixed from the walls and brought a little forward and propped up, the plants with them, when the time for renovations comes.

This implies, of course, that their growth is limited throughout their life. My experience with wall plants has been that one has to keep the secateurs busy on them. Growth that is surplus to the area that can be allowed them has to be pruned away, three or four times a year in some cases, to prevent an unwieldy tangle.

Sometimes, however, the time comes when there is nothing for it but to cut the whole thing right down, back even into tough old wood. Strangely, clematis will suffer this gladly. I have seen a *Clematis montana* that must have known forty seasons, renewing itself from the scaly trunk it had formed. To make rebuilding operations possible it had been sawn through three feet from the ground.

Wisteria has similar powers of recovery in the face of brutal surgery, unlike most members of the pea family to which it belongs. It would be impossible to disentwine the growths that clasp their host supports so desperately. Honeysuckle is similarly responsive under the saw.

A vine is a different matter, however. While it is necessary to shorten all the new side growths drastically every year — indeed to remove all but a few inches of every one — older growth will not endure surgery. It weeps away its sap in a flow that no coaxing or cauterising or tourniquet can staunch.

In this case the only course seems to be to release the 'rods' from their supports and lash them temporarily to a scaffold pole thrust into the ground, or even an improvised system of trellis erected a little way from the wall. For they must not be moved far from the positions they have taken up for fear of causing wounds through which the vine may bleed to death.

Roses, though they may take time to recover, particularly the perpetual-flowering climbers, will spring up anew from sawn-back wood. But Mermaid that infinitely desirable single yellow variety that is near evergreen, is a capricious lady. You have to treat her as gently as a vine, otherwise she is likely to show displeasure at rough handling and leave you for ever. And heaven knows, Mermaid is spiteful enough with those alarming talons when you try to accommodate her.

Roses

A high rate of return: floribunda roses: surgery when in flower:
shrub roses: hybrid musks: rugosas: the pruning controversy:
taking care of the idiosyncracies: pruning on light land: cutting
flowers: feeding: training shrub roses: the pulpit method: a
modification

Unlike most other plants of a shrubby nature, in a new garden, even in their first year, roses will make a reasonable show of colour or yield many blooms to cut and admire indoors. In the effect they make in general and individually, and in the returns they offer for whatever trouble they may cost, roses must stand ahead of all other flowers, provided up-to-date varieties are planted.

Although really enthusiastic rose growers get inordinately excited about new varieties, which are in consequence sold out before the planting season opens, the varieties of the preceding ten years' vintage can be chosen confident that they will flourish, flower abundantly and have a wholehearted vigour that is natural to them. For the raisers are ruthless in the scale of infanticide they practise on new varieties that fall short, if only a little way, of the exacting standards they set themselves. Thus the newcomers that get most of the glory find it hard to oust their predecessors.

Recent rose seasons have seen the most rapid advances in the floribunda group, the roses that bear their flowers in clusters. Individually they may not have the perfection of the stylish, shapely hybrid teas, but the show of colour they offer will continue in a hardly-broken succession from June till October. One could scarcely ask for a more suitable plant for front garden flower beds, where the display must be as long as possible with little labour involved — especially since, when lightly pruned, the bushes will grow three feet tall, often more, and as much through.

The most notable developments have been in the appearance of brighter colours and orange and vermilion tints, but this brings a problem in combining them. Some of their red colourings are so vivid that put together, they quarrel violently. Perhaps the best thing is to plant a patch of the same variety and leave it at that. Fortunately, there are now more yellow varieties which can be used to keep the reds apart, and with striking colour effect.

Their flowering cannot be taken for granted, however. For while some floribunda roses are so eager to go on flowering that, before their first fine careless flush is done, they have produced fresh twigs that show the buds that will keep up the succession of flowers, others are less forward, and need some coaxing to bring them out. My repeated experience has been that all can do with some treatment with the secateurs during the summer as well as at pruning time. Removing the spent flowers is most important in encouraging them to flower later. I do not mean just snipping off the 'deads': it is better to be bold and cut off the whole branching head, right back to a healthy looking leaf from whose joint with the main stem a new flowering shoot will arise.

The response will be all the more thrustful if one of the rapidly assimilated general fertilisers used on vegetables is scattered around them and hoed into the ground, and if this is followed by a soaking with the hose and a mulch of lawn-mowings to hinder evaporation of the moisture.

Shrub roses are often alleged to be no-trouble plants, but I find that those which have it in them to continue flowering after the great midsummer burst need this little surgery just as much. Otherwise they prove as barren in the late summer as the damasks, the centifolias and the gallica roses, whose flowers will be seen no more until another summer comes round.

Whole branched heads can be cut away from the hybrid musks as the flowers shrivel. More will arise from lower down. Similarly, the flowered side-shoots of the Bourbons, that group which includes our old friend without thorns, Zéphirine Drouhin, must be trimmed off.

The rugosas — among them Blanc Double de Coubert and Roserie de l'Haÿ, which have been widely planted in recent seasons — are a different matter. These produce their successional flowers very close to the large hips which quickly follow the first. Left on, these would gradually colour up as the seed ripened, and the plant's work for the year would be accomplished; then it would retire from flowering.

One by one these have to be snipped off between thumb and finger, as tedious a job as soft fruit picking, which I notice the elderly approach with a zest for fiddling tasks that younger people lack. Still it is not a disagreeable job for a langorous summer afternoon when heat has numbed your spirit and the hammock has grown a bit uncomfortable after long reclining.

Pruning roses, indeed, is something that seems all-important in rose growing, especially since experts quarrel so eagerly over it, while amateurs stand mystified by it. With a view, presumably, of driving a coach and pair through the arguments, not so long ago the Royal National Rose Society published a study of the whole subject of pruning hybrid tea and floribunda roses which I suppose we can regard as definitive, produced as a result of an inquiry made to determine the contemporary approach to this thorny topic.

Seven acknowledged experts gardening in different parts of Britain were invited to state the positions they had arrived at after many years of practical experience. Their views were co-ordinated to see if any agreement were possible.

What emerged plainly was that though there were areas of agreement, no rule of thumb would do. The most skilled pruning always takes account of the idiosyncrasies of a particular variety and depends on observation made during the growing season, so that you adjust your pruning to each one individually.

Where the experts were certainly agreed was on the first stage of pruning — when all the weak twiggy growth is removed entirely, as well as any that shows signs of disease. Nothing new in that, but look at the countless roses you see in gardens from the tops of buses. In comparatively few are the pruned roses left as no more than bunches of stout sticks. More often than not they are left to start the season as already dense bushes.

There was also broad agreement on the needs of the newly planted. Pruning to a height of about six inches from the ground was advocated, except on light land where the soil is lean and hungry.

There no such drastic treatment was advised. Discard the weak growth altogether, they said, but only tip the strong shoots left. On light soil the experts' recommended technique was different from heavy land all round, in fact. A much greater proportion of the previous season's wood is retained, but older growths are cut away almost entirely, to encourage new wood to form from near the base. Then the bush will always be replacing itself.

This tendency is encouraged anyway, apparently, by the Superintendent of Regent's Park, one of the team. Except for the first year, he had turned his back on the old method of hard pruning still practised by the professional: 'I see little object in cutting the trees back hard each year when we are trying to provide as good a display as possible over five months of the year.'

Though anyone who wants to grow roses simply for putting on show was told to follow the age-old method of pruning the bushes really hard, there was some agreement on pruning leniently for the best garden results.

In general the previous year's wood, it was advocated, should be cut back to only half its length. Shoots from near the base are to be cherished, for these will become the wood which can eventually replace that already lightly cut back several times. It is here that the individual must have personal consideration. While the rule of the thumb is to 'prune always to an outward-facing' eye and make a spreading bush open at the middle, others already spread too much naturally and somewhere an upward-turning bud must be found on these.

There was a similar resignation apparent in the case of those lanky growers like the Queen Elizabeth rose. Try to keep it low and it grows all the more thrustingly. The only thing is to meet it less than halfway and leave the newer wood at three-four feet. Again varieties differ in their vigour and if they are well-nourished the weaker growers need harder pruning than the stronger plants. This is by no means an invariable rule, however.

So arbitrary is this matter that one of the experts, who grows his roses by the thousand, declared that he worked on the trial and error method. After the first season's hard pruning, he prunes three of his plants of each variety differently — hard, moderately and lightly — before he can decide which they need. Even with one tree, he said, you can prune to different lengths and watch how each responds.

Of course, when an expert has been pruning roses there are no spindly growths to be seen, certainly nothing less than the thickness of a pencil. These have been cut away entirely usually to leave four or five main shoots, sometimes less, on both the hybrid teas and floribundas.

Equally, year by year old, tough and declining wood is cut out entirely. Rough treatment like this helps to promote strong replacement wood that is less prone to disease.

A special word of caution is often wisely given by experts on cutting flowers from our roses. In their first year no stems with leaves should be removed, for a plant needs all it can make to build up its constitution. Even after that, it seems, we should not be too demanding of our plants.

The old advice to cut the flowers with long stems is challenged by the present-day expert on the grounds that there will then be a longer interval before the next crop and the bush will be deprived of some of the food-manufacturing plant it needs. To cut three or four blooms with long stems from the same tree at the same time is simply asking for trouble, is the view taken.

On the time for pruning view-points still differ. While one expert sees no reason to change from the end of March, others find that they are gradually pruning earlier, and the tendency is to get it done in February during the period of dormancy, which seems sound sense. All the pruning cuts are wisely made about a quarter of an inch above each topmost bud which is to grow outwards, in my belief. This is a safe insurance that this bud really will grow and avoids that vexing business of the one below growing out in the wrong direction. Cutting too close to the top bud inhibits it; though, of course, one should not leave a long snag of wood above the bud on which the ever-present agents of decay can settle and multiply.

But vigour is not wholly a matter of pruning. Feeding naturally has something to do with it. The pruning season is also a favourable moment to hoe in one of the proprietary rose fertilisers you can buy in the local shop. It is also a convenient time to follow this by spreading over it a layer of rotted organic refuse.

Hybrid tea roses and floribundas can be kept to garden size by annual pruning but what about the shrub roses of growing popularity? Aside from the romantic overtones they set ringing they suggest a very real down to earth gardening problem, since rain, wind and some warmth combine to make a cat's-cradle of these roses' sprawling growths.

It is a problem that runs through growing most of the so-called 'old-fashioned' roses one orders from catalogues in moments of heady elation. History, evocative names and romantic associations are all very well, but how do you cope in the garden with the whippy branches, heavily armed, that grow five feet long and claw at everything within reach? What you deludedly thought would grow into sturdy bushes become a snare every time you go near them.

Unless you have rolling acres in which to let them go their own way the answer, I am sure, is some form of corrective training. If you have time and patience and not too many such roses, it is best done by tying the growths to staves thrust into the ground. Not just as you would tie in a tomato or dahlia plant, though, but serpentine-like, so that with the main branches near to horizontal the plant is prodded into making many flowering twigs along them instead of only a few at the tips.

In the first year one stake is enough, but as soon as some of those whippy growths arise two are needed and the lax branches are laced to and fro, fixed in place with soft string or pieces of pliant wire, sometimes tying them to one another. In time another must be added, the growths then being trained round them in circles to form a sort of column-shaped plinth, fit to carry a symbolic figure of Flora, the whole set with flowers in midsummer.

Not all the wood is left to develop. Every winter the whole thing is untied and some old wood is removed, together with surplus new growth, which can be too abundant.

Of course, it is a lot of trouble, more than I have time for myself. So I have fallen back on a modification of what has been called the 'pulpit' method of training them. At its best, this consists of encouraging the new shoots to grow up between three or four stakes and to pour their flowers over a ring of wire or withy, linking the stakes at the top. Other plants can be grown successfully between them. But in winter such a forest of stakes can be ugly. My own method aims at reducing their number and employs only one stake, a stout one, to each plant, treated at the end against rotting.

At the top and half way up to this I have nailed four large galvanised staples on opposite sides. Into these are slotted the bent-over ends of two hoops of thick galvanised wire, which can easily be slipped off when the stakes need renewing. The effect is like a sawn-down basket ball goalpost (if that is the correct term) without the basket but with an extra hoop.

Fixing the growth to the wire with small pieces of pliant wire (in preference to string) dresses up the plant and does not severely hamper any cutting out in winter — or after flowering the better time, I believe. All new growths are shortened to just above the upper ring in winter.

I cannot be bothered with a knife and a ball of string for fixing climbers to their posts either, only to have to untie them again when pruning time comes. So at intervals of a foot or so I have stapled hoops of wire round the pillars. The growths can be fixed to these easily, winding the long shoots spirally round, again to try to promote flowering shoots all the way up them.

Trees

Planting a tree: the prunus family: reservations: a laburnum:
a crab like a sneeze: the mountain ash: larger trees: the ghost
tree: the maiden-hair tree: quick growers: the tree of heaven:
conifers: a fossilised relic reclaimed: the coffin juniper

There is something of considerable psychological as well as horticultural significance in planting a tree. It is more than simply that having put one in you are encouraged to go farther in garden-making. One has done something to make a landscape and to perform an act that helps to make life on this planet possible. Without trees there would be no depth of top soil, and without top soil there would be no fertile land on which to grow crops and feed ourselves. One is not immediately conscious of all this, but the significance is there just the same. At the conscious level what one is, or should be, concerned with is making the right choice for the site and for the future prospects of the garden.

For ordinary sites the choice generally narrows down to selecting from the big prunus family, the ornamental crabs and the mountain ashes, some of the birches with the inevitable laburnum always in mind.

About the prunuses one must have certain reservations, or at least plant with an awareness of a possible consequence of choosing those very early ones whose effect can be to bring spring forward. Take the almond, *Prunus amygdalus,* a tree which in fact is best grown in its large-flowered form *pollardii* (actually a hybrid with a flowering peach). You see wonderful examples flowering in March in London, but you can plant one in the suburbs or the country and never see a flower on it, the birds having a great appetite for the buds. The same goes for the flowering peaches. But both have a disorder of which one should be warned: peach leaf curl. This blisters the leaves in late spring and lessens their use to the tree in nourishing itself. To keep it down, spraying both kinds of tree with a fungicide in January or February is essential in some areas where the disease is rife.

I am not arguing against planting these beautiful trees altogether, but simply saying that there are cons attached to them as well as pros. One has to recognise the same in connection with the very early flowering cherries such as the wonderful bright pink Okame; the January-flowering Chinese peach, *Prunus davidiana*; the Japanese apricot, *Prunus mume,* which comes out in February; and that hybrid ornamental plum *Prunus blireiana,* which has foliage of a copper-purple tint. All are highly decorative trees with a compact manner of growth that fits them for smaller gardens and which can be bought 'ready-grown' as 'standard' trees round which one can mow or plant other shrubs. Yet the truth is that the birds may every year rob you of the best of them, an unpallatable fact which has to be faced.

Other small growing cherries which would be desirable if only one could keep the birds off them are Pandora, which has the right upright kind of growth and flowers of palest pink, and Fukubana, whose flowers when you see them are the richest in colour of the family, which has the right sort of twiggy habit. We never see any flowers on ours, but we do watch the bullfinches stripping their buds for much of the winter, which is a sight one must be thankful for just the same.

Fortunately, we do get a bounty of blossom on our Lombardy poplar cherry, *Prunus Amanogawa.* This has completely vertical branches, which means that it can be fitted into a very small space.

The flowers are quite a pronounced pink and are borne in the greatest profusion, in spite of the birds, and the leaves turn to a deep amber before they fall in late autumn. I have read that the name means 'celestial river', the Japanese equivalent of our milky way, which seems to me a very happy piece of imagery, and which always makes one's guest exclaim with delight when you recount it to them while they are admiring the tree in flower.

Our birds seem to have no liking either for a very late-flowering cherry called Shimidsu Sakura, whose blossom dangles in bunches on five-inch long stalks. We also get a good flowering from the 'great white cherry', Tai-haku, whose large flowers are single and purest white. One called Ukon never fails us either; in this case the double flowers are a pale greenish yellow. The tree I cannot abide, though we do have two, planted in a mistaken moment, is the favourite Kanzan. It has been overdone. No one could deny that it is strikingly handsome, but you can have too much of a good thing, even in Japanese flowering cherries, and anyway this is one of the most vigorous varieties.

When it comes to selecting a laburnum, the first choice of course falls on the variety with the longest golden tresses. This is *Laburnum vossii,* a garden tree about which one can have no reservations, except that children must be forbidden to eat the seeds that it bears so plentifully for much of the winter. Another good one, *Laburnum alpinum,* flowers just a little later and its racemes of flowers are not quite so long. Both are splendid small garden trees.

Curiously, the birds seem to have no liking for the ornamental crab apples grown for their flowers and found in catalogues under the old Latin name of malus. The one I am most keen on with red flowers is called Profusion, but one can plant any that are grown with almost equal satisfaction. They tend to have soaring rather than outspreading branches, which is an advantage in a garden. *Malus floribunda,* however, has a rather 'Japanese' weeping look about it, the pale pink flowers falling like water from the arched branches. A pink one called Katherine is rather remarkable in that though the flowers appear double and therefore particularly showy, they are fertile and set a good crop of very ornamental fruits. Other ornamental crabs grown for their fruits, notably the yellow Golden Hornet, the Dartmouth Crab and *Malus prunifolia,* all spectacular in autumn, are not so effective in flower.

One member of this family, with a name like a sneeze — *Malus tschonoskii,* we grow for nothing but this rich autumn colour of its leaves. Indeed, this is a factor of great importance to consider when planting trees, and is often found in the mountain ash group — allied to white flowers in May and showers of berries in early autumn. The mountain ash one could recommend anybody to plant is *Sorbus vilmorinii,* which, flowering, fruiting and colouring its leaves brilliantly, has no tendency to make anything but a dense head of twiggy branches. *Sorbus discolor,* besides carrying a heavy crop of scarlet berries, is specially remarkable for the rich tints of its leaves in autumn, while *Sorbus hupehensis* has large berries like pale pink marble. Not that our own mountain ash *Sorbus aucuparia,* is inconsiderable, especially in its fern-leaved variety *asplenifolia.*

When I noticed *Sorbus scalaris* at a Chelsea show, at first glance I took it for a mimosa, so silvery were the fern-like leaves of the pot-grown tree. I at once ordered it, and if on our heavy soil the leaves have not shown quite the same character, it has proved a most attractive tree, especially in autumn, when the leaves have turned to bronze and it carries its bunches of fruits. But now we are getting up into the bigger trees, which, strangely enough, can only be bought as small specimens which you have to watch grow up, in the way that you do a Judas tree, the red-flowered *Cercis siliquastrum,* quite a small grower but one which dislikes being moved once it has reached any size.

Others with this inclination include *Davidia involucrata,* the Chinese dove, ghost or handkerchief tree. Many seasons may go by before this puts out a first flower, but the excitement will be all the greater when it does. This seems to me an admirable commemorative tree to plant in celebration of some family occasion, for the foliage is decorative and it naturally makes an outline that justifies a solitary place in an expanse of turf. Similarly, one has to wait long for the first foot-long plumes of yellow flowers on a *Koelreuteria paniculata.* But meanwhile the huge compound leaves are satisfying enough, especially when they have turned to amber in autumn.

The maiden-hair tree, *Ginkgo biloba,* is grown for the beauty of its foliage alone, and this is sufficiently distinguished to pay for its garden space, especially as it is a slender grower. The light green leaves, aptly described by the common name, turn to gold and linger for several weeks before they fall. Foliage appeal is all that *Liquidamber styraciflua* has to offer, yet in autumn the huge oak-like leaves take on tones of hectic scarlet and glowing crimson, while it is one of the few trees that does best in one of these problem spots where the soil lies always wet.

On an altogether smaller scale, the much-admired American dogwoods, the white *Cornus florida* and its pink variety *rubra,* grow as inverted cones like hazel trees, branching near the ground. Both flowered first for us after six years, but in the interval gave brilliant autumn colour.

Suppose, though, you want a tall tree, a quick grower, to plant in your garden to make the buildings beyond seem smaller than they are (and the smaller they will seem the closer to your view point you plant it). Well, the 'tree of heaven', *Ailanthus altissima,* will live up to both its common and botanical names and soar swiftly.

Next to this tree with its handsome ash-like foliage and gaunt outline, which thrives so well in towns, as the specimens in the London squares witness, the 'false acacia' has every claim for planting in a new garden to introduce a mature look in the minimum of time. Found in plant catalogues as *Robinia pseud-acacia,* its easy-going ways are evidenced by the tall examples seen in the gardens round the houses of affluent Victorian bour-geoisie fast disappearing from the London suburbs. Perhaps with other Victoriana it is due for being acceptable again. It has an elegant lightness very different from the solid, enduring effects of those times. Its speed of growth can be incredible. An eight-foot plant of the pink-flowering variety *decaisneana* I put in five years ago has more than doubled itself in this time, and has flowered well each year. The most common kind is white. I do not regret planting the pink form, but I wish I had then known of one called *Robinia neomexicana,* which is said to flower rosily in August as well, though I believe only very small trees of this are available.

Of the big ornamental cherries, the quickest growing members of their family though rather less rapid than those I have just mentioned, are two natives worthy of garden planting. The wild gean is best grown in its double variety *Prunus avium plena.* The bird cherry, *Prunus padus,* is seen less often, and is hardly recog-nised as a cherry for it has the distinctive manner of producing its small sprays in tassels like a buddleia.

Among quick-growing conifers our most attractive is the silver-grey *Cupressus arizonica,* not more than a yard through when twenty feet tall. When the lower levels become untidy, as they do, one can remove the branches up to about six feet in the manner of the cypresses in Italian paintings, to reveal the cinnamon-coloured bark.

The most publicised tree of our time has the unwieldy name of *Metasequoia glyptostroboides,* a conifer that drops its leaves for the winter and makes spire-like growth. It made new history when discovered living in China some years ago, after being previously known to botanists from fossil relics. Now it is making up for all its long centuries of obscurity on some remote untrodden hillside. A seedling in Cambridge Botanic Gardens is already thirty-odd feet tall — on limey soil in a low rainfall area!

Cupressus macrocarpa has fallen into disrepute for its inability to withstand frosts, which is no more than one would have expected of a Californian tree. Yet the yellow-leaved variety, *lutea,* which originated in a Cheshire nursery, seems quite hardy, and besides growing two-three feet in a year in good soil, brings life to the garden on a winter's day with its spire of gold.

Winter is a time that lays special emphasis on the effect conifers can make, for it is then that they are most significant in gardens, enlivening an otherwise doleful scene. In fact they can take drabness right out of the winter garden.

Almost all are evergreen, ever-silver or ever-gold, even ever-blue of a sort. Some are so eager to become mighty pillars that they will put on a yard or more in a year. Others will remain with you as dwarfs throughout your gardening life.

Perhaps the fastest grower of all, is the dark green *Cupressocyparis leylandii* used for hedging. As you might expect, in these days when there is so much screening and shielding to be done, against swiftly-rising concrete horrors, it is in great demand, scarce and a bit expensive. Thus one may have to fall back on the familiar Lawson cypress, called *Chamaecyparis lawsoniana* but better known as cupressus. Within the forms of this you could find all the conifers you would ever want, with winter-surviving foliage of rich green, grey, blue, silver or gold. Personally, I specially like the golden ones, *lutea* and *stewartii,* with a growth rate of about two feet a year for isolated planting. I must also put in a good word for the incense cedar, *Libocedrus decurrens,* not often grown by amateurs but slender and slow enough. And for the noble 'blue' Atlas cedar *Cedrus atlantica glauca,* one of the most graceful of all trees.

Not having a rock garden, but not eschewing the dwarf conifers just because of the lack, I find one can use them with effect in a wild garden at the points where the paths turn to one side and at intersections. In these spots the dome-like *Chamae-cyparis lawsoniana minima glauca,* and the mossy *Chamaecyparis obtusa nana* can be shown off in a way they deserve. We also grow the flat *Juniperus sabina tamariscifolia* as a ground cover beneath shrubs.

Of the same family and with outstretched branches, *Juniperus sabina pfitzeriana* is specially suitable for flanking a flight of steps where wing walls would be too expensive or troublesome to build; or, indeed for bringing enduring greenery and an interesting outline to patches of the garden you want to leave to themselves.

Conifers can also weep with more decorum and less obtrusiveness than the willow. One I find especially attractive has the name of *Chamaecyparis nootkatensis pendula.* As our tree grows it is gradually taking on the form of a waterfall reflecting lush grass. For some years I have been watching the slow progress of our 'coffin juniper' *Juniperous recurva coxii,* thinking I shall be in my own before it reaches any size, but this tardiness would fit it as a graceful weeping tree for a tiny garden.

In a winter setting of bare stems and branches the conifers stand out in sharp relief, but none so surprisingly as *Pinus sylvestris aurea,* which obligingly decks itself out in a golden raiment just for the winter months, and grows so slowly that you would never take it for a Scots pine.

Alpines

*The rock garden: modern alternatives: making a terrace bed:
the rock table: the peat bed: creating an opportunity: midget
rhododendrons: shrubs and other plants for peat beds*

Does anyone outside the really high income groups make a
rock garden nowadays? The cost of stone and cartage has
put it almost beyond reach. Besides, changing tastes have led us
to question whether a tiny replica of an alpine scene really has a
place in the smaller garden. But with the miniature in plants still
exerting a fascinating hold on us, it is being supplanted by the
garden of alpine plants made on the flat or a rock table.

Given a choice of the right plants, alpine beds can be made in
the shade as well as in the sun. Broadly, the idea is to choose
kinds, of compatible habits of growth, that will not outrun one
another, and to make the soil congenial to them; then leave them
to cover the ground, excluding weeds with their thick mat of
growth, making a carpet that will yield patches of colour all
through the season.

The chief need of these plants is for soil that drains sharply yet holds sufficient moisture to keep them growing. In the search for ways of gardening taking less labour, I have replaced terrace beds formerly devoted to a wallflower-verbena succession with alpine plants and these have become glowing tapestries of colour, almost maintaining themselves. To lighten our heavy soil I added grit and plenty of the 'pea beach' used on greenhouse stagings, working it in to the full depth of the spade, and putting a layer of crushed rubble at the bottom of each trench as I dug. Then I added a generous helping of the invaluable peat to improve the texture of the soil. When I had finished the beds were four inches higher than their former level, retained by brick-edgings, and this favoured the plants.

Although the ultimate effect sought is informal in character, planting has to be rather carefully planned. I drew up a list of plants and divided them into four seasons of flowering. On a plan divided into areas, each representing the plot to be occupied by each plant, I set down the names, arranging them so that neighbouring plants would flower successively, distributing the four seasons fairly evenly over the whole area.

Many alpine plants keep their leaves in the winter. So even then there is a pleasing patchwork of green, silver and the rufus tints that some plants take on. For the earliest days of spring there should be generous pepperings of the very early flowering miniature bulbs.

By this method one can get colour effects all right, but to savour the intriguing wonder of alpine plants you have to see them close up. And what if you can't bend like you used to? The answer is to make rock tables, like those to be seen in the Savill Gardens in Windsor Great Park (open to the public every day) where the beds are raised to thigh level. These have the added advantage that you can fill the rock sides with plants that in nature hang from crevices, and the height of the beds means that the soil is perfectly drained, nourishing a collection of alpine plants that can otherwise only be grown out of doors in a rock garden if you happened to possess one.

Another contemporary way of growing little plants successfully is in peat beds.

In this fashionable form of gardening, which can be practised on the flat as well as on a sloping patch of land, the raised soil is heavily laced with peat and retained by peat blocks forming walls or outcrops in the manner of rock itself.

Consider the advantages. The lumps of peat are cheap to buy, and light to handle. They do not need manoeuvring into place with a crowbar. Nor are they so difficult to place in a position to satisfy the eye in the way that boulders can be. Beds of this kind can also be quite in character with a small garden laid out in an informal fashion.

Few species of weeds really take to the acid soil built up in a peat garden and those that do are easily pulled out from the loosely textured surface. The peat blocks, bonded like bricks and knitted together with peaty soil in place of mortar, can make retaining walls that ask for no mason's skill to construct. They can be used instead of stone to divide varying levels in the garden, and will offer a congenial home to the plants that insist on the soil containing no lime.

As you explore the world of plants more deeply you soon stand on the fringe of a charmed circle joined by this common loathing of lime. As a group they appear as the most desirable of all plants, and once you experience their lure they present an unending field.

Fortunately, a great number of the huge rhododendron tribe are midget plants, and their variety is as great as the vast upland spaces of the Himalayas, whence they come, might suggest. Many of the other plants that thrive under these conditions are similarly dwarf, which means that here, just as in a rock garden, you can grow a big collection of plants in a small area — even of rhododendrons, for which you otherwise need a country estate.

Some begin to flower in February and the succession can continue well into the autumn if you accept the berries of plants as some of the rewards of your gardening. Moreover, many are evergreen, and so a peat garden will present a living pattern throughout the year.

Where the site slopes, perhaps something approaching a natural scene built up with roughly turned up lumps of peat can be attempted. The larger pieces can form bluffs to support pockets of soil for the plants that like sharp drainage as well as moisture-holding peat, giving way to little dells into which the moisture can drain and where the plants that thrive in soil that is always pretty damp will need no persuading to flourish.

Some of the smallest of the alpine rhododendrons, which make tiny hummocks studded with butterfly-like flowers — often blue and violet as well as endless pinks and reds — come into the first category. The primula family offers many plants for the latter, and here you can grow some of the most desirable of all, for the peat resembles the accumulated rotting vegetable debris on which they subsist in their remote Himalayan ravines. In the peat garden they can be joined by the meconopsis, those alluring blue or yellow, even pink, poppy-like plants once brought from Tibet.

In general rhododendrons are thought of as plants which like dappled shade. The high alpine species, however, need open situations. The answer seems to be to contrive the site for a peat garden so that some of the larger-growing peat-loving shrubs like pieris, the so-called lily-of-the-valley bush, kalmia, with flowers like birthday-cake decorations, and the dwarf Japanese maples, can be included and shade those plants that shun the direct sun.

Besides the primulas and meconopsis, the latter group includes the gaultherias and vaccineums, with tiny urn-shaped flowers succeeded by berries of white or pink or red. To my mind the peat garden is wasted on the ordinary run of heathers, however much they may enjoy it. Here they are better supplanted by a similar but more delicate group of plants, the cassiopes, which will form green carpets over the peat.

However, the tree heathers can be excepted, for the drainage of the site, in addition to holding moisture in just the right degree, offers them a better chance of survival in hard winters than they might have elsewhere. As Mediterranean plants, they like the sun.

In addition to all these comparatively small-flowering shrubs, on its shady side the peat garden offers just the right quarters for several plants that otherwise defy successful cultivation. These are the beautiful violet ramondas and the shortias and schizocodons, the last two with some of the most engaging of flowers, bell-like and fringed but most elegantly poised.

Finally, a raised peat garden standing well above the surrounding level offers a chance of growing all these otherwise unattainable plants even where the existing soil is limy, provided only the smaller growers are planted which are unlikely to send their roots down into the natural level where they will meet the chalk that is poison to them.

Weeds

*Weeds and slugs: the ubiquitous hoe: handweeding: its use:
smoother mulching: paraquat: the simazine weedkiller: bindweed, a method of control: dalapon: the old remedy*

To be told that the leaves of ground elder make an agreeable
substitute for spinach, or that an infusion of them will relieve
gout, is little consolation to the gardener battling with this most
pernicious of weeds. Nor is it in any way endeared to us senti-
mentally if we hear that it may be a legacy from Roman occupation here. It remains the ultimate garden foe against which there
often seems no ultimate weapon. I have even heard of despairing
amateur gardeners moving house away from it!

Weeds or slugs — it would be hard to decide which are the
more discouraging to anyone trying to make his own fragment
of earthly paradise. But strangely, one suggests an answer to the
other. The slug that resolutely bites through every new shoot
put up by the delphiniums you have just planted — shoots that
grow feebler with each attempt — gives the clue to controlling

determined weeds. Decapitate them. Not once, but again and again, until they themselves give up in despair.

For plants cannot live by roots alone. They need leaves for those mysterious processes by which chemicals, light, air and water combine to accomplish the wonder of the growing plant that blossoms. Thwart it in every attempt to make leaves and, as the slugs constantly remind us, it will languish and die.

The weeds that do flourish under constant cutting in lawns reinforce, not refute the argument. They are only the kinds which are able to press themselves flat against the ground to avoid the relentless circuit of the mower's blades. Not many can so adapt themselves. The others quickly fail.

To control the growth of fruit trees you reduce the area of leaves in summer. It is the inexorable law of plant life. The roots may look after the production of new shoots in spring, but later the leaves become the dominant partner and play an essential part in nourishing the roots. By giving a patch of weeds the chance to make plenty of leaves you are also ensuring that the root system is strengthening itself unseen.

One answer, then, to the weed that laughs at expensive easy-to-apply weedkillers is to hoe, hoe, hoe. Just as you would regularly hoe between the rows of vegetables every week, chop the heads off every Sunday morning, wet or fine, with a sharp hoe or even a grass hook. Hydra-like, they will try to raise several new heads where there was one before. But gradually you will get the upper hand.

There are advantages to the soil also. Weed destruction by chemicals does nothing to improve the ground in the way that hoeing does. By hoeing you admit air to the ground and release accumulated carbon dioxide there, with a consequent fillip to plant growth. Ground hoed regularly in summer is much easier to turn over in winter. By hoeing along the rows of vegetables and between flowers you destroy, even before they are visible, the seedlings that are always arising from seeds that lie in the soil in 'numberless infinities' and which are increased alarmingly every time you allow a weed to seed.

It is not as burdensome as it sounds, for modern hoes are made of steel to which the soil does not cling, and they are designed to enable you to reach close to cultivated plants without injuring them.

Though chemical weedkillers impinge heavily on the gardener's perennial concern with weed control, there is still a place for hand weeding, perhaps with an occasional prod of a border fork. Apart from the figure-improving enforced exercise involved, three factors mitigate any tedium. If one does have 'aggression' deep in the soul, some must be dissipated in the destructiveness of the weeding process. Second, you come to know more intimately the plants you grow from the close contact of fussing round them. At a more practical level, the weeds offer a source of organic refuse to rot down into the compost for vegetables and new plantings and of which material there is seldom enough. Some serve to make the loam essential for potting composts. These are any which come up with soil about their roots, and are kept separate and go into a stack of their own. In my experience only the roots of bindweed need be kept out of a compost heap. Others are destroyed and assimilated in a stack made big enough to get really hot.

However, I do burn the pulled-up weeds if they happen to have got left to the seeding stage, but then all the bonfire ash in our garden is put round any frost-tender plants, in the fond belief that its action helps to toughen them.

Some people deal with the weed problem by successfully 'smother mulching' with sawdust, peat or old leaves, drawing more over every shoot that peeps through. The effect of denying the leaves the light is the same. But in some magnificently fitted out back room, scientists have devised a substance that has the same effect with less labour. Poured on to leafy growth of any kind, it drains it of its colour in a matter of hours. Next day, or perhaps the one after, what was the plant lies in a heap of apparently lifeless tatters. They have given it the cryptic name of paraquat.

For annual weeds it is the end; though of course, they will doubtless have left countless seeds behind them to make sure their race is not wiped out. Perennials make a recovery from this plague that passes over them, but weakly, and they fall to a second, third or fourth dose.

This is not one of those scorching weedkillers like, say, sulphate of iron or phenols, which simply burn off the tops, however. It interferes with the vital processes of the plant. Its action is based on this principle, that a plant, even if it is a determined weed, does need its leaves. Roots alone are not enough. The green colouring element is vitally significant. Denude the plant of it and its days are brief.

The beauty of paraquat is that like snow that disappears as it falls, when this stuff touches the ground its potency is lost. In practical terms it means that you can clean a row of raspberries without disturbing their shallow roots and having to spend the next week removing the minute prickles from your fingers. And you can eradicate ground elder from hedge bottoms without the agony of knowing that it will all come back. It may do for a bit, but this time you will be the master.

It also means that those who reject the idea of covering ground between shrubs with weed-proof vegetation can easily keep the soil clean and neat-looking. And in spring the ground you dug in the autumn, then smoothed down in the New Year, no longer requires the removal of that inevitable carpet of weeds by the disturbing hoe. Now you can spray with paraquat and sow the next day. The seeds too prefer it like that.

No one is going to say all the same that this is the ultimate weapon against weeds and that it can take the place of all other means of eradication. We still have reason to congratulate ourselves on the fact that the simazine weedkiller has taken the place of the old sodium chlorate, lasting longer in its effect and staying where you spray it, instead of spreading dangerously into surrounding ground.

Yet though simazine weedkiller has been around for some years now and is sold in every local garden shop, few seem to realise how to get the best from this remarkable substance.

Perhaps it is because it is often described as a 'total weedkiller' that simazine is misunderstood. It is not quick to kill weeds. Sometimes they take six weeks to die after soil in which they are growing has been treated. What it does with unerring effectiveness is to prevent weeds growing in soil to which it has been applied.

Not for just a few weeks either, but for a whole year, as though pronounced upon by a kind fairy. Thus if you do apply it during the winter, soon after the New Year begins when the ground is clean, that bit of gravel path or crazy paving need not bother you for the rest of the year.

Unfortunately simazine, in spite of having a name like an enchanter with a wand and a tall hat, is not able to distinguish between weeds and the plants you want to preserve. It inhibits the growth of them all indiscriminately; that is, if most of their active roots lie in the top three inches of soil. Insoluble, though it is distributed in water, simazine can penetrate no farther than this, or so the theory goes.

Such an inability has valuable practical upshots. It means that you can apply it to paths and between paving stones to keep weeds away without fear that the weedkiller may wash into adjoining flower beds, to the peril of the plants there. It means also that you can use it in those troublesome places where retaining walls and steps abut on to turf and the mower will not reach. If you are not specially tidy-minded you can use it along the fringes of turf where it adjoins informal beds of shrubs. If you have one of those Chelsea-type rock gardens with bluffs of stone protruding from turf you could apply it round these and save endless clipping.

Another use calls for a certain daring. Nurserymen are now applying simazine to their plantations of roses and fruit and certain ornamental trees. I have seen fields of roses untouched by cultivator or hoe but completely clear of weeds. If the roots are well down, runs the argument, why not make the top three inches a neutral zone? There is room for experiment, clearly, but always first on some pilot plot.

A further means of weed control lies in the exploitation of the selective weedkillers sold primarily for use on turf. Their use is not limited to lawn weeds. Applied to the leaves of weeds anywhere, they will destroy the offenders. But while these magic substances can mysteriously and intelligently distinguish between grass and weeds, sparing the one and slaying the other, they are unable to tell the difference between weeds and cultivated plants. So between the latter they have to be applied through a discarded detergent bottle or dabbed on to leaves with a brush or sponge. This is not so difficult as it may sound as these substances are most effective and the weeds most vulnerable when they are in their fullest stage of growth, their leaves offering the greatest area on which to receive them.

The important thing amateurs often fail to realise in using selective weedkillers is that they fail to do their job properly if more is put on than the makers recommend. The leaves simply get scorched then and the roots live to grow another day.

Fortunately the rampageous bindweed is very vulnerable. In

fact, the speed at which it grows is its undoing, for the greater the spread of foliage a weed exposes to the fluid the more it leaves itself open to early death.

A well-tried method of destroying bindweed is to dip the ends of the trails in a jar of the weedkiller, moving it on to a fresh patch each day. During evening potterings I find it better to carry round a bucket of the mixture, uncoil the twining vines of the bindweed, dip them in and pass on to another lot. Where there is room I have simply laid the growths on the ground and poured the weedkiller over them.

Here we must enter the world of chemical terms. Most selective weedkillers are based on substances known as 2,4-D or MCPA. But there is another, much more powerful and more expensive, termed 2,4,5-T. This one will ultimately cope with the more determined weeds like mare's-tail and ground elder. Some now contain a substance known for a special spite against clover, which means that it will also attack other such stubborn weeds also. When you buy a bottle in your local hardware store under one of the proprietary names the comparative prices are an indication of what you are offered or whether one has a little of the other in it.

Another still, called dalapon, kills only grasses and other plants that put up only one seedleaf, like many bulbs, as distinct from the rest of the plant kingdom that in earliest infancy make two leaves. It leaves the latter, the broad-leaved plants, untouched.

Devious, insidious and ruthless though selective weedkillers are, and however many permutations of applications they suggest to the ingenious, they may not be the complete up-to-date answer to the ever-present problem of weeds. Perhaps the humble hoe, dressed up with its silky, stainless steel blade coupled with the gardener's wisdom does remain the ultimate weapon in defeating the annual kinds which always threaten to cover the whole plot with a thick carpet of growth if you leave them to it.

Ground-Cover

Necessity: the weed-controllers: the green or golden carpet:
cherubim and seraphim: London pride: the periwinkles: the
violets: a wild strawberry: the supreme geranium

Necessity first drove me to exploit some of the plants that
spread over the ground freely, even ruthlessly, depriving
weeds of opportunities of founding new dynasties. In the working
out we have found it a very desirable way of dealing with garden
areas on which little time can be spared for upkeep. Ground-cover
plants, in fact, can be employed as full-time gardeners.

They must, of course, offer certain references. While they must
settle down and begin to spread quickly, they must not root so
deeply that where the ground allotted to them is exceeded they
cannot be eradicated. They must make a mat of growth that
weed seeds will not penetrate. The foliage must be decorative
and preferably persist all the winter, bringing life to the garden
even in the dead of the year. They must generally endure some
shade without becoming straggly or losing the colour of their

[124]

leaves. For setting out around flowering shrubs — even some of the more vigorous roses — plants that measure up to these requirements have led us back to some that were formerly discarded by the barrowload.

The impression must not be given, however, that ground-covering plants will destroy perennial weeds already in the ground. Dependable maids-of-all-work for busy and disinclined gardeners though they do become in time, it would be a mistake if they were allowed to gain a reputation they cannot sustain. The trouble apparently arises over the repeated assertion that they will 'suppress' weeds. Eagerly the hard-pressed seize on the notion that you can set a cultivated plant on to a wild one and the patch of nettles or buttercups or couch will be the one to give way. The futility of this is soon shown by the way in which the weeds will declare that they were there first and engulf the interlopers.

To reap the undeniable benefits from ground-cover plants you have to clean the soil of perennial weed roots first. Without this preliminary, putting in any herbaceous plants on land where such weeds have been allowed to have their way, particularly on heavy ground, is invariably followed by anguish. The weed roots interlace those of the cultivated plants ineradicably.

So first the ground must be painstakingly forked over, even combed through, to see that every possible scrap of root of perennial weed is removed. The ground-cover plants are put in during autumn or spring, and for the next season the patches have to be weeded by hand. But after that, save for rooting out an occasional dandelion or dock, the ground-coverers will close over the soil, making a green, grey or golden carpet that will be a permanency. Of course, some of them do flower, but this is regarded as more incidental than significant.

Do shrubs which stand in this groundwork of foliage suffer from the competition for nutrients and moisture? Provided the soil is properly enriched at planting time, there need be little fear of this. They actually benefit from the moisture retained by the living 'mulch', and the roots of the shrubs generally strike deep down, far below the level of those of the ground-cover. Even with evergreens, there is a discarding of the old leaves and renewal going on season by season, and as those cast off decay they add to the fertility of the soil.

One of our most efficient gardeners of this school has proved to be the creeping Caucasian comfrey, *Symphytum grandiflorum*, which I once saw in a garden labelled 'cherubim and seraphim'. At the first intimations of spring it scatters its olive-green carpet with flowers of ivory tipped with apricot, which quality I suppose gave rise to the name. The leaves are fairly well polished and the network of foliage and stems it makes is so dense that I believe it would be a plant for very ably retaining the soil on a sloping bank and would need no clipping over like grass or St. John's Wort, another good ground-cover, does. Having worked up a stock of it, I am now resolved to plant this wherever we have a bare patch of soil and where weeds would otherwise take up residence. The St. John's Wort, *Hypericum calycinum*, of course has a special value in flowering in August and September, which can bring a burst of colour to shrub borders that are otherwise devoid of it after June.

One of the most determined of all plants sold for ground-covering purposes is an ornamental-leaved nettle, none other than a relative of the wild archangel, called *Lamium galeobdolon variegatum*. This will spread far and wide, rather in the manner of the old creeping Jenny, *Lysimachia nummularia,* also enjoying a return to vogue as a ground-coverer, especially in its golden-leaved form *aurea*. While the latter does no more than spread, however, covering the ground very neatly, the lamium is a plant to set between shrubs that have a fairly tall 'leg'. Otherwise it is inclined to run up into them and entwine their lower branches, which I admit is not very sightly. Though one must not deny that it is an excellent plant of this type.

In complete contrast, London pride, *Saxifraga umbrosa,* now back in fashion too, is as well-behaved a ground-coverer as one could wish for: evergreen, dense, not deep rooting and flowering as well in shade as in sun. To make a big patch of it quickly one can pull the clumps apart several times in a season, preferably during a rainy spell. This is what we did with the rare variegated form, whose leaves are marbled with gold and of which we were given a few bits from an old garden where it had been treasured. In no time we had a big patch, and on the most dense clay, too.

Few gardeners of my acquaintance seem to have heard of the London pride whose leaves turn to crimson in autumn. Its name is *Saxifraga geum*. It is not so quick to increase but eventually makes the same impenetrable mat that defies weeds and does even gobble up some kinds. Another saxifrage, the bergenia, is a ground-cover plant of such distinction as to deserve a special chapter of its own later in this book. I have seen broad areas of this very happily contrasted with patches of *Pachysandra terminalis,* which has intricately fashioned leaves to set off against the rounded ones of the bergenia, and which are even more effective visually in a silver-variegated form one can sometime acquire.

A very special word must be said for the periwinkles, the lesser and the greater, called botanically *Vinca minor* and *Vinca major* respectively. For our purpose the little one is to be preferred, keeping closer to the ground in a tight network of growth. I collect all the forms I can find, whether they have single or double flowers, of the common blue kind or white or liver coloured varieties, while some have golden-marked leaves. Heucherella and tiarella are two others: the latter rescued from old gardens where it has become so rampant that it is cruelly trodden underfoot during demolitions; both are also mentioned in the section of 'Special Pleading'. Allied to them are two plants whose generic names are an anagram of each other, mitella and timella. As well as getting the letters mixed up, you can hardly tell the two apart; but this does not matter, as either is worth having, both as ground-cover and as a source of leaves and strange greenish flowers for vases.

Though I have said that one of the main qualifications of a successful ground-covering plant is that it should be able to endure some shade, I do include among those I grow the wall-germander, *Teucrium chamaedrys,* which really must have the sun if it is to give its pink flowers in August. This is a little shrub, a resolute one that in our garden has even smothered that vile creeping speedwell that defies selective weedkillers. In some gardens, in fact, open ground-loving alpine plants of a certain tenacity can be made to do service as ground-coverers if they can be kept in the sun. Usually they are the kind of plants generally recommended for planting between paving stones. For our purpose they are more practical. I would have no hesitation in letting loose in the forefront of shrubs the bluish acaenas, with such exquisite little leaves; nor the fern-like but unhappily named *Cotula squalida,* which looks rather like the yarrow that creeps about in lawns. Neither has flowers of any account, but they are

[127]

none the worse for that and they do have a decoratively functional value.

Many other plants which remain equally lowly while spreading far and wide do bear pleasing flowers, often on a scale out of proportion to their individual size. The flowers of *Mazus reptans* are like tiny snapdragons. Both *Dianthus neglectus* and *Dianthus deltoides* produce tiny pinks. The flowers of *Erinus* Dr. Haenaele are like stars of bright carmine. All the creeping thymes which flower in pink or red or white, and the alpine phloxes in pink and mauve and blue, will fulfil our labour-saving purpose in small gardens in the sun, and one might even use the trailing soapwort, *Saponaria ocymoides,* which is as persistent and determined as a detergent. To this list one must also add all the sedums and sempervivums, the creeping *Veronica prostrata* with blue or pink flowers and the blue skullcap, *Scutellaria indica.*

Really lowly plants that hug the ground which will put up with shade include the violets, the wild *Viola odorata,* and the purple-leaved *Viola labradorica,* and a little-known plant which, called *Waldsteinia ternata,* honours the same family as the Beethoven sonata bearing the name. It is like a strawberry plant that keeps its leaves above ground the whole year, as though the lacquer that seems to cover them might be a preserving agent.

Indeed, in some gardens planted to save labour which I have visited the wild strawberry has been used successfully as a ground-coverer. The wilding I have made most of myself is the common bugle, *Ajuga reptans,* which produces blue flowers in May as beautiful in their effect as any cultivated ground-coverer one might buy. It has many forms and one is led by its all-round appeal to collect all one can find. The same happens with the dead nettle, *Lamium maculatum,* whose deep green leaves are marked with a bar of ivory like a badger's snout and which bears mauve or pink or white flowers according to the form on which you might lay hands. Perhaps best of all the wild plants used for these ends is the common lady's mantle, *Alchemilla mollis,* whose flowers are green but whose leaves are some of the most exquisite one could ever find in a garden, soft to the touch and a refreshing soft green that will complement almost anything around which you may plant it.

Supreme among ground-coverers as a family, however, are the true geraniums, those robustly hardy plants whose name has been usurped by a family with a good deal less to offer. For the plants everyone knows as geraniums and which flower so generously in formal garden beds, in urns and window boxes, have no right to the name. By one of those tiresome pieces of botanical confusion the name geranium got attached to them when they should properly be called pelargoniums. It would be all right if it could be regarded as their common name alone, but it belongs to a group of plants that have everything the busy gardener can ask.

Related to the wild blue meadow cranesbill and our magnificent-leafed herb robert, the hardy geraniums now being given honoured places in the more skilfully planted gardens will often flower for several months on end, and certainly offer ten months of decorative foliage that alone would put them among the élite of plants. They need no staking, and will so densely colonise the places where they are planted that they will soon bar the way of any weeds seeking a foothold there. Moreover, they will endure shade, dryness and damp soil with equal fortitude.

For several years I have been eagerly acquiring every species and variety I can find. I began with *Geranium endressii* and have yet found no better. It opens its first soft pink flowers in June, and still, as autumn gives way to winter, the plants carry their successors. Year by year the first single plant has spread until it now occupies a patch six feet square, a mat of shot-silver leaves that could stand by itself as a decorative feature. It seeds itself about admittedly, but the seedlings are gladly welcomed to make new plantings between shrubs, for planting with other hardy border flowers, whether conditions are favourable or not.

Except that it bears its pink flowers only in June, *Geranium macrorrhizum* has equal qualities. In autumn the foliage takes on rich tints like the maples. Winter may destroy it all, but by February replacements are well on the way. Crush the leaves and they emit a refreshing scent. Only the limits of its June flowering detract also from the superlative merits of the violet-blue *Geranium ibericum*, but this too has introduced rose and crimson shades to its splendid leaves.

Perhaps *Geranium psilostemon*, more familiarly known as *Geranium armenum*, is a little hard to place in the garden, for the flowers have that deep magenta colouring that swears at other shades, and they have sharply defined black eyes. I find that silver-leaved plants combine happily with it, and grow it in company with one of its own kind with this quality, *Geranium renardii,* a most attractive plant whose palest pink flowers have intriguing violet markings on them.

The meadow cranesbill itself is sufficiently decorative to admit to the garden, though its hybrid Arthur Johnson excels it, for it keeps up a succession of those exquisite salvers of blue. We also get many weeks of flowers from *Geranium wallichianum* Buxton's Blue. This is said to be 'doubtfully hardy', but it has survived nine winters for us in wet soil, spreading all the while.

Geranium lancastriense has the distinction of being a native plant found wild only on the island of Walney off the Lancashire coast. It is a form of the familiar 'bloody cranesbill'. *Geranium sanguineum,* but with pink flowers that are veined with crimson instead of the vivid violet-magenta. *Geranium sanguineum* also has a valuable white form which goes on and on, hugging the ground in the same manner, and equally redoubtable in the face of threats from other plants.

If *Geranium nodosum* is less showy than others it compensates by the shiny leaves which do their best to emphasise the long succession of lilac flowers, while *Geranium punctatum* is also grown mainly for the foliage, which is marked with maroon spots. Both are excellent as ground coverers in shade.

Though the hardy geraniums are a little difficult to eradicate altogether once you have planted them, I have never yet heard of anyone who wanted to. They are like the best of guests, whom you are glad to have with you, who accept the garden as they find it and enhance it with qualities of their own, yet never attempt to occupy the place and submerge others.

Surgery

Tailoring to fit the garden: enhancing the outline: cutting out leaders: training: corrective surgery: binding up the wounds

Shrubs that are planned to furnish a labour-saving garden cannot be allowed to go on extending in height and spreading sideways for ever. They must be curbed occasionally with the knife — tailored to the garden, if you like, perhaps in winter when one is frustrated by the weather and the state of the soil in attempts to get other kinds of gardening work done. By emphasising the silhouettes of shrubs and trees winter often reveals how crowded we allow them to become.

When a bush begins to decline in its 'yield' of flowers this is usually because too many shoots are straining after the light, in consequence growing weakly. The bush with branches among which the air can circulate freely is always the more healthy, better-looking and more generous with its flowers.

When all is leafless it is easy to distinguish between the old and the new wood from the colour and texture of the bark and while

[131]

the soil remains unworkable pent-up energies can be released by removing an old branch bodily, right to the ground from such shrubs as mock orange, weigela, deutzia, escallonia and the stronger-growing summer roses.

In theory this is the wrong time, I know. Correctly it should be done just after flowering, but there never seems time then. The sacrifice of some flowers in the following summer is easily justified by eventual results.

In winter it is also easy to decide on the crossing branches of ornamental trees whose outline would be enhanced by their removal, or those which mar the symmetry or detract from the upward reach of the leaders. Even young trees benefit, I find, from a few awkwardly growing branches being cut out each season.

The tool I find most convenient for this work, is a pair of long-armed secateurs with jaws like a parrot's bill. Old branches have to be removed with a saw after being temporarily roped to stronger ones so that they can be lowered gently. Then no damage is done to their parent wood, and this is, of course, aided by first making a saw cut on the underside of the branch.

Certain shrubs are always pruned in spring anyway, and are dealt with summarily — those which flower in summer on the wood which will be made in about four months. The commonest among them is the buddleia which produces mauve or violet plumes in August. Unless you have once done it yourself it is hard to believe that if you cut the six-foot stems almost to the ground during late February, more will grow again and be just as tall in time for the ensuing summer's flowers. *Hydrangea paniculata,* the blue caryopterias, fuchsias and the deciduous forms of ceanothus are all cut back just as hard, right down to a few inches from where their last year's growth began.

It is important to distinguish between this hydrangea and the mop-headed hortensia type which flowers on shoots made from old wood. The method of pruning which suits the latter best is simply the removal in early spring first of weak, slender shoots made from the base, and then, when the bushes are crowded, one or two of the oldest branches to enable those that remain to wax fat and enjoy the ripening influences in summer of light and air.

Those splendid long-flowering evergreen ceanothus, like Autumnal Blue and burkwoodii, often prove perplexing, for they seem to fit into neither the spring nor late summer group. But they can in fact be lightly pruned in February — they really need it if they are not to become lanky bushes that are easily blown out of the ground. Their loss from this cause, incidentally, can often be prevented also by pegging down into the ground some of the lower branches to give greater anchorage, an attention which brooms might be given occasionally, though these are not pruned.

Experience has taught me the wisdom of cutting short the display made by the winter jasmine by pruning in late February, while it still carries the last of its yellow flowers. The tangle it is inclined to form can be avoided and one can be sure of a full show of flowers next winter which you cannot rely on if you prune it later. Invariably grown against walls — often very suitably facing north — it is not a climber, as it lacks means of self-support. Any long growths needed to extend the framework must therefore be tied to wires or trellis or tucked into the mesh. Next you take the secateurs and snip away most of the pendant side growths, right back to a couple of buds from the point where each arises.

Another kind of surgery that can be practised in winter before the birds begin to nest concerns the selection or preservation of leaders of trees. Contenders for leadership are treated with less finesse in horticulture than in politics. They are executed, summarily, for rival leaders can upset the elegant poise of a tree. Deciduous species suffer the threat as well as conifers, though these can suffer most — certain species in particular.

The well-known silver-leaved form of the Lawson cypress known popularly as *Cupressus fletcheri* is commonly a disordered battleground. Leave it to itself in the hope that the shapely little sapling you put in will maintain a narrow, conical outline all its days, and you are likely to be severely dismayed after a few years. Not one, but four, five, and perhaps six, main growths will soar and jostle one another for supremacy. You have to be ruthless with them and cut back, if not cut out, all but the one that has got a little ahead. Sometimes, in some varieties, one does not notice the progress of the rivals and there may be only one, proceeding by stealth but resolutely, until one day the tree looks lopsided. The offender is best cut out just the same and the gap left concealed by tying other branches over it.

Certain conifers, however, seem reluctant to reveal a leader at

[133]

all. When natural selection fails, one has to be appointed. You have to put a cane beside the tree and tie to it, season by season, an important-looking shoot until it has grown into the leadership. Otherwise such trees make little upward progress. The particular offender needing this treatment is the splendid blue spruce, *Picea pungens kosteriana*. I have found that some weeping conifers can be helped on their dolorous way by offering them an arm similarly. A weeping spruce I once planted just stood there sorrowfully, doing nothing but moping, until I was moved to provide for its support and give it some encouragement.

Sometimes the leading shoot of, say an Atlas cedar is broken by tempest or mishap. The technique to repair the harm done is not to make a side branch serve in its place but to slice off the damaged top and allow a main shoot to grow afresh from the old wood. Side branches tend to be unwilling to serve and prefer to go their anarchic way.

Some of the deciduous trees grown as standards in gardens have a natural tendency to make broad heads composed of outstretched branches. This must be accepted. But more often appearances and practical considerations are best served by encouraging a system of branches to radiate from a spire-like leader. Of course, training is advisedly done in the early stages, when the stake should be long enough to hold the leader exactly perpendicular. If this has to be pulled up later it will have to be done in stages to avoid snapping the wood.

Allowing a forking rival leader to go its own way in a deciduous tree is sometimes the cause of its untimely death. Leaves are caught in the narrow crotch and rot prospers there. Or else splitting occurs due to stresses set up during uneven movement in the wind, allowing an entry to disease spores. Of course, an evenly balanced, symmetrical tree casts less shade than one with a dense, tangled head and, due to the free circulation of air between the branches, is healthier and flowers better. One never has any doubts about removing crossing branches from it, either.

Of course, all wounds caused during corrective surgery must be pared clean and painted to seal them against disease. If any incipient buds round it break in early summer, they must be rubbed out. All the wood removed can be burned and its ash used between rose bushes to help them produce more and better flowers.

Tubs

*Gardening for the gardenless: shrubs: the fragrant box: yuccas:
the Mexican orange: camellias: fuchsias as town plants: winter
protection for the half-hardy: concealing the tubs: the practical
details*

The possibilities of gardening without a garden are enhanced
and stimulated when you sometimes find that in the larger
stores you can buy Italian decorated pots and urns, glass–fibre
troughs that look like unobtainable lead ones, and tubs that put
to shame those graceless receptacles painted a harsh green that
could never harmonise with the subtle tones of nature. But the
basic materials are still the plants will thrive in them in town
conditions.

The most general idea is to find shrubs that will give plant form
to the balcony or porch, courtyard or backyard, or even terrace,
all the year. Perhaps they will flower, and they must preferably
have evergreen leaves. Usually they have to put up with lack of
sunlight. They must not mind some dryness at the roots.

Conifers, for all their formal outline and tones of olive-green, silver, blue and gold, though often planted in tubs, seldom seem much of a success for long. Think of the places where they thrive best, in high rainfall areas where the atmosphere is always moist, so unlike a dusty town atmosphere where the heat-radiating stones help to dry the air.

Bay trees would be excellent were they not rather vulnerable to frost, especially as they survive spells of dryness. A light overcoat of polythene in the coldest weather, though, is enough to protect them from harm; they will not suffer, either, for a couple of weeks or so in a shed or outhouse.

Tough, drought-resisting and yielding to clipping and training into pyramids and pillars, birds and spirals, box holds all the court cards. Not the least considerable of its qualities is the fragrance it gives off on hot days.

For architectural effect the spiky yuccas, whose sword-like leaves develop in rosette fashion, are naturally formal. The common belief that you have to wait half a lifetime or more to see flowers on the plant you have put in is disproved by the number of plants noticed bearing their tall spikes of ivory bells in gardens every summer. The smaller-growing *Yucca filamentosa* flowers more regularly for us than the bolder *Yucca recurvifolia* more often grown in town gardens.

If a flowering evergreen is to be used it must have a long season. In the limited soil of a tub, the so-called Mexican orange, *Choisya ternata* goes on flowering for several months. The blossom is sweetly scented and the light green leaves release an aromatic fragrance when crushed. Similarly, *Skimmia foremanii*, of rounded outline and attractive in foliage all the year, keeps its scarlet fruits like cherries the whole winter.

While camellias are successfully grown in tubs, giving a two months' succession of flowers of such waxen beauty that they deserve to be brought close to eye level, they need some care in positioning. For the summer they must have semi-shade and frequent watering from a lime-free source, but need some sunshine to ripen their new wood if they are to flower abundantly the following spring.

Among the deciduous shrubs the Japanese maples are of such delicate outline that they are attractive in themselves as foliage plants and need no flowers to embellish them. The varieties burdened with the names *Acer palmatum dissectum* and *atropur-pureum,* with leaves like delicately-worked lace, have the greatest appeal and are the slowest in growth.

As town plants in tubs, urns or window-boxes, fuchsias have hardly a rival, for they flower almost as well in sun and shade and put on a continuous performance from June until October, and you get the best from the flowers if you have to peer up into them. A large proportion of the varieties generally sold are hardy, but in any case fuchsias need only to be kept dry indoors for the winter.

Hydrangeas are equally generous with their flowers, and per-haps it is when they are grown in tubs that one most appreciates the changing tints of their flower heads.

Tub gardening offers opportunities for growing some of the half-hardy plants successfully in the open, giving them some winter protection indoors. I would not be without our oleander, which flowers for four months at a stretch. In the winter it is kept without harm in an unheated greenhouse. Nor would we part with our lemon-scented verbena plant, *Lippia citriodora,* grown for no more than the refreshing scent of the leaves which you pick and crush as you pass.

Fortunately, we can grow myrtles in the open, but in less-favoured gardens they make tub shrubs that are pleasing in out-line, evergreen foliage, flowers and the scent of the whole bush, in bloom or out. Though the Mediterranean *Myrtus communis,* has all these qualities, the Chilean species, *Myrtus luma,* is even more attractive, since the young shoots, stems and leaves, are suffused with purple.

What about the tubs and urns that are planted with bulbs for the spring, with petunias or geraniums for the summer . . . must they stand empty all the winter? They can give a garden some-thing of the chilly atmosphere of a holiday resort on which the visitors have now turned their backs. But one has only to tuck a rooted sprig of ivy in them to transform it.

Any ivy will do. Could you wish for anything more decorative than the patterning of bronze and many tones of green that embellishes the younger leaves of the ivy that appears apparently from nowhere in shaded spots in the garden and in hedgerows? The most rudimentary root system provided by pieces pulled up during autumn renovations will sustain them.

For town courtyards where something green is needed in winter much more than in the country, one might prefer something more sophisticated. The silver-marked Canary Island ivy grown indoors gets frost-seared in the open, but any of the smaller-leaved varieties grown as house plants will laugh at the cold. For all their high-born looking elegance, they are simply forms of the old ivy that will always try to conceal crumbling masonry in castle grounds or slum.

If all this seems a little sombre, one might try plants of *Euonymus radicans variegata,* whose silver-splashed leaves also have pink tones in them. Or one might pull up some bits of one of the variegated periwinkles, preferably the form of *Vinca major* known as *elegantissima,* whose gold leaf markings bring a touch of illusory sunshine to the winter scene. One periwinkle even sets out on its flowering career in winter and might also be used. This is *Vinca difformis,* which needs a rather sheltered place.

All these trail, flinging arching shoots about with a certain unruliness. Those who feel all should be tidy for the winter might keep handy in pots a few plants of the neat evergreen *Skimmia fortunei,* whose scarlet berries, so vivid and unmistakable, are unaccountably shunned by birds. Of course, all this means that the spring bulbs would have to be started off in pots, plunged in ashes and be transferred to the urns just as they were coming into flower.

Extending the idea of keeping a reserve of plants specially for the purpose, one might have one *Viburnum davidii* stallion plunged in a seraglio of females and bring the odalisques, adorned with their blue berries, on to the stage for the winter, leaving the gentleman to gather his reserves in the meantime.

Perhaps, though, the supreme winter delight to enjoy in an urn or a pedestal would be to have a potted plant of the common winter jasmine tumbling from it like a fountain pouring out golden stars for weeks at a stretch.

The inescapable practical details of tub gardening are that every container must have drainage holes at the bottom. These should be covered with bits of broken pots or stones so that they remain free. The best soil to use is turfy loam, mixed in the proportion of three parts to one each of peat and sharp sand or grit, and rammed firm round the roots with a broomstick or the handle of the trowel.

Indoors

Cossetting the pot plant: origins in the tropics: watering: azaleas:
the bromeliads: overpotting: renewing plants: the return of the
conservatory: climbers from warm countries: the exotic jasmine:
the bougainvillea: return to Victoriana

W hen wind, rain and frost have brought the leaves down and
reduced the garden to disarray, our preoccupation with
planning and planting, with pruning and pricking out, gives way
to cossetting indoor pot plants. They can be rather more encouraging then.

Cosseting them? That's the trouble most of the time. They get
too much. They quickly become besotted with the zealous care
they get. The foliage plant whose leaves turn yellow and fall or
develop brown shrunken patches is usually suffering from a
surfeit of good things — usually too much to drink. In winter the
same sad tale is heard again and again of a sickness creeping over
the plants that have been coaxed so carefully only to show resent-
ment by discarding the very leaves for which they are grown.

This would be avoided if their natural inclinations were better understood. Most of these which are made to serve as pot plants in the house are of tropical origin. Picture what it is like for them at home. They live permanently in the steamy forest or on wooded hills in competition with the roots of mighty trees. Often they drag out an existence as epiphytes, making roots along the stems that find their way into accumulations of rotted vegetation where branches of the trees they inhabit fork. The temperature, by all accounts, is fairly stable and the length of daylight hours too. Inevitably they show distress in our homes on occasions and sigh for the forest. We might be surprised that they thrive at all.

Central heating may produce a steady temperature to their liking but not an atmosphere congenial to them. This problem can be overcome by plunging the pots in some kind of moisture-holding material. The happiest house plants are always those whose pots are sunk in another container filled with peat or vermiculite which is damped frequently and keeps the atmosphere immediately round the plants moist through evaporation. Standing them on a tray of pebbles over which water is poured has the same effect. The pots must never stand in water, or not for long. That would be the surest way of making them lose their leaves.

No one can tell you exactly how much and how often pot plants need water. Here we might usefully take another look at them in their native homes. There the rain, it seems, comes copiously but fitfully. The soil is stacked with humus but is loose in texture and water drains away readily from it.

Accordingly, it is better to keep foliage plants on the dry side rather than wet, giving water only when the soil is almost dry. This is particularly important in winter, when short days cause a hardly perceptible rate of growth. But it is equally important to moisten the leaves frequently and to make sure that dust does not clog them. A weekly shower will be their best tonic, and this perhaps arranged most easily by standing them in the kitchen sink and flicking water on them with a brush.

On the other hand, the plants forced into flower in winter, like the Cape heathers, cyclamen, azaleas and primulas, are in the full lusty growth of their prime then and require water every few days. But not so much that the soil becomes sodden. Nor must they stand in a saucer of water. The best test for moisture needs is the old gardener's habit of rapping the pots with the knuckles.

If they answer with a dull sound they have enough already. If you get a ringing tone, water them and later pour away the surplus that drains through the pot.

Azaleas are a special case. Since they are grown in a block of peat rammed tight and heavily interlaced with roots, it is almost impossible to water them adequately from the top. It is necessary, then, to stand them in a bowl of water up to the pot rim, and let them slowly absorb it. I find this is required about twice a week and that a shower as often is also advisable. Yellowing leaves and prematurely falling flowers are almost always due to the same causes: too much water, too little light, cold draughts or an unfortunate spell of neglect with consequent dryness.

A sickly, flagging azalea plant, or any other in fact, can often be restored to its pristine vigour by standing it on a upturned pot or basin in a bowl of boiling water, to give the plant a kind of Turkish bath. Of course, the hot water level must not reach the plant's pot.

There are other special cases, too. One group of house plants, the bromeliads, members of the pineapple family, are singular in that water can be allowed to rest in the 'vases' made by the leaves. The most familiar of these is *Aechmea rhodocyanea,* whose leaves being dusted with a silvery 'meal' suggest that it may be a drought resister.

This you water by keeping the 'vase' full, just as the rains do in the sub-tropical forests where it grows on trees. Another familiar plant so treated is the scarlet-centred, star-like nidularium.

The best hope of keeping that tantalising plant aphelandra flourishing seems to be in plunging the pot in another of a large size and filling the space between with peat and sand. This is kept moist by watering, and the plant will receive most of what it requires through the porous clay of its own pot.

Or take the case of the plant disrespectfully known as mother-in-law's tongue, which compensates for this indignity by enjoying the official title of *Sansevieria trifasciata laurentii.* You have to tread very carefully here. It is so easy to offend innocently. In fact it is advisable to treat it like a succulent plant. Which means that it is quite capable of looking after itself for quite long periods.

A fallacy that must be guarded against with this, and most other house plants to a lesser degree, is what gardeners refer to as 'over-potting'. It is tempting to believe the plants need plenty of soil in which to thrust roots, but in practice you often find that they do best with their roots cramped, nourishment being provided from a bottle, though only when they are growing strongly.

Can an azalea be kept to flower again another year? Most likely. All you have to do is continue giving it rain water until about the middle of May, when it can be put out of doors sunk in the ground in a lightly shaded place to take a rest.

Early in September you take it up, give it a pot a size larger and pack it in with peaty soil, giving it a fortnightly dose of liquid fertiliser and every few days standing it in a bowl of rain water up to the rim rather than attempting to water it from the top.

A season may be missed before this is the happy result of such care, however. The plant may decide that it needs a sabbatical year to recover from being forced.

Similarly, cyclamen can be made to go on from year to year, the tubers growing fatter all the while. Reduce the watering gradually when flowering at last comes to an end, but substitute for it an occasional dose of liquid fertiliser to add to the store of nourishment the tuber husbands for the following season. Gradually the leaves will go, and the tuber can be left dry for a couple of months' rest.

When the summer holidays are over it will need a pot of fresh soil and spraying every few days, which, together with a little water at the roots, will prod it into life. On a light windowsill, but free from draughts, it will grow under the stimulus of increasing water, and more doses of the magic liquid manure.

When bulbs raised for the house go out of flower, after having drawn on their own resources since they were planted, they can be restored and made to serve as garden plants, though they will not suffer forcing in bowls again. The technique is to keep the leaves as long as possible by continuing to water the plants, using fertiliser concentrate in the water every now and again. When the leaves can endure no longer and show that the plant is growing sleepy, watering must be reduced gradually.

The same technique can be applied to those expensive bulbs of amaryllis, correctly but less attractively called hippeastrums. Only they are not hardy enough to grow out of doors. When they have had two or three months' rest they can be given some fresh soil replacing the top inch with this and some water, when they will begin all over again.

The return of the conservatory, in the shape of easily-erected timber-framed 'home extensions', means that many former outer walls of ordinary houses are now protected by glass and offer hospitality to some of the most desirable of climbing plants. They are the enviable climbers of warmer countries, which can be brought into our homes.

Most of them are remarkably long in flower, a quality not asked unreasonably of plants which become part of the furnishings. It happens, however, that they are also plants which can be grown successfully in pots on any flat windowsill.

Foremost among them I would put an exotic jasmine, *Jasminum polyanthum*. I know no climber which has a more delicious scent, not of the kind that cloys and which you grow tired of, but a refreshing, sweet perfume. The pink buds form in prodigal masses, and as they unfurl the white flowers cascade over whatever the plant is trained, or rather encouraged to scramble. Its only basic need in the way of artificial warmth is to be kept just above frost level.

According to the degree to which the room is heated, it will flower in winter or spring. In a temperature that does not fall much below 50° F. the first flowers will appear soon after Christmas. If you rely on the increasing natural warmth of spring to stimulate it into growth after its autumn rest, it will not burgeon until later. In either case you can expect a performance lasting nearly three months.

As a pot plant on a light windowsill in the home this jasmine has sinewy growths which can be twined round three or four canes in serpentine fashion. This will produce a column of blossom almost concealing the foliage, with just the right balance of root cramping and feeding with liquid fertiliser.

With plenty of vacant soil for its roots to explore such a plant may wax fat and fail to flower. Keep it on edge, though, doubtful about where its next meal is coming from, and it will express its anxiety about survival by flowering freely. But you always save it from disaster by just enough liquid nourishment to keep it going, if on short commons.

If the jasmine leads because of its scent, *Plumbago capensis* is a near rival with its length of flowering season. The plant begins in early July and goes on until early December, all the while giving a succession of delicate blue flowers in airy clusters. Again it needs only the minimum of heat. It is always better for severe pruning in spring, cutting back all the sideshoots to a framework of main branches.

A bougainvillea is a plant you either abhor for its crude bright magenta colouring, or delight in, perhaps because of its associations with holidays in warmer places. Actually the salmon-red variety Mrs. Butt is a much more agreeable colour. Both are hung with their highly coloured bracts, the showy leaf-like features which enclose the inconsiderable flowers, for several months. The other plant I suggest for the shelter of the well-lighted inner walls of one of these glass surrounded rooms, or as a summer pot plant that will give a show as long as a primula in spring, is the bright orange *Streptosolen jamesonii*.

If there is any doubt at all about sufficient artificial heat to comfort them in winter, they must be kept fairly dry then, on the sound principle that a tender plant brought near to being desiccated will endure low temperatures more bravely than it would if it were heavily charged with moisture. In a state that will only barely ensure their survival they will come safely through cold.

Accordingly, rather than plant them straight into beds let into the flooring, I think it is better to set them in large pots sunk in the ground. The water they need then is minimal, and they need receive hardly any in winter. Of course, an occasional venturesome taproot will stray into the soil below, but this can easily be snapped in autumn without harm to the plant by giving the pot a sharp upward tug, so that the plant is deprived of this natural means of taking up some water. As room plants they can be treated less severely in the off-season, but still kept rather dry.

In company with camellias grown in tubs, the usual run of foliage plants for the house, even a gardenia in a large pot, any of these climbers adorning the wall help to extend the garden as well as the house.

The tradition of growing plants under glass is peculiarly English and belongs particularly to the Victorian age, when countless new plants were sent home by our traders abroad, with a consequent stimulus to the technique of persuading them to grow in artificially contrived conditions. Never have these conditions been better supplied than today, which is why so many Victorian plants are right up to date.

★

Asters

The Michaelmas daisy: replanting to avoid mildew: the novi-belgii type: the Aster amellus: transplanting in the spring

Mildew, you might think, is a disorder that goes with damp. Not for roses and Michaelmas daisies. They get it worst in the best of summers. You expect to have to spray roses for this or that and keep it up all the summer. But you ought to be able to let Michaelmas daisies get on with it and look after themselves.

This is the trouble. They can do it too well — for a time. They increase exuberantly, flower prodigally. Then comes the reckoning. Burnt at both ends, their candle is reduced to a flicker due to soil exhaustion and overcrowding.

To save them from themselves, the perennial asters that most commonly go by the name of Michaelmas daisies need pulling apart and replanting every couple of years, every third year at most. Then they maintain the thrusting vigour they show at the outset. Only the young outward-reaching growths of course, are good for replanting. They will not be saved from mildew in a dry summer, but it won't matter quite so much. A puff or two of karathane fungicide will stop it getting a hold.

Now the Michaelmas daisies treated in this way are the so-called novi-belgii type of American origin. They offer the greatest colour range and we could not do without them. But a European type, bred from *Aster amellus*, is neither so forward nor so vulnerable to trouble when it comes. The best known of these are the violet King George and the pink Sonia. Besides having a resistance to disease, they wisely keep to themselves and need dividing only at much less frequent intervals.

Others that can be found by shopping around hardy plant nurseries, through the agency of their catalogues, are Lac de Genève, a lavender shade, Jacqueline Genebrier, brighter in its pink than Sonia, and the self-describing Blue King and Mauve Beauty. All have the single flowers currently in fashion.

Another merit which gives them a high rating among hardy plants is a longer flowering season than the novi-belgii varieties can provide. Those already in general distribution begin their season in late August, continuing until well into October.

The season is begun even earlier by a bluish hybrid known as *Aster frikartii*. If one is inclined to say that Michaelmas daisies are not wanted till the autumn, the cogent retort is that gardens of diminishing size need plants that will give the maximum effect for the longest period. Anyway *frikartii* has an elegance that sets it apart from the other perennial asters. Its supremacy is now challenged, however, by a mauve-blue variety called Junifruide, which starts to flower in late June, ceasing in September just as one is getting anxious to clear up the garden for the autumn.

Now the amellus type, for all its qualities, has one defect. It can only be transplanted satisfactorily in spring. For this reason, some sensible nurserymen are now growing them in pots.

Obviously they are not going to oust the more familiar type, which is so easy to propagate. But anyone impressed by the displays of Michaelmas daisies in a genial autumn, where mildew has been kept at bay, and encouraged to plant more, might decide on the earlier amellus kind, as an addition to their range of asters.

Autumn Cherry

Storms and blossom: a legend of Japan: outline like hawthorn:
its position: growing

Although equinoxial gales and rain may be savage they never
seem to be able to mar the astonishing beauty of the so-
called autumn cherry. When the storms subside and the sun comes
out there stands this redoubtable little tree proudly bearing its
cloud of white blossom against blue sky on a November day, as
immaculate as a film actress who has just passed through a jungle.

Ordeal by tempest does not sweep the flowers from it as the
winds of March will shatter the almond blossom. And even if
frost sears them another crop soon takes their place, in accordance
with the nature of the tree. This capacity for renewal all through
the winter is scarcely hinted at in the botanical name of *Prunus
subhirtella autumnalis*.

True, the main flush comes in autumn and later bursts are less
impressive, but they are abundantly welcome in the mild spells
our winter usually brings.

According to legend, we owe this tree to a fragrant little incident in Japanese history, fifteen centuries ago. During a rout in a Kyoto garden the Emperor noticed a single petal carried on the breeze into his glass of rice spirit. Reassuring himself that it was not the drink playing tricks with his vision, he summoned attendants and bade them seek out the strange tree that bore its blossom on a November day. It was this flowering cherry.

Even the bullfinches, which have an appetite for the buds of most ornamental cherries, stand in awe of this one. I have watched them in the branches of our tree, so decorative amid the white blossom that we should not have minded if they had taken nips here and there. But they have left the buds untouched, apparently just delighting in the sight of it, too.

Fortunately, the autumn cherry is not a big grower, though it does in time develop the rounded outline like a hawthorn that fits it for a position, say, at the end of a garden vista. That is, if you allow it to develop fully. Where it is grown in gardens it is rarely allowed its head, secateurs constantly keeping it small.

Like the winter jasmine, this is one of those plants of which you can cut budded sprays, bring them indoors to stand in water and watch the buds open.

If I have convinced you that it is a tree worth growing within view of a window in any garden, it only remains to add that it will grow in any soil, likes a sunny place and that a standard tree bought on a six-foot stem and planted between November and the end of March should set out on its flowering career a year hence.

Bark

The tracery of twig and branch: coloured stems: the dogwoods: willows: whitewashed brambles: the bark of trees: the lime-green maples and the silver birch

Etched against the whiteness all round, the tracery of twig and branch is all the garden may have to offer in snowbound days. But the bare sticks of some plants can be brightly coloured, their tints enhanced by the pale winter's sun, and these are worth planting for this feature alone when the garden is otherwise desolate.

Indispensable in a garden made to yield something every day of the year, they deserve a patch to themselves within view of the windows. Close companionship strengthens the effect they make, though they could well be planted between other bushes in temporary retirement at this season.

The most striking are the most easily grown of all. These are the coloured-stemmed dogwoods that you cut right down in spring to gain the exuberant response of a multitude of young twigs, which are most highly coloured. The brightest and best is *Cornus alba sibirica* often called the Westonbirt form, whose stems are scarlet. In *Cornus stolonifera flaviramea* they are gold.

Pruned hard in the same way every spring, several of the willows can safely be planted as garden shrubs, for they too have shoots highly coloured in the first flush of youth. Like the plumage of water fowl, they seem brightest in winter, though they will flourish away from water.

Having egg-yolk-yellow stems itself, *Salix vitellina* has a variety called *britzensis* whose young shoots are orange, while those of *Salix daphnoides* are the colour of a ripe damson.

These tints can be made even more conspicuous if among the bushes are a few plants of the so-called 'whitewashed brambles', of which the best is *Rubus giraldianus*, whose detergent-white stems rise eight feet high.

Have you noticed how the stems of the familiar *Kerria japonica* remain apple-green all the winter? This could also be grown in a patch devoted to such plants, and here, too, I would put in a bush of stephanandra, whose rusty brown stems will contribute to the general effect and which will offer an almost endless source of foliage for cutting in summer and autumn.

The bark of several small-growing trees can be even more appealing than that of, say, a pine or an ash. The polished chestnut-like bark of *Prunus serrula* never fails to intrigue our visitors and abundantly compensates for its insignificant show of flowers.

Every year the bark of *Acer griseum* peels away to reveal beneath a smooth rust-coloured layer. Again the flowers are of small account, but the autumn foliage is brilliant. Several of the maples, indeed, which form little trees have bark of lime-green striped with cream. In our garden there is little to choose between *Acer davidii* and *Acer grosseri hersii*: both are equally striking. They are as remarkable if less familiar than the silver birches which are so well worth planting for the whiteness of their bark.

That of *Betula papyrifera* is even whiter than the native birch, while the bark of *Betula albo-sinensis septentrionalis* has a distinct pinkish touch. The trees are slender enough for garden planting but the surface roots are inclined to be greedy. A fall of snow, throwing them into relief, seems to enhance all these, decorative enough as they are without it and they have the added advantage that they need very little looking after to achieve their effects.

Bergenias

*Polished leaves through the winter: 'elephants' ears': early
flowering: divide and increase: the Ballawley Hybrid: protection
from the wind: the thuja hedge: new varieties from Germany*

Frost and snow cannot dim the lustre of one of the garden's
most precious assets, a generous patch of the large-leaved
plant known as bergenia.

In the plant catalogues that gardeners study with an ardour
others bring to closing prices, racing form and pools prospects,
this plant is lumped with the herbaceous perennials. Perennial it
certainly is, even deathless, but to style it 'herbaceous' is to slander
it. For the polished leaves persist all through the winter, shining
with all their might in whatever sun we get then.

Some people might call them 'cabbagey', though if you have
eyes to see the beauty in a cabbage leaf this is no defamation. I
have heard them more endearingly referred to as 'elephant's
ears'. In fact, the bergenia is a plant justly raised by the flower
arrangers to the height of fashion for the sake of its foliage.

Not only does it enliven the garden out of season, but it is one of the best weed suppressors and is also impatient for the spring, thrusting up its flower stems weeks in advance and opening its red or pink hyacinth-like clusters even in February. The chill favours rather than harms them, allowing them to remain there for several weeks, just as daffodils last longer when the spring weather is dull.

No wonder, then, one is greedy to increase this plant and make bold drifts of it, especially as it grows contentedly in whatever soil or site you choose to plant it. This is a quite simple process. It suffers division at any time. In fact when our cats' sporting round it result in bits being broken off at the woody stems, I simply push these into the ground and they grow, just like stems of a succulent plant will.

Once I was offered a forkful of a certain variety by a characteristically generous gardener. I broke it up into as many bits as it would make then and again a year later. Next season we had a hundred plants to put out.

Unfortunately, I have not been able to put a generally recognised name to this form, which is by no means uncommon. Its distinguishing feature is that the leaves turn the colour of well-rubbed mahogany for the winter, when those of others keep their lustrous green, while its flowers are magenta rather than pink, and the stems taller.

But I collect all I can. The common species unjustly taken for granted in old and uncared-for gardens in what were fashionable Victorian suburbs — look how well it grows under the dusty laurels! — is *Bergenia cordifolia*. When encouraged its leaves can be nearly a foot across, though not tropical-looking and out of character. A neater species with leaves of lighter green is *Bergenia schmidtii*, which is even hastier to get into flower.

If you are properly up to date as a gardener, you will want to grow the splendid but fey Ballawley Hybrid, or Deelbees. With true Irish unconcern for moderation, its leaves will exceed a foot across. At the approach of winter they turn a rich, bright red. And just when you expect them to retire and give place to new leaves, one spring morning you suddenly find they have changed back to green again. The flowers are better than any others.

This strange behaviour, however, does not go on in full exposure. Leaves of such extravagance are inclined to get tattered unless the plant has a bit of shelter. Protection of a slight degree is also needed by one called *Bergenia ligulata,* whose leaves are strangely hairy, suggesting the mystery of its native Nepal.

I grow this one in the shelter of a thuja hedge, where like other kinds it seems indifferent to the competition from the stronger roots, and it is equally unaffected by the resinous fallen thuja leaves that make the soil inimical to other plants.

Others have their origins in Siberia, which no doubt accounts for their redoubtable toughness and powers of survival. In Northern Germany, indeed, they have received the attentions of the flourishing hardy plant breeding industry there. The result is a widening of the flowering range.

Those circulated here are Morgenrote, which has been found to produce rose-pink flowers in late summer as well as in spring and to have a less expansive manner of growth, and Silberlicht, which lives up to its name and gives almost white flowers. Aberglut also deserves a place here, for when I first saw it growing in Northern Germany it was defying bitterly cold weather, blowing down from the Baltic, with sprays of flowers of a distinct crimson.

Box

Weakness and merit: rich green in winter: scent on a summer's day: controlling the roots: refurbishing: front hedging in small gardens

When, in the company of other gardeners, I sometimes express a liking for old-fashioned box edging, up go the cries of horror. It is time-consuming, anachronistic and encourages pests, so they say. And I have to admit the weaknesses that underlie its merits.

Of course it needs clipping. Of course slugs seek its shelter to breed. Of course its roots stray and suck the goodness from the soil. As for its being out of date — well, cypresses were grown by the Greeks and peonies by the Chinese before that.

When it is nearly winter and much of the garden is being cut down for burning, I am glad that within view of the house windows we have trim little beds edged with box. They give form to the garden when it is in danger of losing it, and draw outlines in rich green that remain all through the lifeless months.

Not that this is all there is to it. The finish it gives the rest of the year to beds outlined with paving, for dry walking, flower tending and admiring whatever the weather, offsets any sense of harshness in this part of the garden.

Above all, though, in summer we relish its scent. Just the scent released by the leaves on a hot day. A whiff of it and one is transported back to holiday visits to hotter places, to cloister gardens, where we have lingered. Sometimes, strangely, the memories flash across the consciousness before one has really noticed the scent, and its appeal is enhanced by its elusiveness.

In particular, box seems admirable for edging rose beds filled with those new varieties of such powerful vigour. The lusty, healthy varieties of today need something about their lower parts to offset the lankiness they develop. Perhaps this is why the shrewd Dutch growers propagate it on such a large scale.

The roots of the box will do no harm to the roses if once a year, perhaps during the autumn clean-up, they are cut short in their wandering by the spade being thrust down into the soil fairly close to the edging. Indeed, this is a worthwhile practice to follow annually wherever hedges abut on to flower beds.

As for the slugs that will always be with us, box edging or not . . . well, there is much to be said for knowing just where to find them. By laying the deathly pellets there they can be slaughtered in their beds. In gardens where box edging is cherished but has become bare in patches, it can be refurbished by lifting it in autumn, pulling it apart like any herbaceous plant and replanting the pieces, just touching, in soil enriched with bonemeal.

Unlike the *Lonicera nitida* so often planted in small gardens, box needs clipping only once a year. Besides being used sculpturally for edgings and figures, spheres and cones, in the conventional but highly pleasing manner, it makes excellent front garden hedges up to four feet high that long retain the shape into which they are fashioned with the shears. In the small gardens now being made round new houses the loose informal flowering hedge of recent years' fashion would take up room that could ill be spared. Box may not only be a better choice on practical grounds for these gardens but also more in character with closely built houses and their style.

Camellias

A gardening volte-face: conditions for growth: protection from late frosts: camellia or cameelia: the flower of Traviata: Camellia williamsii: the autumn cousin: Flying Dragon and Snow on Peak: tea

If the name camellia still suggests Edwardian opulence, steamy conservatories and serge-aproned gardeners with a faithful old-retainer look about them, it is only the exotic appearance of this shrub and its waxen flowers that preserves the illusion that it needs special care in a greenhouse. The fact is that it is just as hardy as a great many other shrubs we grow out of doors — and considerably more satisfactory in the long run.

Although camellias are seen at their best in gardens on acid soils where rhododendrons flourish, a neutral soil free from lime will support them provided that plenty of peat is worked in before planting. In any case camellias make a tight mass of thread-like roots which find peat congenial.

Since the roots lie close to the surface, an extra annual layer of old leaves or peat over the area they occupy keeps them from harm. But this liking for having their roots moist must not be taken to mean that the plants will grow in permanently damp soil: the other thing they insist on besides an absence of lime is free soil drainage.

Once established and with enough growth to sustain them, camellias are prodigal with their flowers. To help them meet the demands they thus make on the resources around them an occasional dose of liquid fertiliser is well worth the trouble during the time they are in full growth, when the buds for next spring's flowers are being made, perhaps when vegetables or chrysanthemums or dahlias are being fed in this way.

Unlike the steady-going mulberry, said never to venture a leaf until all danger of frost is past, camellias are usually foolish enough to open their first flowers in those beguiling early spring days when anyone might be misled into thinking there could be no more bad weather, and thus they often stand in danger of losing their precocious blooms. Do not worry if this happens as these are surely followed by more.

However, the sovereign method of avoiding frost damage to early flowers is to put the plants where the sparkling early morning sun cannot reach them. It is for this reason that camellias are frequently grown safely against north walls, where special beds must be made for them, replacing soil possibly containing lime from builders' refuse with peaty loam. They also grow particularly well under the high canopy of branches of tall trees, in the woodland soil made by generations of fallen leaves.

The one contentious matter about camellias is the pronunciation of the name, whether the 'e' should be sounded long or short. The plant was named in honour of a Jesuit missionary, one Georg Joseph Kamel, who combined a study of the natural history of the Philippines with his ministry there in the seventeenth century. Camellia is simply a Latinised form of his name, and what justification is there for pronouncing it 'cameelia'?

The plant itself is native to the Far East, and the most easily obtained type, as well as the most varied, is *Camellia japonica*, prolific in its named forms and colourings. The colours stretch from white through countless pinks to blood-red. The forms range from singles, each with a shaving brush of golden tipped stamens in the centre, through different degrees of doubling until

the multi-petalled type is reached that is surely the flower celebrated in the Dumas story, in 'Camille' and 'La Traviata'. This
association, it is said, is what led to the mispronunciation of the
name.

Almost all japonica varieties are suitable for the garden, perhaps
the more formal varieties as wall plants or for the town courtyards for which they are appropriate shrubs, especially as the
foliage remains a highly-polished rich green all the year.

While most of the japonica camellias originated in the last
century, and are now restored to the honoured place occupied
today by other Victoriana, in recent years a new type has been
bred from a species found in 1917 in the region where the
Himalayas protrude into China. Grouped under the name
Camellia williamsii, they have a singular and convenient way of
casting their flowers as they wither, to make way for the long
train of succeeding flowers, whereas others have to be removed
by hand if they are not to disfigure the bushes while more are
opening. So far these flower only in shades of pink and rose.

To some growers, the semi-double form of *Camellia reticulata*
grown apparently for centuries in Chinese gardens, remains the
finest of all and often tantalisingly unattainable. When the parent
was at last discovered wild in 1924, at altitudes with other plants
that are hardy when brought here, it was hoped that this would
be found hardy too. But the wild form proved disappointingly
tender, unlike the magnificent japonica varieties. Still, it is
worth trying on the west wall in sheltered gardens where it gets
afternoon sun to ripen and firm its wood.

Once you have set out on camellia growing, indeed, you
develop a collector's mania. Soon one is led to try the still more
challenging kinds, for cutting the flowers for the house from
mature bushes keeps them within bounds and makes room for
more.

Japonica camellias have a cousin that flowers in the autumn
and winter, *Camellia sasanqua.* This plant is also native to the Far
East, and centuries of cultivation have produced hundreds of
varieties with such fairy tale names as Bundle of Fortune, Scarlet
Bird Brocade, Playing Butterfly, Sword Dance and Beautiful
Peacock. Like the japonica camellias they produce a succession
of flowers, and are thus able to take advantage of the mild spells
our winter so often brings.

Shelter and sun are needed by this type of camellia, and thus they make specially admirable plants for town gardens which can provide such conditions, while they have a neat manner of growth and can be trimmed and trained. In gardens where walls and fences would shelter them from strong winds, but given a southern exposure, they should prove adaptable bushes to lengthen the flowering season. In addition, as they grow six to eight feet tall, they could be used as supports for some of the more slender growing clematis.

The first I planted was the old *Camellia oleifera,* more correctly called *Narumi-Gata,* Narumi Bay, whose white scented flowers are flushed with carmine. I was soon encouraged to add the rose-coloured *Hiryo,* Flying Dragon, double white *Mine-no-Yuki,* Snow on Peak. *Mine-o-Tuke,* which is a kind of fuchsia-pink and semi-double, Crimson King, and *Hiodoshi,* which is apparently translated as Scarlet-threaded Suit, though the flowers are red splashed with white.

Fanciful though these names sound, and exotic though camellia flowers are, the plants are not so very far removed from everyday life, for the tea we drink is nothing but the dried leaf of a camellia.

Clematis

Perverseness of this esteemed climber: hot head but cool feet:
wilt disease: 'stopping' new growth: spring varieties: Clematis
jackmanii: Nelly Moser: using trees as hosts: later flowering
varieties: on a balustrade

In general esteem clematis surely stand ahead of all other
climbers. Yet for perverseness they have few rivals among
commonly grown plants. They are plants that demand understanding from you.

They like a limy soil but it must have plenty of humus in it
too. It must drain freely but hold moisture. They flower best in
the sun but the roots must be kept cool, perhaps by the shade of a
bush or under a covering of stones. They need a trellis for support
but brush aside your attempts to train them over it.

The best hope of accommodating these fastidious plants lies in
digging twice the depth of the spade, putting rubble at the
bottom of the hole and adding compost or peat, lime and bonemeal as the soil is returned. The other main practical detail is that

planting must always be followed in spring by cutting back the top growth to the first pair of good buds left above ground. At once a short pea-stick must be put in place for the new shoots that will quickly appear to cling to as they begin their ascent.

In spite of their notorious capriciousness, only one disorder seriously afflicts clematis, the wilt disease peculiar to them and which, quite in character, defies cure or palliative. One day a plant may stand proud and full of vigour, the next something may have taken hold of it that will cause it to hang limp and expiring.

However, now that clematis plants are more frequently grown on their own roots by nurserymen, who formerly grafted them on to the vigorous stock of 'old man's beard', in consequence of which the plants advance with less abandon, clematis wilt is a scourge of lesser importance. Yet it remains a troublesome malady for which there is no chemical remedy, only the knife. Swift surgery may save part of it, but you have to cut away every fragment that is turning black, burning it as though it were plague-ridden. As it is believed that the plants which are allowed to have their heads and race up their supports are those which are most susceptible, it is much better to 'stop' the new growth of young plants occasionally in their first season to toughen them. The tips are simply pinched out when each new shoot has extended to about eighteen inches. This will encourage branching and help avoid the distressing habit clematis have of going bare for the lower four-five feet as summer reaches its height and all else in the garden has a rich fullness about it.

If they do have a certain waywardness that quite often troubles those who attempt to grow them, clematis also have redoubtable qualities. In the winter of early 1963, our plant of the beautiful evergreen *Clematis armandii,* which wreathed the upper windows, was cruelly struck down. We thought it was lost and had begun to consider a successor. Summer turned into autumn without a sign of fresh growth appearing from below ground. And then this determined plant suddenly, in February of the next year, put up two new shoots three feet long in as many months, and now it has replaced itself entirely.

This is strange behaviour I have noticed in clematis before. Now I would not think of pulling up an apparently dead plant. Another of our plants, this time the lilac Comtesse de Bouchard, fell sick from wilt disease. We could not stop it. Every scrap of growth was afflicted and there was nothing that could be left above ground. It slept for a season and then began life all over again.

The flowers of *Clematis armandii* appear in the spring and are white in the form called 'Snowdrift', pink in 'Apple Blossom'. They are not large and bold like those of the summer-flowering varieties but their profusion makes up for this. The foliage is handsome in itself. Highly polished and deeply engraved by the veins, each leaflet is about five inches long and half as broad. Its effect is of tropical luxuriance, yet not out of key with our landscape. To this quality must be added perfume.

Unfortunately armandii insists on being given the comfort of a south or west facing wall, which it will eagerly cover with its vines, reaching the eaves in three or four seasons. I have heard it said against this clematis, that the lankiness it then takes on, leaving its lower parts bare of foliage and flowers, is its disadvantage. But what this characteristic does is leave room for you to grow something else at its foot. This serves to shield the roots from hot sun in the classic fashion and from frost damage too.

Splendid though the armandii is, however, it could not hope to usurp the position of admiration enjoyed by the large-flowered clematis typified by the purple *Clematis jackmanii,* which is all that many people know, but not all they need to know, if they are to enjoy the full beauty of the clematis family. Even this is advisedly planted nowadays in its *superba* variety.

The softer coloured Comtesse de Bouchard which I have just mentioned is one of its aristocratic relatives, though it has another kinsman, perhaps from the wrong side of the blanket, in the richer violet Gipsy Queen. For situations where even these may seem a trifle ordinary, one might choose the deep red of Mme. Edouard André, the light blue of Mrs. Cholmondley, the shell pink of Hagley Hybrid, or the violet and carmine of Star of India.

These jackmanii clematis are the varieties you are always bidden to cut down hard, as far as to the first pair of buds above where last year's growth began, every year in February. Hard though it may come to do this, removing all that proud growth that bore so many flowers, I am sure it is wise to avoid the tangle the plants otherwise become.

Next to jackmanii the most celebrated of the clematis is the famous Nelly Moser. This comely lady gets herself up in lilac marked along the middle of every sepal (the correct name to botanists for what the rest of us regard as petals in this flower) with a bold brush stroke of bright pink. This typifies a group of large-flowered varieties which start to flower months before the jackmanii type and go on for nearly as long. Obviously, you would not cut these right down altogether if you wanted to get the full value from them. You would hardly be likely to, for the group includes the red Ville de Lyon sold on every market stall, white Marie Boisselot, light purple Lasurstern and a violet one called The President which has a lighter marking where Nelly Moser has her bar of pink.

Yet I must admit that when these are allowed their own way they too become a tangle. All will flower late in one big flush if they are cut down like the jackmanii type, but there is a stratagem by which one can get the best from them both ways. This is to cut through near the base half the long growths, leaving the other half to flower early and also leaving the cut stems in position. The following year the growths that were left to flower early are the ones to prune. All of which means that the main shoots are left to endure for one whole year in addition to the season in which they are made.

Certain clematis are plants to set the imagination alight — when you meet them for the first time — as mine was when we picnicked one day in the Alpes Maritimes, where the air was heavy with the scent of *Clematis flammula*. It was growing wild, entwining every bush and sapling on the scrubby hillside and offering any gardener a clue to the best way of cramming more and more of these plants into the garden.

This is the way to grow all the small-flowered clematis — scrambling over bushes, and leaving the walls for the buxom and more stylish large-flowered varieties.

I admit, however, that you need a fairly big bush, even a tree, to play host to *Clematis montana,* that easiest and perhaps most rampant of the whole family, grown almost as frequently as jackmanii. What is not generally known about this favourite species is that when it was first brought to this country it had a scent. It was even known then as *Clematis odorata*. But as the original stock died out, to be replaced by its own seedlings, so did the scent. Now one can buy a scented montana again. Its pet name is Elizabeth and it has the pink colouring of the well-known rubens form.

One of the most intriguing of all the family, is *Clematis macropetala,* in either dusty mauve or dusty pink, both forms with nodding flowers like stars that are a little weary of trying to please so intensely. One of our plants uses a Mermaid rose as its support, and as neither needs much pruning the partnership seems a happy one, on a north-east wall too. All the spring and early summer clematis species, by the way, belong to a class that you can leave to themselves until the tangle needs drastic surgery.

The later flowering varieties include a series also that appeal to those who appreciate a certain airiness about their plants. Perhaps the most striking of these is the pink Duchess of Albany; Gravetye Beauty has a ruby tint about it, and Etoile Rose is a rather paler red. In botanical language these are hybrids bred from *Clematis texensis,* itself the only red species. They are slender growers rarely seen more than ten feet tall, dying right back in winter to save you the trouble of pruning them. They mostly bear the bell-shaped flowers of the parent.

Rather taller but still carrying small flowers, are the hybrids bred from *Clematis viticella.* This is the small flowered purple one sees during the holiday season flowering so prodigally but uncared-for in French villages. Abundance is light red, Little Nell white shading to mauve as the petals extend, and *alba luxurians* white tipped with green.

More rampant still but also eligible for this purpose is a singular clematis called Huldine. This one is two-faced. Seen from the front when in full flower it presents a galaxy of opalescent stars. Only when the flowers are seen from behind, against the light, are the carmine markings that lie concealed within revealed. Thus it is the perfect clematis to clamber over a balustrade. It also has as long a flowering season as any I know, continuing from the midsummer until the frosts put a stop to it. In appeal and the rewards it gives it sums up all the qualities that make this great family of climbing plants so desirable and so well worth trying to satisfy.

Cypresses

The slim dark pillar from the Mediterranean: an accent plant:
the Arizona cypress: winter flowering: hardier alternatives

At those times when the inescapable talk of holiday travel
surrounds one, the vision evoked of shimmering heat,
peopled by nymphs in bikinis, is pierced by a slim, dark tree, the
characteristic cypress of the Mediterranean. Nostalgic holiday-
makers, their imagination struck by it, repeatedly ask nurserymen
if it can be grown at home.

Though in the wild it is said to spread through many lands,
it is too closely associated with the Mediterranean to be added to
our own scene without offending the eye as much as highly
coloured roofs. Yet its slender outline makes it an important
accent plant to keep in the garden-maker's pattern-book.

In our own garden we have grown a pair as twin pillars where
a hedge would otherwise be abruptly interrupted. They were
grown from seed extracted from cones we once picked up in some
sunnier garden. The text-books say this tree is frost-tender in

youth, but ours certainly suffered nothing in the dreadful 1963 winter, by which one always measures hardiness nowadays.

In plant catalogues this tree is found as *Cupressus sempervirens*. As well as remaining 'always green', just like the botanical name says, it is known to be very long-lived. Planning his road over the Simplon, Napoleon is supposed to have deflected it to spare an ancient specimen. A couple of centuries before, like an idle misunderstood teenager with a flick-knife, Francois I had thrust his sword into the same tree in a moment of despair. The former doors of St. Peter's, made of redolent cypress wood, are said to have lasted more than a thousand years.

A similarly erect tree, but with pewter-coloured foliage, is also admired on the Continent, where it is now being planted on a large scale in gardens, often as a thin but dense screen. This is the American cousin, much more recently brought to the civilised community of garden plants, called *Cupressus arizonica*. In spite of its origins down there in the heat and dryness, the Arizona cypress proves quite hardy and curiously enough this tree bears its sprays of yellow flowers in winter. We planted two some time ago and found that it grows rather more swiftly than its Mediterranean cousin. In ten years one of our unclipped trees exceeded twenty feet; then it got a little shabby and the day came when the lower branches had to be removed. But making it a standard tree with a bare trunk carrying plumes of leafy shoots, like one of those trees lining the oxen tracks in Renaissance pictures, only enhances it. For the trunk has a reddish bark that proves an attractive addition to the garden scene, especially in winter, when it has weathered.

Like other fast-growing conifers, the Arizona cypress is sold as a pot-grown plant and therefore quite small. But by avoiding root disturbance during transplanting this also means that it will start to soar its first spring in the garden.

Unfortunately, neither is likely to be stocked by the little local nursery. You would have to send away for them. But on a midwinter's day fifteen years hence you would hardly regret having planted the narrow green *Chamaecyparis lawsoniana erecta-viridis* or greyish *Chamaecyparis lawsoniana allumii* as alternatives. Both are sold everywhere, though more often called by the generic name of cupressus, from which they are distinguished only by a botanical difference in leaf shape.

Daphnes

An early awakening: the scarlet berries: companionship with
winter heathers: the daphne laureola: prince of a noble race

Driven on by an impulse no cold weather can bridle, daphne
bushes are seen resolutely fattening their buds in the
dead of winter. Then, when all else (or most of the garden) is
still asleep, indifferent to what may come, the daphnes break into
full flower. . . . Or they should do.

Unhappily, this is one of those treasured plants that sometimes
fail to appear on time. The trouble is not cold or disease, but
nothing more than premature senility. It is, in fact, a plant to
whom, like our pets, we have to concede a limited life. But it
does not leave you long bereaved. The scarlet berries that daphne
bushes carry in autumn, and which are so eagerly seized by the
birds, are a natural means of replacement. They are also a means
of growing this plant in the grand manner, in the banks in which
it is seen, and smelt, to the best effect.

Enthusiasm for 'clearing up the garden' on a bright, brisk

winter day should be severely curbed when you get near a daphne bush, alive or dead. The chances are that fairly close to it you will come across several little light brown sticks standing vertically in the soil which you could easily mistake for unwanted seedlings of tall trees. A close look will disclose their relationship with the daphne.

If they are taller than six or eight inches, it is better to leave them to mature where the seeds have fallen or been sown by the birds for you. If they are less it should be possible to transplant them, provided they are taken up with as much soil as possible clinging to the roots.

One daphne bush cannot reveal adequately the charms of this perfumed, winter-flowering plant: you want at least half a dozen. Such a lordly planting is not difficult to accommodate in a small garden. Rarely seen more than three feet tall — usually only two — the bushes have a conveniently upright manner of growing which allows you to tuck low-growing, later-flowering plants between them. That is, unless you can afford space to let your winter heathers run between them to make a self-maintaining patch that yields its total effect in one go for the three worst months of the year.

While both will endure lime in the soil, they also share a common liking for plenty of peat or leaf mould around the roots and, ideally, sun.

You will see from all this that my subject is *Daphne mezereum*, the native mezereon that you might look for wild for a lifetime and never find. Yet did not Gilbert White report finding it in Selborne Hanger in 1778? I hope some bird will one day enter this National Trust property with seeds from a neighbouring garden and re-colonise it with daphnes.

But one must not talk as though this were the only daphne to which one should give garden room. I would not want to be without our colony of another native species, *Daphne laureola*, whose scented flowers, not out till spring, are the green of a greenfinch's breast. It is evergreen, too, even in winter still a soft green that does not need the sun to highlight it. Growing to about three feet, and spreading by means of suckers, this one does seem well content with shade.

Other species come from much farther afield. These are mountainside plants that are more difficult to please. The species found in catalogues as *collina, retusa* and *neapolitana,* all compact little bushes with purplish mauve flowers in late spring, want it both ways. They ask for good drainage and decayed leafy refuse that holds moisture.

Prince of a noble race, however, is *Daphne odora.* When I first tried this against the south-facing wall it is said to need, it fell victim to the first cold winter. Then I heard that its variety, *aureo-marginata,* with its golden-edged leaves, was hardier. Our plant has now gone through many winters unharmed. The cold has hardly receded before it opens its flowers, which last for weeks, releasing a scent that each year we say is finer than any other plant can offer.

Eucalyptus

The height of the eucalyptus: gunnii: the disc-like leaves of
perriniana: creating a firm foothold: planting: a garden screen

'Eucalyptus trees,' I declare with lamentable pride, slapping
the donkey-coloured bark of one of them. The fact that
they are dead doesn't lessen the awe of those I am showing round.
The corpses of the trees still stand thirty feet tall, to which proud
height they grew in less than ten years from two-foot seedlings.

These were the victims of that cold winter of nefarious
memory, and the tallest of them. Others, which were growing in
less well-watered soil and were not so thrusting, came through
unscathed. The survivors stand there brazenly, a monument to
the cold-resistance of certain members of this fascinating and
enormous family of trees from the southern hemisphere.

One of our trees began to flower at the age of ten. Each flower
consists of a fluffy tuft of stamens, rather like a mimosa but much
bigger. So tall is it now that I watch the progress of the buds
through binoculars from an upper window.

This one is the famous *Eucalyptus gunnii,* renowned as the hardiest of them all and reputed to grow to a hundred feet in this country. Gunnii, as it is referred to in the parlance of gardeners with pretensions of horticultural learning, expecting their listeners always to know that it is a eucalyptus, reaches the same climacteric as the whole family early in life. In infancy the leaves are round. As the tree passes from the cherubic innocence of childhood to gaunt teenage-hood, the leaves become slim and elongated.

This characteristic is most marked in a species called *Eucalyptus perriniana,* and in youth this tree's disc-like leaves have the additional advantage of being strung along the stems like a kebab. Our tree, a sad case of retarded development, was not destroyed by frost: it was swept out of the ground by tempest. Used, I suppose, to poor soil in Australia, eucalyptus don't trouble to take a very firm roothold. So you must not let them have their head for some years. Instead you must cut them down by half every year, about September, until they have fattened their trunks sufficiently to resist strong wind.

The only one which I have not had to treat in this harsh fashion has the curious name of *niphophila.* I first saw this sunning itself on the Riviera and living up to its common name of 'snow gum'. It was so enchanting that I bought a plant, only to be disappointed at first. For its leaves were not snowy but grass-green on our soil. Since then it has shown compensating qualities: toughness, fairly slow upright growth and such a convenient way of making its new branches that you can always cut bits off and not notice next day where they came from. This is done often, for the leaves are shaped like praying hands and therefore like those of the *perriniana* in constant demand to go with flowers.

Set out from pots in spring, eucalyptus plants have the whole summer in front of them to get used to the garden. But for the first winter they must be wrapped up. Standing enclosed within polythene fixed to canes, perhaps with some fallen leaves packed over their roots, they will not be reminded too forcefully that they are far from home.

But would I really plant such a mighty grower in quite a small garden? Yes, anywhere large enough to take a single birch. For although they grow at the rate of four to five feet a year they have a similar airy lightness of form and have the added advantage of keeping their silvery leaves all the year round.

[171]

Gentians

Instruction from the Alps: perennial species from further east:
plants for balconies: the willow gentian: sowing: Gentiana
sino-ornata: boggy ground: spreading a colony

Not until you have left the tree-line behind on an Alpine
holiday walk are you likely to find gentians growing wild
as once we did on a memorable occasion in Austria. There in full
merciless exposure to sun and wind and snow the gentians grew
like buttercups in an English meadow. Remote, vast and inhospitable though their home was, it nevertheless offered an instruc-
tive lesson on how to grow them in a garden.

Everywhere rock protruded through the shallow soil, showing
what little chance there was of water lodging about the roots.
What soil lay there was made peaty by decomposed relics of the
old wild herbage, annually compacted under snow and com-
posted naturally throughout time. The clouds that so often
overshadowed everything were a frequent source of moisture.

Only those completely lost to the spell of gentians would

bother to try to emulate these conditions for these species. For most of the European gentians are annuals, born to perish in a brief season and maintaining their colonies by the seeds which stay locked under the packed, frozen snow all the winter. But it is well worth approximating these for certain other species whose natural homes lie farther east and which are perennial.

Fortunately, unlike the magnificent *Gentiana sino-ornata,* spoken of in awe, they do not insist on lime-free soil. All they need is the moisture that goes with the free drainage of the terrain in the high places.

To gardeners on the smallest scale they are of immense value since they flower in the late summer when most little plants are long over. In my experience they are happy tucked among their earlier flowering fellows, enjoying the competition for root room.

The species easiest to buy is *Gentiana septemfida* which is also among the most handsome; it needs no cosseting and remains long in the garden. Lasting in flower through August and into September, it bears a specific name, oddly enough, unrelated to the season or to the manner in which the blue trumpets are cleft at the mouth but to the fringe just within them. This is one of the features that helps to make each individual flower so entrancing.

Whereas with the famous *Gentiana acaulis* you may wait a lifetime for the flowers and then not see them, *septemfida* will provide them in the first season in any garden soil. Not un-generously either, but in bunches of half a dozen or more at the tips of stems hardly a foot long.

Equally easy to grow, provided drainage is efficient and moisture adequate, the rather deeper blue *Gentiana lagodechiana,* each flower, standing elegantly on its own stem, pleases some growers more.

One called *Gentiana gracilipes* has a similar elegance to delight the highly critical, the stems branching to bear their several flowers. Sometimes they verge on purple, though on the outsides this tint merges into green.

For sheer lavishness, we relish our plants of *hascombensis* during the summer. The richest sapphire colouring is joined with an exceptional profusion of flowers. All I have against it on our heavy soil is that the weight bears down the stems and meets the convenience of slugs who can't resist nibbling at a bloom and passing on to the next, then the next.

We grow these lime-tolerant gentians in terrace beds open to the full sun (when it comes) and the prevailing south-west winds. The place was prepared for them by adding nothing more important sounding than road sweepings and leaf mould. Aristocrats of the plant world though they may be, they seem to enjoy this plebeian diet.

Suppose, though, you have so thickly planted your garden that you can no longer guarantee anything an open position; you can still grow a gentian. Not an alpine, but a woodland plant. This is the willow gentian, *Gentiana asclepiadea,* which is happiest in the damp soil of light shade.

The stems in this case rise to two feet, capped by the character-istic blue flowers in August and September. In a damp season they flop, as though exasperated by the weather. But they can be made to lean nonchalantly against, say, dwarf azaleas, who, too, enjoy these soil conditions.

When the season of all these is closing, it is not time to put them out of mind. It is in fact time to sow seed of them, though the seedlings will not appear until spring. In the meantime, they can be left to lie close to the surface in pots and boxes, exposed to the worst the winter can do to them, just as they are cast on a cold hillside by nature. Come the spring, their seed coats weakened by being frozen, they will burst and release those tiny flashes of green that betoken the promise of such exciting flowers, the bluest of all blues.

In spite of all these species, *Gentiana sino-ornata* remains, in the estimation of some exacting plant connoisseurs, the finest of all gentians; indeed some go as far as to say the finest plant ever brought from the eastern Himalayas, that remote, inhospitable region so rich in garden-worthy plants.

Its trumpets of sapphire, massive for so lowly a plant, glisten like a peacock's crop. On the outside they are boldly striped with ice-blue like some stage gallant's absurd pantaloons. No wonder it is now grown as a flower to cut, for striking though the effect it makes in the garden may be, it is a flower that insists that you admire it individually. The botanical explorer who found this astounding plant was content with entering in his notes the laconic comment that it grew 'on boggy ground'. He had no need to add more, for it will flourish wherever the soil remains moist all the year.

Like many other garden plants brought from the same distant area it dislikes lime in the soil. But this factor is of less account now that we have the 'sequestrene' product, which, watered on once a year, dissipates the iron-inhibiting power of the lime. The best way of providing a comfortable home for this gentian is to choose somewhere to which moisture drains but does not lie stagnant, and work in peat or old leaf mould copiously.

You may sometimes see this plant in some enterprising and patient plantsman's garden grown in the grand manner, in bold patches with whole beds to themselves which in autumn become sheets of richest blue. It is not difficult to achieve such an effect where space can be spared. The plant you buy in a small pot can be pulled apart in spring to make four or five, each with a tiny tuft of pearlwort-like leaves then, but trailing white roots.

These can be planted several inches apart, firmed with the handle of the trowel and watered every day for the next fortnight, if the weather is dry, to help them get established.

Year by year the colony can be increased in this way, though it will also spread naturally, until in time you have a mat of foliage almost as thick as that made by the common alpine phlox. Then it needs no more than a little rug of leaf mould or peat spread over the patch sometime in winter, when there will be hardly anything to be seen there. In spring, new leafy shoots will push their way through it, the roots enjoying the coolness it induces down below.

Reluctant to give a whole bed to them, however, in return for only an autumn show, I have found that the dog's tooth violet, *Erythronium dens-canis* makes an agreeable companion plant to scatter among the gentians. Its bulbs enjoy the same soil conditions. The flowers open in spring, and after these are over the plants continue for a while to display spotted foliage that is attractive in itself. This shades the soil while the gentian is refurbishing itself. When the gentian is ready to spread its flowering stems again the erythronium gracefully retires.

Perhaps to call *Gentiana sino-ornata* the autumn gentian is a little misleading. The flowers often go on well into the winter, and sometimes we have even been able to pick a few in February. They do need the sun to open them, and if you have time or a leisured approach to life, in winter you should tap them to shake out the raindrops they catch, and so prolong their lives.

[175]

Hardy Cyclamen

Wild plants of the Appenines: conditions for growth: ground
coverers: from Naples to Turkey: decorative foliage

Higher and higher we climbed on a mountain road which
took us on gyrations like a bat's flight. We were driving
up into the Apennines, looking for the place again where several
years before we had found tiny cyclamen growing wild by the
acre. At last a touch of warm pink showing through the undergrowth of the hanging woodlands which the road parted
announced them, and we stopped and got out to admire. So
thickly did they grow that you could hardly avoid treading on
them — thousands upon thousands of miniature replicas of the
cyclamen we try to cosset indoors at Christmas, growing in
prodigal abandon on an inhospitable mountainside.

I had remembered the profusion but forgotten the surprisingly
harsh conditions they had to endure. Perhaps because it was
hardly credible I had forgotten how shallow the soil was, barely
covering the rock beneath, and I had forgotten the fierce

competition from strong growing trees and shrubs which took the light from them and left them little nourishment on which to survive. All the cyclamen had to live off was the annual accumulation of fallen leaves and the decaying remains of other vegetation. Unlike their companion plants, they had no deep striking roots that could penetrate far into the fissures. The tubers hardly had a hold on what soil there was. It was all a living demonstration of how to grow these engaging little plants in the garden, especially as the tubers are offered for sale freely with all the other bulbs for autumn planting.

At least some of the species might be regarded as small-scale ground-covering plants, since they are in leaf for ten months out of the twelve. By planting several kinds you can extend the flowering season of the hardly cyclamen from September till March in a very small area and they might well be planted along hedge bottoms in the dry shade that will support little else.

Of course, they would have to be offered a good start with plenty of leaf mould to make them feel at home, and perhaps some bonemeal to draw on while establishing themselves. But all they really demand is soil that does not lie wet for long.

The wildings we found were *Cyclamen europeum,* but this is not the most adaptable one. The easiest comes from a warmer country still, *Cyclamen neapolitanum.* This species has some rather odd ways. It makes both its roots and stems from the same area of the tuber, and thus you have to be careful to put it rounded side down in the soil, the shrunken part uppermost, under no more than a couple of inches of soil covering.

Even then, in deep Latin dudgeon, it may sulk for a year. So you must mark the spot and wait for the return of an exuberance that may outlive the planter, for hardy cyclamen are among the plant immortals. I have read of an ancient tuber growing larger than a bowler hat and going on for its century!

It is surprising to find such an enduring plant so anxious to provide successors. But it does seed itself freely, even sowing on its own crown, from which the seedlings must be carefully lifted.

The flowers of the other hardy cyclamen that do well in gardens differ botanically rather than in the effect they make, except that they follow one another, varying in colour from carmine to white. After the Neapolitan comes the Turk, for *Cyclamen cilicium,* native to Asia Minor, flowers about November.

Soon after Christmas it is the turn of a group now known as *Cyclamen orbiculatum,* which in the botanist's reckoning includes those found in the autumn bulb catalogues under the names of *coum, atkinsii* and *hiemale.* It is always surprising to find their apparently delicate little flowers out for weeks on end in weather shunned by most of us.

The hardy cyclamen season ends at Easter with *Cyclamen repandum.* But still there is the attractiveness of the leaves all through the summer. These are some of the most decorative of all miniature plants. Crimped at the margins or heart-shaped, they are often marbled and mottled on their deep green with silver, while underneath they show crimson.

Heather

Courage of winter flowering heathers: erica carnea: clipping:
autumn heathers: a disturbance of blackbirds: how it was curbed:
feuding clans: calluna vulgaris: its varieties: native heaths

By the time autumn arrives in the garden the winter-flowering
heathers are well set with buds. But it is best to avert one's
gaze then from these unwelcome reminders of the close of
summer. Yet one cannot resist a sideways glance or withhold
admiration from such determined plants.

By December some varieties will be in full flower. And whatever weather may follow after that, there they will lie, patches
of pink and ruby and white, even of a salmon tint and near-
purple, for the three worst months of the year.

Such a valiant plant, some gardeners would say, in their well-
worn jargon, 'ought to be in every garden'. I do not wish to be
different just for the sake of it, but I cannot take heathers to the
heart myself. They lack the magic of, say, a Christmas rose, even
of the winter jasmine. Though I am always adding to our

collection of them, my interest is largely utilitarian. We make them work for us.

Of the heathers we grow the winter-flowering *Erica carnea* comes nearest to taking a hold on the affections. Without it the scene we look out on would be nothing but russet and green for three months of the year. With it the winter days are made to seem briefer and less as something to be endured.

The plants are cheap to buy and spread over the ground quickly, making an evergreen covering weed seeds find uncongenial. But do not be misled by the sophistry of those who might try to make you believe heathers suppress weeds. I have frequently spent an afternoon removing a fine stand of creeping thistle or couch from one of our plantations of them.

In the parts of the Alps where *Erica carnea* is a wild plant, you might reasonably expect to find its environment so much to its liking that it would be seen at its most lusty. It is, I have noticed when seeing it there, entangled with a lot more plants which are wild there too — but garden treasures in this country. In our own garden, I notice that the crocuses on which it has encroached have no difficulty in penetrating it when they thrust up towards the light.

What I have been surprised to find is that whereas our native British heathers grow wild on open land, *Erica carnea* at home prefers light woodland. Indeed, I think it is about the only heather you can expect to grow successfully with some shade. Another point to be chalked up in its favour. Then it has no aversion to lime in the soil, something from which most others of its kind shrink in horror. One more factor which brings it within the scope of every gardener. And then, I find it grows satisfactorily on heavy clay with only a little peat added.

By a strange perverseness of nature the winter heathers which grow best in this country all come from a single colony once found on an Italian mountainside — a white form found by a lucky Scotswoman — and named Springwood White. It has produced a pink form, but there are plenty of others in varying tones of the purplish pink which led to the plant being endowed with its rather distasteful name. Of these, the bright rose Winter Beauty, carmine Vivellii and deep pink King George are all easy to get. Fewer nurseries stock a carmine one called Eileen Porter, yet this has the longest flowering season of all.

The same eagerness to outdo all the others in span is shown by a hybrid which once appeared in Derbyshire from an unplanned union of *Erica carnea* with the misnamed *Erica mediterranea.* (The latter actually grows wild in south-west France, Spain and Northern Ireland.) The hybrid grows twice as tall as the carnea varieties and fortunately shows a similar tolerance of lime.

When the plants are sent out by nurseries they are often in bud already, so you can see what you are getting in the very first winter. Planting rather deeply will encourage the plants to layer themselves, and by increasing the range of their root system, spread quickly.

Spreading in this case does not imply invading. If a heather seems to go too far it is no trouble to curb, while a clipping over with the shears when the winter flowering season is at last over in spring keeps the plants to a state of neatness to satisfy the most tidy-minded of gardeners.

If you live north of the Border or have roots there, however, most probably you think romantically of the autumn heather, forgetting the mists and midges of the Highlands that go with it. You may even feel that your 'filial bands' are being treated a little disrespectfully at the suggestion from down south that heather can be employed as a garden boy to help keep the place tidy. Yet it does have such a menial use as well as bringing a touch of its revered beauty of the hills to the garden.

When we adopted the method of mulching shrub beds in our garden with the fallen leaves of autumn, as an alternative to constant weeding, we didn't allow for the views of the blackbirds on the subject. As fast as the leaves were put on and as fast as they were swept back the birds pecked them all over the surrounding turf. So some barrier was needed, some edging plant to form a pen within which the blackbirds could scratch for worms as hard as they liked. The ordinary heather was the answer.

Fringing the beds with it not only helps to keep a 'weed-free garden' less like the implications of this foolish term, it also brings early autumn colour to an area which lacked it previously, as most shrubs are well over by then. I don't mean edging them in the ribbon-like alyssum and lobelia fashion, but running irregular patches back towards the shrubs as well. Besides holding back the dead leaves that nourish the shrubs and suppress the weeds, the heather fringe has other values, both practical and aesthetic.

First, edge trimming is all but eliminated. Heather and grass tend to treat one another like feuding clans and reluctantly respect each other's territory. The mower can be run right up flush with the heather, even into it sometimes without causing any harm. The heather makes patches of bright green or gold, even silver, the whole year, which gives a special flash of delight on a winter's day. Unhappily, this is not a plant for anyone whose soil contains lime. But those unfortunates could produce the same effect with *Erica carnea*.

The most effective of the autumn heathers, varieties of *Calluna vulgaris* in general, is called Mrs. H. E. Beale, whose sprays of flowers of bright pink, double when you examine them closely, are often eight inches long. But its supremacy is being challenged by Peter Sparkes, a rather brighter shade of pink. Likewise, another favourite, *alportii* is giving way to the brighter crimson of C. W. Nix. I have seen no reason yet to dig up the older varieties stocked by most nurserymen but have contrived to find room for the newcomers too. This is getting a little difficult now, as all these have a vigour that prompts them to grow to two feet if you let them, though the clipping with shears after flowering which is advisable does keep them from expressing themselves fully, and mulching with peat does help to create a cushion-like effect.

Another reason why they are making demands on space is that only in sunny places will they flower well. In the shade they straggle and flower only hesitatingly. Fortunately, there is a series of compact growing autumn heathers which are suitable for those getting limited on space. Of these I think I like County Wicklow best. It is neither purple nor white, but shell-pink and grows to no more than a comfortable nine inches. The flowers of J. H. Hamilton, the same size, are a brighter pink. Ruth Sparkes has white flowers that are double and these make a bold effect for the small area occupied.

Most of the white heathers, of which there are many, are vigorous and as importunate with their flowers as the gipsies who try to thrust bunches on you in the street — at least in our area — in autumn. One called *serlei* has long spikes of flowers that ought to bring one a great deal of luck, especially in its golden-leaved or *aurea* form.

By contrast, Sister Anne has only silver to offer, but it is an engaging little plant dusted with fine down over the leaves, which turn a rufus shade for the winter. Growing less than six inches high, it spreads outwards, not thrustingly but contorting its stems as though it had misgivings about its place in your garden at all. Eventually it overcomes its agonies of shyness and you find you have a charming ground coverer decked with purplish pink flowers in autumn.

One strange variety called *tricolorifolia* is even more curious. From a heap of brown foliage looking like some sleeping creature's winter covering, in spring it breaks forth with young shoots unable to decide whether they want to wear pink or red or bronze or gold and in fact dolling themselves up in all three at once. Later it sobers down and in autumn is a dark green and purple as the heather of the moors (and heavy clouds) should be.

Fortunately for romance, the practical details can be dismissed summarily. You can plant at any time in autumn or winter, and peat must be worked into the ground plentifully to simulate the soil of their native heaths.

Hellebores

The lenten rose: the right hospitality: the Christmas rose: endur-ing foliage: Helleborus argutifolius: planting

Only their season of flowering justifies the name 'lenten roses' given to the plants called botanically *Helleborus orientalis*. They are not roses at all, but buttercups, and instead of suggesting any kind of spring spell of penitence it is a considerable luxury to have them flowering away in the garden all through the pre-scribed forty days of self-denial.

For most of this time they do demurely hang their heads. But just about when Easter arrives, they lift them and stare at you as though to announce that fertilisation has been accomplished and that their immortality is certain.

Long before then, you will have been admiring the maroon markings the hearts of the delicately chiselled flowers bear. If you grow a batch of seedlings each will be different in the degree of greenness or soft pink which suffuses their pearly whiteness. You might even get a plant with the highly prized rose or ripe plum coloured flowers, though to be sure of these tints you would have to buy plants with individual names and perhaps pay half a guinea each for them.

You would have the satisfaction of knowing that they would accompany you through much of your gardening life if you offered them the right hospitality. As we have seen this would be a shaded place where the ground remains fairly moist. Here you would have to dig the soil as deeply as one's energy will allow and work in a large bucketful of leaf mould for each plant.

It might be a couple of seasons before you saw a flower, but in the meantime you would have the pleasure of the ample foliage, which is handsome in itself and lasts nearly all year.

The flower stems arise in January, reaching eighteen inches when they have branched, which helps to show the flowers to more advantage than the fashion in which the Christmas rose, *Helleborus niger,* displays its blossoms. Not that this is to denigrate this more familiar plant, which enjoys the same environment.

A most admirable plant of the same family which also bears its flowers on stems less than a foot tall goes by the name of *Helleborus atrorubens* in plant catalogues. In this case the flowers are purplish red, appearing first in November and continuing until they can join hands with the lenten roses, of which it is probably a separated brother, so to speak.

A plant of this species which I have known for some years seldom has less than fifty blooms on it at one time and it keeps this up for four months of the year. What other hardy plant can outrival this, while demanding no lifting and separating for a generation? All the plants need is a handful of bonemeal flung round them occasionally and a soil covering of leaf mould every spring before warm weather causes some of the moisture, with which they like to hug to themselves, to evaporate.

One could hardly classify all these hellebores with the general run of herbaceous plants, though they renew their leaves every year. But they do not cast off the old until the new are almost ready to take their places. Thus they add an enduring foliage effect to their other qualities.

Indeed, the species admired by gardeners of discernment and found in catalogues as *Helleborus corsicus* would be worth planting for its leaves alone. Its name is now declared officially to be *Helleborus argutifolius.* The change in the specific epithet is to be welcomed in this case, because it tells you something about the nature of the leaves.

They are made sharp by the decisive way in which they are slashed, and by the rows of teeth (no more fearsome than a puppy's) which fringe the segments. The plants stand two feet tall, a bright green all through the winter, each a sturdy little bush that demands your attention. But this is not all there is to the Corsican hellebore.

At the first intimations of longer days, but while it is still winter, this plant proclaims the approach of spring with a peal of bell-like flowers. They are not white or pink or maroon this time, but green — pale apple-green, and scarcely believable the first time you meet them. They are not the bells on a fool's bauble either, foolhardy and likely to be dashed by the next cold spell. Once opened, they defy whatever may come, needing only wind protection.

Opinions differ on the exact time for planting hellebores, but broadly it falls as the flowers decline.

If you have the patience you can raise the plants from seed yourself. This is sown in early spring, preferably under glass. It is generally slow to germinate and the seedlings usually progress slowly at first. They might be hastened by sowing them individually in the compressed fibre pots. Those we raised some years back are now big clumps. Growing in moist clay and having seen no more direct sunshine than hapless broiler chickens, they demonstrate how adaptable are the hellebores to garden problem spots, especially as they now propagate themselves by means of their own self-sown seedlings.

Heucheras

Foiling weeds: perennial: garden counterpoint: spring planting:
crocheted foliage: Bressingham hybrids: annual mulch: foam
flower: summer flowering: setting off snowdrops: Bridget Bloom

During a spell of replanting one spring, casting about for
some plant to complement a collection of penstemons and
relieve their lankiness, I hit upon the heuchera. Thus I was led to
exploit the garden value of a herbaceous plant which recent
breeding has elevated to high status from one formerly associated
with such horticultural horrors as clinker rockeries. Its merits
deserved its release. What I was looking for was some plant whose
foliage would spread about over the ground and foil weeds, yet
let the scillas of early spring pierce it, and which would itself
flower between the tree peonies that make a flattering background
for the penstemons.

That the heuchera is perennial at all is surprising when you find
that it has its native home in Mexico. Yet robustly permanent it
is. In five years I have had plants grow eighteen inches across,

and I have then been able to divide them into many rooted pieces to play an under part in our garden counterpoint.

Spring is the time for this and for buying new plants when they are making a fresh relay of foliage, having kept the old all through the winter. In themselves the leaves make them quite pretty plants. They are round and neatly scalloped, a rich unashamed green, furry to the touch. In one species, however, they are the classical ivy shape and marked with copper and bronze. I have used this one, *Heuchera rubescens,* as a ground cover round those rather disturbing orange floribunda roses.

In this case the heuchera flowers are of no account, but in other varieties they are some of the most charming and individual June has to offer. From the hassock of foliage each plant makes, the stems rise eighteen inches, perhaps two feet, swinging tiny bells of coral, pink, carmine, cherry or scarlet, according to which variety you buy. When you order the Bressingham hybrids you get a variety of colourings, all of which merge and have been selected for their quality. Graceful is the term used repeatedly of the effect they create, and no other will do.

The long and patient survival of this plant on those clinker rockeries shows that it is patient under neglect, poor soil and drought, making a woody stem with which it can provide for its own survival. Such thrift, however, can be its undoing, and flowering can tail off when too much energy is spent on it. So the plants like an annual mulch of peaty, sandy soil, to prod them into making new fibrous roots.

Heuchera has a near relative called *Tiarella cordifolia,* living wild in a more northerly latitude. By contrast to the sun-loving heuchera, this is a woodland plant and a most valuable one for shady spots, whose frothing mass of white blossom has earned it the name of 'foam flower'. Again it forms a leafy hummock, never completely disappearing below ground, and it spreads well enough to be regarded as a ground-coverer.

The two plants have been combined to produce a bi-generic hybrid, not common among plants, on which the musical name of heucherella has been bestowed. The best of this new race is called Bridget Bloom. She has the eagerness to adapt, that enviable ability of the young. Not content with the month-long flowering season of her parents, she goes on from early June all through the summer, producing sprays of pink flowers all the while. She has the same attractive foliage of the race that can be a distinct garden asset.

While heuchera is a sun-lover, as you would expect of a Mexican, heucherella finds shade more agreeable. I regard Bridget Bloom as one of the best of hardy plants, and use it in woodland to link the azalea and hydrangea seasons. Here it sets off snow-drops well too, for the foliage is visible when they are out. Beware, though, of a cousin, *Heucherella tiarelloides,* reared from crossing the same genera; it is shy to flower and really good only for its foliage, which, like that of its relatives, can be agreeable as well as useful in an informal garden scheme.

Hibiscus

*Flowers to decorate a South Sea maiden: the tree hollyhock:
need for an open site: favourite varieties*

Watching hibiscus bushes come into bloom in summer one
could easily think these must be the self-same flowers
smiling South Sea maidens are supposed to wear in their hair
(when they know American tourists are about). Tropical looking
in full blossom in August and September, this shrub nevertheless
fits happily into our gardens.

In London parks I have seen people stand and stare in amaze-
ment at the bushes set with their funnel-shaped flowers of blue
or white or red, unlike those of any other shrub grown out of
doors. Their shape has earned them the name of 'tree hollyhock'.

If the appearance of this bush gives a false impression, so does
its name. *Hibiscus syriacus* suggests that it is native to the Middle
East, and few plants from there are reliably hardy in this country.
In fact it is one of the great number of shrubs of Chinese origin,
which at once puts upon it the stamp of winter toughness.

Flourishing in what is known as 'ordinary' soil, it does need a good deal of moisture-holding matter worked in. Otherwise, just like a hydrangea, it will hang its leaves in the warmth that favours its flowering, and just when it should be enjoying its hour of triumph they may turn pale and perhaps fall.

The site must certainly be an open one, though. In dull weather or partly shaded spots its buds refuse to release the flowers. Given sunshine, they burst in succession over about six weeks in August and September, when few other shrubs are in bloom.

Apart from insisting on this, the hardy hibiscus is pretty easy going. While in time it will grow into a little tree ten or twelve feet tall if you let it, you have only to prune it fairly hard in spring to keep it to a comfortable four feet. Thus it is among the more suitable of shrubs to grow in tubs in a town courtyard that catches the sun in summer.

For this purpose its only disadvantage is a certain reluctance to come into leaf in the spring. Sometimes a newly planted bush will not even break at all in its first season, feigning death when it is actually settling in at the root.

The star variety is called Woodbridge, a light purplish red and notable for the boldness of its flowers. Of similar poise, those of Hamabo are white marked with red at the throat. An all-white variety has the unromantic name of Totus Albus, while a blue one is called with equal directness Coeleste.

Some have double flowers, though these do not enjoy the approval of some discriminating gardeners on the ground that the effect of the doubling is a muddle, when much of the appeal of the plant lies in the simplicity of the single flowers.

Two varieties which yearly give us special pleasure in our garden lack even names. They are forms of a species known as *Hibiscus sinosyriacus*, which I have been told was one of the last plants to be taken out of China before the work of Western botanists there was brought to a halt. Each flower is more cup-shaped than the familiar kind. Those of one bush are white with maroon at the heart, in the other they are a light mauve with a deeper centre. At present, this species is a great rarity, but when it has been propagated and distributed more freely, it could challenge the hibiscus that has been grown in this country through three centuries and remains one of the most desirable of the few shrubs that flower in late summer.

Hostas

Companions of a damp summer: foliage desired by flower arrangers: creation of colonies: toughness and adaptability

For a damp summer such as we get three times out of five, those fashionable plants the hostas are particularly apt. Lush, luxuriant growers, they look much more at home under the grey skies and through the rain than unhappy salvias and geraniums, or even those highly coloured roses, all standing there forlorn.

Botanically, hostas are lilies, and their flowers, a dozen or so on each stem, though small and nodding, have the characteristic lily form, standing poised two or three feet tall. Usually they are some shade of mauve, sometimes white. But it is not for their flowers that one grows hostas; it is for their leaves.

Look at *Hosta sieboldiana* (also known as *glauca*), most common of the family. You could hardly have a nobler or more robust hardy perennial. In the best forms each leaf, never less than six inches across, often eight or nine, is dusted with a greyish bloom that seems to throw into relief the prominent veining.

No wonder flower arrangers scatter slug pellets round the plants to save the leaves from being punctured by the plants' only pest: tiny snails. No wonder they cut them in their prime and hang them up until they have dried to tawny and amber shades.

Even the plain green leaves of the next most common one, *Hosta fortunei,* have such distinction that one would take endless trouble to make it comfortable in the garden. In truth, I don't think I could stop our plants flourishing if I tried.

During the summer its varietal form *albo-picta* loses its yellow tints, as a cat's eyes change colour when it leaves kitten-hood behind. But up to this stage in the season the broad leaves are a primrose shade, only gradually overtaken by the green of its maturity, though always remaining a fresh tone.

As its name implies, the species sold as *Hosta albo-marginata* has leaves outlined with white, a contrasting tone which they retain through the season. The name also describes, if rather less accurately, the foliage of one called *lancifolia.*

The same might be said of *Hosta plantaginea,* but there is a word more to say about this one. The leaves are a delicate green and it bears some of the most beautiful flowers of all, white in this case and not until the autumn. For this reason, it is the only hosta one needs to put in either a sheltered or sunny place. The rest show their pleasure in shade by the splendour of the foliage they make there.

They not only wax fat but can be used to cover the ground most decoratively around such shrubs as rhododendrons and hydrangeas (though they don't mind lime), most of them flowering in the interval between these two and always looking well-dressed between spring and autumn. Then, it must be admitted, their decline is not very pretty, but by that time bad weather has usually driven one from the garden for anything but work.

Just like peonies, these plants are happy to stay just where they are put, year after year. Yet to make the bold colonies in which they are seen at their most effective (and at their most effectual as weed smotherers), they can be divided any time in winter. A sharp knife is needed for this as the clumps are dense.

The toughness and adaptability of these plants are also shown in the way they endure being transplanted bodily. In a wild moment of gardening inspiration I have lifted and moved an ill-placed plant with a foliage spread of a yard. A crowbar and a brick were needed to lever it out of the ground in Archimedian fashion, but from that day to this it has not turned a leaf.

Of course, in its new hole I surrounded the exposed fleshy roots with plenty of peat and washed it in before returning the soil. For this is all these well-behaved, long-suffering plants ask of you — to be given the decaying vegetable refuse which gardeners, always preoccupied with Latin terminology, dignify with the name of humus.

Hydrangeas

Division of varieties: value as a hardy plant: flowering season:
prize of floral artists: the electric blue: northern exposure:
hortensias: the bohemian relations: lacecaps: pruning

Perhaps the number of disappointments over hydrangeas one
hears about, the non-flowering, the bushes cut back by frost,
derives from a lack of clear division between those suitable for
planting out of doors and varieties better adapted by their nature
to being grown as pot plants.

The blowsy plant bought as an oversized flower in a pot and
put out in the garden when you have grown bored with it
indoors is hardly likely to repeat the same performance outside.
The likelihood is that it is not only frost-tender but belongs to the
group that flower mainly from buds at the tips of the branches
and only meagrely from sideshoots.

On the other hand, a whole group of hydrangeas are both
reasonably, if not altogether reliably, hardy and do flower mostly
on lateral growths, whose buds are less susceptible to frost.

[195]

In fact, the hydrangea is certainly one of our most valuable hardy shrubs, if one can divorce it from its conventional associations. It does not have to look like a sugar icing round the platform at school prizegivings, half overhung with palms and asparagus fern.

The varieties most suitable for planting in the garden often have subtle tints in their colouring that invite you to look closer at them. And they have a season of flower far longer than their artificial appearance decorating the stands at Ascot might suggest. As they age the flowers take on the mellow richness of maturity instead of fading. When their time is long past they are treasures eagerly pounced on by floral artists. Then, even those chemically produced electric blues become acceptable, and you will have the flower heads to decorate the house all the winter. This they do without their stems being stood in water.

The blue colouring so deeply desired in hydrangeas by some who grow them will appear only on acid soil. Elsewhere it is wasted endeavour to apply the colouring powder conveniently bought in packets. You can put round them all the old nails, hinges and rusty tins you can lay hands on in an attempt to add to the soil the iron they need, which the lime locks up, but you will only succeed in turning them into a washy mauve, if they make any response at all.

Though they will thrive on chalk with plenty of decayed organic refuse added, hydrangeas will flourish and oblige you with what colours you want of them if you are lucky enough to garden on acid soil.

Before we took over the land that has become our garden, sick horses were sometimes put on it, and I often turn up their old, rusty shoes. Lacking someone like the gravedigger in Hamlet to muse over them, their only memorial is the blueness of the hydrangeas round which we place the excavated shoes to continue rusting away.

However, those denied the desirable acid soil have hope in the sequestrene product now available for supplying iron in an assimilable form to plants which are otherwise unable to get it from the soil. But treatment must be repeated every year in late winter.

Whatever the soil, though, one can safely plant hydrangeas with a northern exposure. They flower well there, and they do not flag in heat as they are inclined to do in sunny places.

As for varieties for our purpose, on any soil one might plant the bright pink 'Altona', glowing crimson 'Westfalen', and rose 'Ami Pasquier'. On acid soil 'Altona' turns from blue to crimson as the flowers age; 'Goliath' can be almost violet and 'Westfalen' the colour of a loganberry. Any colour description, however, is arbitrary, for it varies from garden to garden, and specialist firms, who list many others, are reluctant to be precise.

All these are the familiar hydrangeas of a rather formal character which fits them best for courtyard or close-to-the-house planting, and they are attractively grouped as the 'hortensias'. I think their somewhat artificial look, relieved by their billowing manner of growth, is exactly right for flower beds at the foot of walls.

The hydrangeas that serve this rather formal purpose so admirably have a whole company of relations which are more bohemian, better adapted to patches of wild garden where they can be set between rhododendrons and azaleas to give another show of flowers in late summer and autumn when otherwise there would be none. The most familiar is the frothing *Hydrangea paniculata*, producing great plumes of ivory flowers. Another called *Hydrangea quercifolia* is grown partly, as its name suggests, for the oak-like leaves which turn to rich colours before they fall. *Hydrangea arborescens* might be mistaken at a glance for a guelder rose strayed out of its own season.

But the most intriguing are the 'lacecaps', so called from the curious formation of the flower trusses. In these a display of broad sterile flowers attracts insects to the cluster of fertile flowers they surround.

They bring a little tension, too, for the colours are inconstant. When the flowers begin to show they appear white or a blush pink, and for a week or two you are filled with anxiety. Aren't they going to be blue or rose or carmine this year? But as the days grow shorter the pigments emerge, and then well into the autumn you have a display that grows richer day by day.

Their names? Blue Wave, *mariesii*, White Wave, *thunbergii*, *lilacina, acuminata, serrata* — you start with one and soon become a collector when you realise their dividends. Most of all, though, I think I like *Hydrangea villosa*, for not only does this give us many weeks of blue flowers that, however close our acquaintance with them, intrigue us as much as they do our friends, but it also offers light green leaves with the texture of velvet that you must always stroke as you pass.

This fascinating quality is most developed, however, in one grown for its foliage alone, *Hydrangea sargentiana*. So splendid are the leaves of this one that it is advisedly grown in the shelter of a wall, a west or north-facing one for preference, where they will be safe from the danger of being torn to tatters by gales; and where, indeed, they grow more splendidly than they would in the woodland the plant otherwise likes.

Pruning? All you need to do is remove weak, unpromising growth and cut away some of the oldest wood now and again in spring.

Lilacs

Exuberance of lilac bushes: the small varieties: syringa micro-
phylla superba: elegance from Canada: how to prune effectively:
need for the sun: the planter's indulgence

Looking up at the abundance of flowers produced by the lilacs
in suburban gardens regularly every year as spring gives
way to summer, the fellow making a new garden on a necessarily
midget site might admire them and decide that a lilac bush must
be forgone on the account of its size. They always seem to be
ten or twelve-foot bushes when mature, altogether too massive
for the tiny plots that go with houses being built now. But wait
a moment, before they are written off.

Just as they will obscure all else round them with the amplitude
of their foliage, the many forms of the common lilac have been
planted so freely that they also overshadow kinds which are more
graceful and less robust, and keep to scale with small sites. One
is even sold to grow on a rock garden.

This is the plant offered as *Syringa palabiniana*. In its three-inch pot when bought it looks as though it will remain a stunted dwarf. In fact it will grow four feet tall, and bear plumes of purplish-pink flowers with the characteristic lilac scent.

Perhaps, at this stage, to remove any quizzical looks I should repeat the old explanation that the name syringa, wrongly bestowed on the mock orange bush, called botanically phila-delphus, is in fact the lilac's correct botanical title. The error was first made early in the seventeenth century and has not yet been erased from everyday talk.

Attempts have been made to change the name of *Syringa pala-biniana* to *microphylla,* but it would be sad to lose a term which slips so easily off the tongue. Anyway, it serves to distinguish it sharply from another miniature lilac which deserves special approval for small sites. For not only does that four-foot bush called *Syringa microphylla superba* flower in late spring, but it puts on a second show in late summer.

Again the flowers are perfumed and though there is only the one shade of rosy pink, it is an immensely pleasing little shrub. Someone with a gift for 'improving' plants, by the way, might try getting some of the other colourings found in the common lilac into these two plants.

The Persian lilac, *Syringa persica,* which does grow a little bigger, already has a white variety in addition to the lilac coloured form in which it is most often seen. The flower panicles in this case are rather small, though to some tastes this is an advantage.

Indeed, the bounteous heaviness of the trusses in which the common lilac forms its flowers is regarded by many gardeners of discrimination as not fitting them for the informal type of garden anyone with a fairly ample site makes these days.

They prefer varieties with more elegance which comes from single flowers each having longer and more slender tubes and more space between the clusters. Several of this type have been bred in Canada. In their production the scent has not been sacri-ficed and the colour range is widening. Bellicent, for instance, is a flesh pink and you can find the purple admired in some common lilac varieties in either Donald Wyman or Hiawatha. The growth habit of the pink variety called Fountain in itself commends this one.

Unfortunately, these all have the same vigour as our admired common lilac, but this factor does mean that either type can be used effectively to make a tall solid screen for the garden where defence in depth from the outside gaze is possible.

In any event annual pruning is both practicable and desirable to put off the day when lilac bushes outgrow their environment. They are inevitably pruned to some extent by the inroads made on them by cutting sprays for the house, and once flowering is over the secateurs should be used on them with forthrightness.

All the spent trusses are cut away to spare the bushes the strain of seeding and as this is done strong shoots already produced lower down the branches are selected and preserved to bear the following season's crop. Weak shoots are best removed.

Indeed, the failure of lilacs to flower well can often be attributed to too many shoots having been promoted by hard pruning without reducing them to allow the selected few to gain all the ripening effects of the sun and of air circulating freely round them.

Lilacs do need the sun for their well-being. Deny it them and the bushes 'go all to leaf'. Also, as an aid to producing tough wood that flowers well, it is worth putting bonfire ash round them. Their other need is for the indulgence of the planter's patience. Sometimes not until the third year after planting will they flower at all.

Magnolias

*A garden fantasy: Magnolia soulangeana: red flowers: careful
positioning: confidence in the future: trees and shrubs*

A garden fantasy I have nourished for a long while and have
tried to bring to reality is a grove of magnolias. These are
surely the most noble of trees, making an appeal to the imagination (and demand on the pocket) no others can match. Close
familiarity through seeing so many examples flushed with
blossom in so many gardens in the London suburbs cannot
diminish their status, even though in stature they eventually
become an increasing embarrassment in such a setting and a
greater temptation to passers-by to pluck one of those huge waxen
flowers.

In one way it is fortunate that you normally cannot buy a
magnolia as a ready-grown standard tree, like a cherry or a
laburnum, though I did hear of one going for £75 not so long
ago. It means that you have to watch it grow from a bushlet a

couple of feet high into a mighty tree, and this helps to enhance the mystique that surrounds magnolias.

Perhaps it is their astonishing splendour, which places them among the élite of all plants, that has won magnolias a reputation for being difficult to rear. The fact is that the right situation is more important than the soil they are given.

Those examples you see from the tops of buses in Streatham and Putney and Finchley (enjoying them in a way their owners presumably never do) prove how easy they are to grow. They deny the classical theory that the plants need peaty soil that is well-drained. Still, this is what one would choose for them at the outset.

Unlike other trees commonly grown in gardens, the magnolia has fleshy roots. Not only does this mean that they like the soil to be on the loose side rather than compacted, but also that they are easily damaged if one applies the advice always given to 'tread firm' too literally in this case. It also explains why the plants take to a new environment with more alacrity if they are planted in spring rather than autumn. Some damage during lifting is un-avoidable, and a root so affected is inclined to die back at a time when the growth impulse is dormant.

In any event a cushion of damp peat round the roots, and plenty more in the soil which they will later explore, help to avoid damage during firming after planting and promotes progress. A little stake to prevent rocking in the wind is essential in this case. The inevitable and indispensable bonemeal, of course, will help to feed the young plant.

Progress from the start is usually fairly certain from the magnolia that graces the suburbs. This is the hybrid called *Magnolia soulangeana,* after the Frenchman in whose garden in the environs of Paris it arose from two Asiatic species a century and a half ago. What is most curious is that though the flowers of the hybrid are heavily stained with purplish red at the heart, those of one parent have a mere flush and the others none at all.

The degrees of redness in the flowers is of considerable concern to magnolia fanciers. The soulangeana form in which it is most developed is one which carries the third name of *lennei*. Meeting it for the first time, one hardly recognises its kinship with the well-known hybrid. The flowers are flatter and broader, deep rose on the outside and lined with ivory within. I have found the bush rather more open in character too, but perhaps this is because we have ours in shade, where fortunately it does flower well. It follows the parent, often going on into June.

Incidentally, this tardiness means that it escapes the frost that is the peril of most magnolias and which they share with camellias. But the danger of damage to the flowers can be minimised by planting them, just like camellias, in some position where the early morning sun cannot reach them.

The much desired red colouring is most advanced — that is, in a magnolia on which one can expect to see it within 20 years — in one called *Magnolia liliflora nigra*. The last name must be taken as it applies to tulips and read as 'purple' instead of 'black'. This is a rather smaller grower. Our plants have progressed at half the rate of the soulangeanas, flowering from their first days in the garden.

The smallest of magnolias, slow enough in growth for the smallest garden, is *Magnolia stellata*. As the name implies, the flowers are like stars, and pure white. They come out earlier than all the rest of the family and therefore this one must be particularly carefully placed.

Another specially good species for gardens is the small growing *Magnolia sieboldii*, sometimes offered as *parviflora*. This may not be able to compare with some of the others in majesty, but it has an appeal of a different kind. Opening after the others, the chalice-shaped flowers of pearly white nod shyly, and as you lift them you find they enshrine a boss of claret-red stamens. Then you get the drift of the rich, fruity fragrance, like some rare liqueur. This alone would make it worth growing.

Perhaps it argues confidence in the future to plant the kinds that have to grow into trees before they begin to flower. But gardeners do not think about these things. Anyway, some tree-like species are not so slow in showing what they can do. Our tree of *Magnolia kobus* hung its branches with its big white stars before it was a teenager. Nearby in our nascent grove the red-flowered *Magnolia mollicomata* seems intent on catching it up. This is the best one to plant if you have a fancy for growing the celebrated red *Magnolia campbellii,* which people will go miles to see in flower and stand before in silent awe.

If you have to hurry to see the show this makes, when you hear of it, before frost turns the lot to a brown pulp, one called

Magnolia obovata will look on you with a reserved smile. He —
for gardeners are inclined to personalise such trees — he will be
saving up till frost danger has passed. Only then will you see the
massive white flowers high up there, and perhaps notice the ring
of stamens of crimson which they enshrine.

What it is important to realise is that not all magnolias are
billowing shrubs like the soulangeana everyone knows. Some are
trees that can be coaxed into pyramid-like growth and perhaps
have greater garden potential than the over-done cherries and
laburnums.

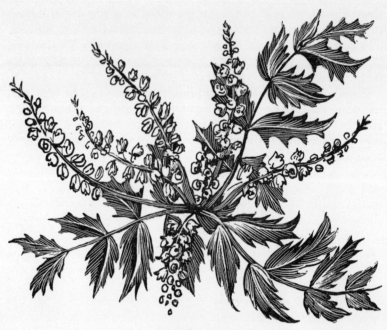

Mahonias

The many advantages of this family: use as a low hedge: the Mahonia japonica: elusive scent: the autumn flowering lomarii-folia: bronze-red leaves

This single genus of plants deserves a second and third glance from garden-makers, however limited their scale. For the bushes are tough, adaptable, evergreen, highly decorative whether in flower or not. They number among them several that definitely and regularly take it on themselves to blossom when the year is at its lowest ebb and the weather likely to be the most unkind of the whole twelve months.

Once they were grouped by botanists in the great berberis family. This immediately suggests that they are prickly, but the spines barb the leaves in this case rather than the stems. What it does indicate is that they will endure shade as well as sun and that they are not in the least particular about the kind of soil they are offered.

Almost everyone knows *Mahonia aquifolium,* by sight if not by name also. This is the plant you see about in gardens with sprays of holly-like leaves which bears tight bunches of yellow flowers. The fact that it suckers is not to be held against it. This can be put to advantage by using it as a ground-coverer, especially under trees, giving an all-the-year-round effect there.

If the plants get lanky and unsightly, the tops can be removed and all begun again with new growth from close to ground level. But the upright-striking nature of the main growths means that this mahonia can also be put to good purpose as a low and neat hedge.

One is less inclined to curb the splendidly attired *Mahonia japonica,* however. This is the pearl of the family, though we have had to endure some confusion over its name. Sometimes it is still and erroneously called *Mahonia bealei,* but this in fact has stubby, erect plumes of flowers, while those of *Mahonia japonica* are formed in sprays, lax and arching. Sometimes they are a foot long. Their pale yellow colouring, their disposition on the bush, and their indifference to wet and cold would be enough. But they are scented too, quite heavily, and of lily-of-the-valley.

For its leaves and stance alone, coupled with the fact that it is evergreen, it would be worth planting in a corner of the smallest garden. The leaves, as botanists say, are compound and therefore composed of many leaflets, again forming elegant reflexing sprays. They are fashioned into giant posies, big enough to fling at the feet of the best-loved prima donna.

Making comparisons between the scents of those mahonias which have this quality is a subjective business. To some eyes the hybrid called Charity is an even finer plant than *japonica,* for it has a better-dressed poise and the flowers approach a golden-yellow. But I did not think its scent nearly so good.

Unfortunately, the splendid *Mahonia lomariifolia* has none. The flowers really are gold in this case and open in November in the most astonishing cluster of spikes. Another of its characteristics is that it has a tall, lean, gaunt, aristocratic outline. Which means that you can tuck it in almost anywhere. If it is a little on the tender side, having come from not quite so far up in the Hima-layas as the misnamed *japonica,* this is of no account in the sheltered confines of a town back-yard-become-patio, where it would be in character.

Old Roses

The distinction of old roses: their 'subtlety': profusion of blooms: rose of a hundred leaves: moss roses: the rose from Damascus: attar of roses: the white rose of York: Fair Rosamond: the apothecaries' rose: Tuscany

What is it that gives the 'old' roses their distinction, that enables them to survive through generations of changes in gardening fashions and to retain their hold in an era of new rose production on such a scale as never known before? In a word I can describe it only as 'subtlety'. Yet they have a simplicity of the kind admired in a plain Georgian house front. To some gardeners their appeal is so strong that they will give garden room to no roses but old ones, or at least roses grown as shrubs.

Beside old roses, they will tell you, the hybrid teas of recent raising which we all grow, even some floribundas, are 'obvious'. I cannot go all the way in this over-simplification, but growing both I can see the point. Whereas the old roses we are able to cut so lavishly from a handful of bushes have a touch of mystery and sentiment about them, the hybrid teas in the same room can seem simply stylists by comparison, for all their magnificent splendour. Certainly the old ones are much less trouble. You do not have to worry much about pests or diseases afflicting them, or even pruning them very often.

The notion that only the old roses are scented will not bear sniffing. Many of our hybrid teas have a fine richness of scent, and in some old ones it is faint. One of the qualities, however, which has led me to devote a whole little garden to old-fashioned roses is their generosity with their flowers during the month that is their only season. Then the bushes are garlanded with bloom in abandoned profusion.

There is nothing heavy or ungainly about them during this time. The flowers are beautifully poised and the bushes take on a form which happily supports this out-pouring of blossom, a quality which, say the critics, hybrid teas lack.

Strangely, the blue tints which some modern rose breeders seek to isolate in some rose of the future, and which others try to breed out of their varieties in favour of clearer pinks, are often present already on the old-fashioned roses, and sit happily on them. Several varieties are prized for the mauve and violet colourings which overtake the flowers as they age. Some, indeed, are at their most attractive just before they fall. Then, not only are the colour tones most subtle, but the beautiful form of the flowers, often 'quartered', is revealed. Thus the rose that usually excites most comment in our garden, if not general admiration, is one named Tour de Malakoff. In one single flower and at one time you get rose, purple, mauve and lavender tones. This is one of the old *Rosa centifolia* varieties the 'rose of a hundred leaves' of such sumptuousness that it inevitably appears in countless old masters.

Another of this group which seems to be equally intriguing bears the name Chapeau de Napoléon in reference to the cockade-like wings of the calyx from which the pink flowers thrust forth. Of the pink centifolias, though, my own vote goes to Fantin Latour, a rose of such beauty as to deserve a painter's name.

The moss roses, which derive their name from the moss-like excrescences on the calyx, which invite you to stroke them, are centifolias with this added quality. Again we can find among them touches of violet, most pronounced, I think, in one called William Lobb, a six-foot bush in our garden, though it is run close by the smaller-growing Capitaine John Ingram. I only wish they bore as many flowers as our heavily laden bush of the striped moss rose, whose multitude of flowers are each flecked with rose on their blush ground.

So formal are the flowers of the damask rose Madame Hardy that most who see it immediately liken it to a camellia. It is certainly the most handsome white rose I know and has the fullest share of perfume. By contrast, Hebe's Lip is simply a single rose with two rows of petals, one of which is touched with red at the edges, but it is a flower of exquisite perfection. The term 'damask' associates the origins of these roses with the crusaders, who are said to have brought the first from Damascus for their ladies at home in the north. But it must have spread east too, for one of its group called Kazanlik is supposed to be grown in the Balkans for attar of roses, though when I repeat this story as I point out our bush to visitors I often detect a response of disbelief, for it needs a good deal of credulity to find much scent in it.

The two varieties of the white rose of York, *Rosa alba,* I grow are Celestial, which adds to the beauty of its soft pink flowers the distinction of bluish foliage that is a rare quality in a rose, and Great Maiden's Blush, a soft pink rose.

Of all the striped varieties the old-fashioned roses can offer the one I prefer most is Commandant Beaurepaire, whose crimson flowers are splashed with pink and sometimes deeper shades than the ground, and the apple-green foliage shows them up particularly well.

If you like such markings in a rose you find them specially pronounced in *Rosa gallica versicolor,* also called *Rosa Mundi* after the Fair Rosamund. Red and white in motley splashed, it arose as a sport from the old 'apothecaries rose', *officinalis,* said to have once been grown around the French town of Provins for the potions industry there. It is a specially generous rose of bright pink whose many suckers are never unwelcome but are encouraged to form low thickets.

One velvet crimson rose will do the same. Called Tuscany, and heedless of the troubles which afflict roses commonly, rich in scent and colouring, it seems to enshrine all the qualities for which these old roses have been rescued from ill-deserved obscurity and make them some of the most prized of the sophisticated gardener's plants.

Penstemons

The patrician elegance of the penstemon: mysterious caverns:
new plants from cuttings: colour tones: growing from seed

Beside the commonalty of summer flowers, with daisies of
one sort or another in the kind of majority that would be
ecstasy to a politician, the penstemons have a patrician elegance
that makes them look almost frail. This is simply the diplomatic
deception of the well-bred, concealing inner toughness.

When the collection of varieties we have built up is coming
into blossom, I think I prefer penstemons above all other plants
loosely grouped as 'herbaceous'. Even though they go on flowering until October, one never grows bored with them. Airily
poised on their stems, in spires that produce still more buds each
week, the flowers might be fairy trumpets hung there at a
Titania's bidding. They have the faintly furry, dusty texture of
moth's head, and are so mysterious and cavernous within that
even a bumble bee exploring them is lost to view.

The toughness is seen in the wiriness of the stems. Other plants may be dashed by vexing summer gales, but the penstemon stems simply bend a little, though never allow themselves to be part of the disarray all around or discomfited by it.

They are really sub-shrubs. Often the stems survive the winter well set with leaves. But they renew and increase themselves from the base just the same.

In the belief that the top growth gives the rootstock frost protection I leave it to stand through the winter. If the weather is mild I let it develop again and flower. If the winter has been harsh and it has got bedraggled, then I remove it in spring and make do with the new shoots that arise. Penstemons, it must be admitted, for all their virtues, are frost tender. And, like most plants that flower away for weeks with all their might, they have a limited span. Lived flamboyantly, their lives end early. Three or four years, perhaps five, and all is over. But they are as easy to increase as pinks and violas.

Once you have acquired your plants and got them growing strongly with an occasional draught of liquid fertiliser, you have only to break off some of the side shoots that sometimes appear on the main stems — but more often some of the unflowered shoots that come from ground level — and use these as cuttings, rooted in a frame or polythene-topped box.

Here they must stay for the winter, covered with a sack during very hard spells but otherwise exposed to free ventilation most of the time. They are planted out in May, like summer bedding plants, as they are often regarded.

The penstemon which has lasted longest for us is Firebird, more often catalogued as schönholzeri. It is the colour of a Frensham rose seen in full sunlight. Newberry Gem is a deeper tone, Southgate Gem brighter. In Castle Forbes there is a sharp contrast between the crimson ground colour and the white throat.

Of course, the easiest way to acquire a stock is from seed, when you get a mixed bag with some of the most striking of all the flowers, though my experience has been that the plants are not quite so hardy as the selected varieties with pet names.

The seed can be sown in April without heat; otherwise it is done in February. Hurried along in fibre pots each seedling in its own one, they should then come safely through the spring in a frame and make plants that will show what they are capable of in their first season.

Philadelphus

Reckless profusion: the syringa usurpation: the Chinese wilding:
Albatre and Belle Etoile: dwarf oranges: layering: Gerard's
warning

The mock orange bushes seen and smelt in gardens in the least likely places show how adaptable a plant it is. In town and country, suburb and subtopia, it flourishes and flowers with the recklessness of midsummer. It is equally indifferent to the nature of the soil, and is seldom too shy to flower the first season after planting.

Like the hazel or a black-currant bush, it is blessed with perennial youth and is capable of replacing itself from below ground in a few years. In practice this means that it can easily be kept within average garden size by cutting out one or two of the oldest branches every year, right down to the base, and leaving the younger growth to take over.

Indeed, when flowering declines it is usually because young and old wood are trying to co-exist in a thicket of growth which

[213]

prevents fair shares all round of the air and sunshine that promote ripening and consequent flowering. Accordingly, this drastic pruning has to be done as soon as the flowers wither and drop.

In plant catalogues and text-books they appear under the prosaic name of philadelphus, yet are commonly and more attractively known as 'syringa', a botanical name usurped from the lilacs, to whom it properly belongs. In spite of the confusion which results, they bear it shamelessly and no one but the pedants seems inclined to deny them it.

For some years I collected all the mock oranges I could find for planting, not in a bold group in the way that most plants of a kind look best, but for scattering throughout the garden so that we could extort the maximum from their scent potential. Even the roses have to accept them as companions.

Scent being tantalisingly fugitive, coming and going with the breeze and the temperature, I would not like to say which variety has most. Though I am right outside that breed of gardeners who hold that the natural species are always more desirable plants than the man-made hybrids and varieties, I must own on this occasion that the mock orange in our collection which we cherish most, for several qualities, is a Chinese wilding, *Philadelphus delavayi*.

The big but well-poised flowers hang in bunches of a dozen at a time, each as exquisitely shaped as a tiny piece of Meissen porcelain, the blackish stamens emphasising the whiteness of the flowers. This is a tall bush, I do admit, but lanky enough to put other plants under. Anyway, its proportions can be kept down by cutting out some of the old wood each year, and in this instance this yields an extra bonus, for the younger wood is a mahogany shade marked with cream, a valuable garden asset in winter.

Personally, I much prefer this among the tall growers to the celebrated Virginal, which hovers uncertainly between being double and single. The doubles lack the individual perfection of the singles, but perhaps they have an advantage in lasting in bloom just a little longer. My choice of a fluffy-flowered variety would be Albatre. After a dozen years our plant was still not more than four feet tall, having had some old wood cut out every year when flowering had finished. The beautiful Belle Etoile proves similarly accommodating, and is much admired for the purplish flushes seen at the heart of each flower.

If, as a race, mock orange bushes are a little undistinguished out of flower, one variety, *Philadelphus coronarius aureus,* has the added merit of golden leaves for the early part of the season, though they deepen to green as it advances.

Even tiny gardens, where everything has to be scaled down, can have their mock oranges. Two are dwarfs, content to grow only three to four feet tall, offering themselves for the mixed borders of shrubs, bulbs and herbaceous perennials which have supplanted the splendid but hard-to-maintain herbaceous borders that now rarely survive at their best outside public parks. Sybille has the fashionable purple stain at the heart; Manteau d'Hermine has fluffy double flowers.

The ease with which these shrubs can be reproduced is characteristic of most plants that show a powerful will to live by renewing themselves from the base. Often you can pull off a naturally rooted branch to offer a friend. Or if you peg down some of the younger branches in spring and cover an incision in the bark with soil these will make new plants by the following spring. Cuttings made from shoots that have grown this season, pulled off in July with a tag of the old wood, take root in light soil in a month to six weeks if they are kept in the close atmosphere of a polythene-enclosed box.

If you find that mock orange quickly flags when you attempt to transfer its perfume from the open garden to the house, try stripping off the leaves. Sprays often last longer under this treatment.

But take warning from old Gerard. In a famous note in his 'Herbal' written over three hundred years ago, he complained that some picked philadelphus flowers 'smelled more strongly after they had laid together a few howers, but with such a pontick and unacquainted savor that they awaked me from sleepe, so that I could not take rest till I had cast them out of my chamber.'

Pinks

Mrs. Sinkins: the briefness of her span: blood of the carnation:
varieties: pinks for rock gardens: sowing from seed: 'perpetual'
pinks: 'show' pinks: 'imperial' pinks: lime for the soil

Ever since I learned that the fragrant white pink known as
Mrs. Sinkins once grew in the garden of the workhouse at
Slough back in the last century and was named after the wife of
the master there, Oliver Twist has lost some of its horror. Life
couldn't have been all cruelty and institutional drabness in those
places if they had time then for such a sweetly-scented flower
worthy of being cherished in gardens ever since.

But when I watch the buds of Mrs. Sinkins release their flowers
in our garden, and the clove-like fragrance arises again every
season, I wonder if the time has not come to take leave of the
lady and give her a decent burial.

For though she has persisted all these years, like many other garden pinks with sentimental associations, her annual span is too brief. Barely a month of flowers is too short a time for the pink season when by means of other varieties we can grow it can be lengthened to nearly half the year.

And then she is a slovenly matron, bursting out of her seams. A pink, though it may bring echoes of jumbled, fragrant cottage gardens, is a stylish flower that has always engaged the 'florist's' enterprise. A flower to pick and put on show, to peer into closely and sniff the scent.

The newer pinks have all the qualities asked of such a flower and the varieties are endless. Perhaps to suggest that they are new, though, is misleading, for the original crossing was done half a century ago. Then the blood of the so-called 'perpetual' carnation grown in greenhouses for cut flowers was introduced to the garden pink. The upshot was that the pink, while retaining its compact form of growth and its hardiness, took on the long-flowering capacity of its big brother. Since then crossing and selection has gone on and on, and today the 'perpetual' pink has an unimpeachable reputation as a top garden flower.

Queen of them all is called simply Doris, salmon in colour and with a red eye. Her daughter, Doreen is a deeper colour and as prolific with her flowers as her parent, though less well scented. Pearl and Swanlake are both particularly richly scented though simply white flowers. Sunset is what might be called a soft red, while Portrait is the crimson so greatly admired in any flower of the carnation family; though, it must be said it lacks scent. So does one called Prudence, which compensates for this failing by flowering for as long as Doris — from May till November — showing its beautiful lace-like markings of purple on a white ground through all those months.

The long flowering ability has even been brought to the cushion-forming rock garden pinks, which entitles them to the name *Dianthus allwoodii alpinus*. Thus you have a race of pinks from whom you can expect the very maximum returns in flowers.

Although you cannot rely on all the flowers from seedlings to be of quite the same quality as from named varieties, which are the result of selection from many thousands, you can grow the 'perpetual' pinks from seed with as little trouble as is entailed in raising any hardy annual. The results can be very satisfying indeed, especially if you want a quantity of plants. I can imagine kitchen garden patches lined with them in the same way that they are often edged with Mrs. Sinkins.

The seeds of pinks are large enough to space out a couple of inches apart in the seed-box, by-passing the need for pricking out. If you sow in spring, by the autumn you will have plants large enough for planting (though you can do it later). They will begin to flower in the following June.

The named varieties are increased on the home scale by pulling out 'pipings' or tufts of leaves and pushing these into sandy soil in July, preferably under a polythene covering but even in the open ground with the prospect of a high proportion taking root.

Once the possibilities of 'perpetual' pinks were realised and the plants had proved themselves, it seemed that there was no reason why the long-flowering capacity should not be allied to the ultra-stylishness of the kinds grown specially for exhibition. Accordingly, a dynasty was founded in which all the names of the scions are preceded by the term 'show' to denote their aristocratic perfection of form. Crimson, white, rose, salmon, scarlet — all the colours you can expect in pinks are available, which you can enjoy again and again in one season.

Side by side with them, another race called the 'imperial' pinks was being raised. Bearing their fragrant flowers on lengthy stiff stems, they might be grown specially for cutting alone. Again, the skill of the plant raiser has led to many colourings.

Pinks have the extra merit of flourishing in almost any soil. While they certainly do like it light, they will also thrive on clay if a little sharp sand is worked in at planting time and more added each season. And if they are grown on the poor land, feed them a few handfuls of organic refuse like hop manure.

Their chief need, however, is lime, which you cannot remove to accommodate rhododendrons, but which you can always add for the comfort of these highly bred but nevertheless robust pinks.

Pomegranates

*A tree from history: the Carthaginian apple: its attractiveness
as a shrub: flowers of crumpled tissue paper: the dwarf variety:
use as a pot plant*

The pomegranate trees known to flower in London, and not
only occasionally either, are living testimony of the hardiness
of this romantic plant whose branches enfold legend and history.
In how many eastern tales, as well as the Bible, the pomegranate
appears. How often it is seen on ancient fragments of sculpture,
in decoration on vases, urns and carpets. The name by which
botanists once called it, *punica,* recalls that the Romans knew it
too, and perhaps it was preserved from Carthage, for they called
it *Malus punica,* the Carthaginian apple. Perhaps some legionary
thirsting in the desert was grateful for the refreshing soft pulp
that the highly coloured rind, like polished leather, encloses.

Here we may never see the fruits ripen, though I am told that
at Hampton Court they colour sufficiently to attract the predatory
attentions of young visitors. But as a flowering shrub it is one of

[219]

the most attractive that can be grown in the shelter of a south-facing wall.

The flowers are of that luminous vermilion that rose growers are so excited at having bred into their roses. From buds of the same leathery texture as the fruits they push forth petals like crumpled tissue paper stained with the juice of some tropical fruit. Not all at once, though, like an apple or pear, but more like a citrus fruit, the flowers opening successively over two or three months.

While I have not known the wood damaged by frost, I am sure the wall shelter is needed to radiate on summer nights the heat collected during the day and so help bring about the ripening that in turn helps to promote flowering. I have tried it against a wooden fence but never a flower appeared. As for soil, some richness may be needed to encourage growth in the early years, but later, like most hot country plants, I would expect more flowers on poor soil than from good land.

If you do need a wall for the pomegranate it need not be high, for there is a dwarf variety which, close to the Temperate House House wall at Kew, can be seen only a couple of feet tall in spite of some age. In fact, you don't need a garden at all for it, since grown as a pot plant indoors the dwarf pomegranate can be even more attractive than in the garden. Here I have found it will sometimes go on flowering into early winter, and you can watch intrigued the swelling of the buds, hoping one day to be there just as one bursts and releases the delicate flower within.

Seeds of this shrublet, *Punica granatum nana* are available from several firms and the plants can easily be raised by sowing these in spring. They are like cucumber pips and are therefore big enough to place individually in tiny fertiliser-impregnated fibre pots, in which the young plants will develop swiftly.

Perhaps a couple of seasons will have to go by before the first buds appear, but from then on if they are kept on the sunniest windowsill they should put on a show every year. If tiny seedlings are planted out of doors it would be unwise to let them take their chance unprotected for the first few years. Not until they have made some hard wood can they be allowed to go without their winter overcoat of polythene, anchored perhaps with stones and tied to a circlet of canes round each plant.

So unusual and so striking is the pomegranate in this country that it is a plant to treasure, even though absurdly simple to grow.

Primroses

The abundance of wild primroses: the railway embankment:
primula vulgaris: marriage with the Alpine primrose: many
varieties: petulant doubles: lifting and dividing: raising from seed

Every year in late February primroses by the thousand burst
forth suddenly on our railway embankment and other places
where the gipsies cannot get at them to pull up the roots for those
enchanting little baskets they sell but which shame such vandalism.
So abundant are their flowers again after all they have gone
through since we last saw them that the question inevitably
arises: what place do primroses have in the garden?

The treatment they get in nature itself suggests the kind of
places where they can be fitted into the garden. Once their season
is done and the wild herbage grows up round them they are quite
concealed. They do not suffer by it, but wait there consolidating
the gains of their brief spell of full exposure. Our railway embankment gets burned over every summer — but still the primroses
come up undismayed in spring.

Accordingly, in the garden, I see no reason why they should not be scattered among taller growing plants which are cut right down in autumn and only reach their full height again in summer. Provided the soil gets its annual layer of hop manure or old leaf mould every year, resembling the decaying wild herbage from which they would benefit in the wild, they will flourish and give an earlier show of colour on ground that would otherwise offer only one in summer. Then the primroses lie concealed, but not totally obscured from the light.

The primroses we cultivate in this way in our garden include several of the pink and red kinds besides the beautiful pale yellow hedgerow plant that has to suffer the indignity of being known to botanists as *Primula vulgaris*. The primrose of the Alps, however, was more thoughtfully treated and bears the name *Primula juliae*. By crossing this with our own, many hybrids have been raised and none of the robustness of either has been sacrificed for the new colours.

The best known, of course, is Wanda, sold, I suppose in hundreds of thousands every spring. As a garden plant it is almost indestructible, always coming up again to produce a long succession of its purple flowers every year. The variety Jewel has more red in it, while Pam is a distinctly maroon, both having the same easy-going ways of Wanda.

For several weeks on end one can enjoy the lilac flowers of Wendy on vigorous plants, and for an equal period the glowing crimson Betty Green. Rose Brazier and Prince Purple, which describe themselves, we have found as robust as the wilding too.

Once you begin to acquire named varieties of primroses you develop a collector's zeal for them, for you can always find odd spots to plant them and each new name encountered in catalogues is a spur to acquire it. Soon you go on to the doubles, and then you are lost. For these are fugitive and tantalising, flourishing one year, petulantly threatening to expire the next, and keeping you frantically pampering them and always seeking just the right conditions for them.

One grower will advise plenty of cow manure in the soil, another will recommend chaff, and someone else the damp atmosphere of the west of Ireland. And then you will hear that they must be divided up every year to maintain their vigour — which I think is very near the truth. Certainly, like all other primroses, they take best to heavy soil well-enriched with old manure if you can get it, but otherwise generous helpings of peat and hop manure.

For all their abundance in nature — there are over five hundred species scattered round the world — primroses do get tired of the same ground and like a change. For some years I have grown the pink-flowered, bronze-leaved Garryarde Guinevere (actually a polyanthus) on the same site, but now, divide them though I will, they remain debilitated and indicate they need a change.

The time for lifting, dividing and replanting is immediately the flowers are over, just when we usually get an inconvenient dry spell. Flooding them before and after is better than delaying the job until a heavy shower comes, in order to give them the maximum time to build up for the following season.

If you are not particular about the shade, however, coloured primroses — even rich blues — can be raised from a packet of seed sown in early spring. The seeds are tiny and need shaking out only very thinly on the surface of a box of peaty soil, covered by the merest scattering of sand and watered by holding the box in water up to its top edge until moisture shows on the surface. If it is then placed in a polythene bag, kept closed, you need not look at it again for a month or so. Soon the seedlings will be ready for pricking out, and later a second time into a bed of leafy soil shaded for most of the day. By autumn they will be ready for planting where they are to flower.

Silver

Leaves of silvery cast: lightness in the garden: shrubs: the shrubby groundsel: lavender cotton: herbaceous plants: artemisia: anaphalis and immortelles

Dismay too soon follows the excitement of discovery when one gets caught up by the vogue for growing plants whose leaves have a silvery cast about them. After an exuberant performance in their first summer, too often the first winter sees them perish. By nature they are generally plants that have had to adapt themselves to drought, shallow soil, hot sunshine and decided winters — can they be expected to enjoy our wet ground and alternations of cold and damp winter weather? But there is hope.

If you are gardening on light soil, or close to the sea, or even in a low rainfall area, most of these plants will flourish for you and burst into new growth with the spring. But even where the ground lies wet and cold much of the winter, the garden need not be deprived of these so-called 'silvers'; they then only have to be chosen rather carefully.

Their foliage is some of the most pleasing of the whole plant kingdom and can help relieve the heaviness that begins to creep over the garden in high summer, when everything is in its fullest maturity. Like white-flowered plants, they are also masterful in keeping warring colourings at a safe distance.

Gardening on clay myself, and having tried many of them in twin borders which were to be devoted to shrub roses rising from a shimmering silvery groundwork, I have been able to sort out some of the possibles from the hopefuls.

First among them I must put that cherished shrubby groundsel *Senecio laxifolius,* often sold as *Senecio greyii,* which you see in almost every seaside garden. Though we are frequently reminded in horticultural comment that it is a plant native to New Zealand, I have never lost it. When a plant has grown too big I have hacked it about mercilessly and it has always recovered. I do not care much for the yellow ragwort flowers, but it stands there silvery the whole year, as pleasing in winter as at any other time.

We have had our bushes of *Phlomis fruticosa* just as long, and they have had the same rough treatment on soil on which you can hardly stand up in winter. Yet they go on happily. In this case the hooded sage-like lemon-coloured flowers in chubby clusters are much more agreeable, and the big leaves are rather like a rabbit's ears and as furry to the touch.

While we have had to replant low hedges of lavender in which the winter wet leaves ugly gaps every year, never has the same fate overtaken one of *Santolina chamaecyparissus,* or lavender cotton, a dome-shaped little silvery shrub that always smells to me like a Christmas dinner. When it has got too floppy we have cut it to the ground about August and like the senecio it has sprung up again as large as life. It is one of the most silvery of all.

An even more pleasing plant than this, though, but offered far less frequently, is its cousin *Santolina neapolitana.* The foliage is much more feathery in appearance and almost as soft as that of the favourite 'southernwood'. In spite of the origins suggested by the second name, a plant we had survived more than ten winters in wet soil, to die eventually of decrepitude.

This is often what happens to plants of this kind; or else they get so contorted as to be too grotesque to be allowed to survive. So it is worth providing successors from cuttings every four or five years. One can simply push these — taken during August or

September — into the light, fairly shaded soil close to a hedge and leave them uncovered with the reasonable expectation that more than half will 'take'. This goes for lavender, rosemary and sage, too.

Among herbaceous plants, *Artemisia ludoviciana*, one of the wormwoods, has long been a flower arranger's favourite. Encrusted though the grey leaves are, as if they had had to adapt themselves to very frugal living, the plant does go on from year to year, throwing up more three-foot stems each season.

Growing other members of this family, I have had two big surprises. We cannot stop *Artemisia maritima*, a foot tall, growing in a patch of wet soil. Not that we would really want to, for the leaves are as exquisite as the filigree patterns made by frost on a window in a cold night in the pre-central heating days.

The behaviour of the artemisia known as Lambrook Silver has surprised me even more. This is a form of *Artemisia absinthium*, the source of the flavouring of absinth. From the smell of the plant I cannot think myself why any Bohemian would want to sit sipping it in the old Café Royal, even for effect. Unless you were worried by botanical exactitude, you might take it for a much bolder version of *maritima*.

When I first planted it, I thought it would be one of those kinds that have to be replaced annually from cuttings. But it has come happily through severe winters heedless of the wet condition of the clay. In early autumn we cut the flower stems to dry them for the winter. Rather feathery, they contrast well with dried hydrangea heads and the carcases of teasels picked when the goldfinches have done with them.

Fortunately, we have found that all three species of the silvery *Anaphalis* will endure the ground we can offer them. As a ground cover *triplinervis* is excellent, as good as the argent *Stachys lanata* itself, resisting weeds with clumps of foliage that are rather like sorrel with frost on the leaves. *Margaritacea* has more lightness about it.

While both produce flowering stems a foot or so tall, *Anaphalis nubigena* stands more than two feet high when in flower. All are crowned by clusters of *immortelles*, which can also be cut, this time in late summer, for drying for arrangements that preserve something of summer in the home through the winter.

[226]

Tree Peonies

A golden opportunity: 'the most overpoweringly superb of garden shrubs': the need for careful siting: proletarian support: tantalising vagaries

Intensive production of the plants in Japan and swift transport here have recently brought the opportunity of growing the tree peony, once a rarity, within the scope of anyone with a garden. It is a golden one of high carat, for this is surely one of the noblest plants the garden lover can cultivate. Beside the well-bred tree peony, with its even more splendid foliage, the herbaceous type looks just a little bit brash.

What is there about it that leads one to squander money, garden space and time on plants that are foolhardy enough to put up shoots that can hardly hope to avoid being nipped by frost?

Listen for a moment to Reginald Farrer, prince of earlier garden writers and one of the few ever to see tree peonies growing wild high up in the western provinces of China:

'That single enormous blossom, waved and crimped into the

boldest grace of line and absolutely pure white, with featherings of deepest maroon radiating at the base of the petals from the boss of golden fluff at the flower's heart. . . . The breath of them went out upon the twilight as sweet as any rose.'

Brocaded language like this, with a touch of gush, is needed to describe the sumptuousness of the tree peony, 'the most overpoweringly superb of garden shrubs', as Farrer decided.

Listen also to some of the names the Japanese have bestowed on them: Lion in the Cherry Orchard, Temple of Good Fortune, Imaginary Heaven Bird, Flight of Cranes, Palace of Violet Light. Only such fanciful names could suggest the nature of their flowers.

The flowers seem to be made of the finest silken damask of every rich and subtle rose and crimson with which Titian ever robed his Venetian prelates and patricians. They appear in tones of purple, white and amber too.

Under the skilled touch and discerning eye of the Japanese, the wild moutan, as it is called, which Farrer saw, has been transformed into a plant which offers countless varieties. Some are single, others are composed of multitudes of petals folded one upon another, but all opening out at last to display the golden diadem of stamens they enshrine. All are massive but saved from coarseness by their texture and the delicate bluish tone in the green of the antler-like foliage, like the patina copper takes on in the open air.

Inevitably the favours of these plants are not to be won lightly. Careful siting and patience are needed. But once they are established you can bequeath them to your successors, for they have the indifference of the East to time.

The kind of place they like is somewhere with a north-western exposure, and the very best site is something few can give them: the northern fringes of a patch of woodland sheltered by overhanging branches, although this does give a clue to the site that many gardens where there are trees can offer. Not that they are, to my mind, wild garden plants. They are too sophisticated looking and highly bred for anything but a fairly formal site. Though they survive generations of the same family, one rarely sees a plant more than about four feet high and five feet across, but it would have taken many years to reach this size. Usually they are about as big as a well-nourished floribunda rose, breaking forth into their incredible splendour every year about the same time as the lilacs.

Like other plants that are long-lived, tree peonies must have a spot prepared for them by draining the soil so that later in life the roots will not stand in wet. They also like plenty of old compost in the ground and an annual scattering of bonemeal.

Longevity also rightly suggests that the plants are rarely beset by troubles. The only disorder that does occasionally afflict them while young can be discouraged by how they are planted.

For the tree peonies are really an aristocracy depending for their existence on the dubious support of an unseen proletariat. Like introducing serving wenches into the genealogy of a ducal house, to propagate the plants the scions are grafted on to a stock of the herbaceous type. They cannot stand alone in infancy.

This means that when you plant a tree peony you must bury the union of stock and scion, as though to conceal this regrettable necessity. The joint is easily discernible as a swollen lump just above where the roots start. Buried about an inch below the surface, it will be safe from harm during hard weather, which might cause it to open, while in time roots will form from the scion. It is exactly the reverse of planting a fruit tree.

I have found that when you buy a plant or two in winter, when they arrive from Japan, it can be worth the trouble of growing them in pots under glass until the end of May to hurry them along. This lengthens the effective growing season and provides a better chance of encouraging scion rooting than the plant would have in open ground in the first season. Actually, I have put them in deep fibre pots so that there is no planting out disturbance.

This practice also avoids the possibility of a setback due to frost nipping prematurely expanding foliage. Some growth will have been going on within the polythene covering in which you get the plant and a check is almost unavoidable if the plants are put out at once.

Even when tree peonies have been growing in the garden for years they never adapt. Always they show their salmon coloured shoots too early in the year. Then comes a cold spell and, having been seared, they have to try again. This is why they are most satisfactorily grown in a north-west facing position, with shelter to the east and south. It is a vagary that makes them more tantalising and therefore more desirable.

Weepers

The temptation of the 'backs': the full grown willow: the
willow-leaved pear: ornamental cherries: Buddleia alternifolia

Passing along the 'backs' at Cambridge and watching the
weeping willows gently flicking the water with their slender
wands, I have wondered how much gardening folly a scene like
this, so English, so affectionately held, has inspired. To see these
superb trees anywhere in their full pride, especially just as the
leaves are unfolding, or on a languorous summer's day, is a
temptation to plant one in the garden. But it can be a temptress
that will lure you into a situation from which you cannot
extricate yourself. Her graceful tresses will ensnare you!

The sapling that will arrive in the autumn in response to the
order you sent off in the high summer moment of inspiration
will all too quickly lose its winsome youth and become a mighty
tree. In five years you will have doubts, and bitter regrets in ten
when it will occupy half the garden.

Even if you can bring yourself to the point of resolve to cut it down, your hand will be held back, if not by other members of the family, then by the neighbours. A neighbour of mine who after several years of oscillating between destroying and sparing a willow he had planted with his own hands in his own garden let it be known round about that his mind was made up. There was a public outcry. It had become a landmark — which we are all fortunate to enjoy still.

No one thinks of planting an oak in a small garden, yet wherever I see new gardens being made, inevitably, however small the plots, there are the weeping willows. If only the willow-leaved pear, *Pyrus salicifolia pendula,* took their place. This is a much more garden-worthy tree. Even more silvery, the leafy branches hang vertically in the same airy manner. Its flowers are not worth mentioning and I have never seen it fruit, but as a foliage tree of graceful form it amply justifies itself.

Not so slow growing, though, that it takes several years to show its characteristic form, when it does tend to outgrow its site it can be curbed without fear that it will respond with the embarrassing exuberance of the willow. Perhaps the best place for it is as the centre of focus at the end of some vista, preferably before a backdrop of foliage of deep green against which it will seem etched. Here it could shelter a seat and in time become an arbour to shade those rare outdoor meals we dream of.

Our tree also provides an endless source of exactly the right foliage to set off the carnations of coconut-ice pink or bright cerise which one buys, only to find them hard and uncompromising colours in a vase at home.

Weeping trees, indeed, seem to have a special fascination. Besides the weeping pear, several ornamental cherries have the same manner of growth. The branches of *Prunus yedoensis per-pendens* sweep down to the ground, in early spring trailing almond-scented blossom of palest pink.

Usually this tree is sold grafted on to a stem six feet tall. This is not tall enough for its beauty to be displayed worthily, however, and it seems important to me to tie some of the branches upright for several seasons to lengthen the trunk.

The slender *Buddleia alternifolia* makes an exquisite little weeping tree for the smallest garden, gracefully hung with lilac flowers with the scent of honey in summer, while the foliage has a silvery cast which also helps to simulate the willow-like look.

Weigelas

A good tempered easy-going shrub: planting with other shrubs:
pruning: Eva Rathke: competition with a thuja hedge: a golden-
leaved variety

One of the shrubs almost everyone starting a garden begins
with, the weigela has such qualities that it is hardly likely
to outgrow the affections. As with so many of the best known
plants there is a little confusing bother about its rightful name.
For a time we were bidden to call it 'diervilla', but this name now
seems to be reserved for a few esoteric species.

This good-tempered, easy-going shrub seems to offer most of
what is asked for in bushes for no-trouble gardens, whether in
town or country, even though the connoisseur may look a bit
disdainfully at it. It flourishes equally well in shade or sun, poor
soil or rich. Its flowering season, which lasts a full month — does
any rhododendron last longer? — comes just at the time of that
uneasy spell when you are still sorry to have seen the last of the
spring flowers and await the overwhelming richness of the roses.

The range of colour may not be very great, varying from pink to deep red, but you can use it to contrive striking effects by planting it in company with other shrubs whose flowering season coincides. For instance, the red varieties and the white guelder roses set off each other, and sometimes in our garden the deutzias and weigelas flower together, to the enhancement of both.

The pink varieties look surprisingly well with those precocious shrub roses of soft yellow colouring that precede their kind in flower, like *Rosa cantabrigiensis* and Canary Bird. For weigelas complement the rather gaunt form the roses take on as they age, as they can be kept to a rounded shape by annual pruning.

This should be done immediately after flowering is over. Every season the bushes make new wood plentifully from points close to the ground, and it seems desirable to cut away the branches that have borne the flowers and to allow this to take their place.

Of the pink varieties Conquete is perhaps the finest, bold in flower and a pleasing shade. The colour of Bristol Ruby is fairly accurately denoted by the name, while I would describe Newport Red as garnet. But I could not myself cast out the old Eva Rathke, a deeper colour than either. For though the criticism that its crimson is a dull shade may be justified, placed where the afternoon sun can strike through the flowers it glows brightly. It also has the advantage over the others of continuing in flower for so long that eventually you have to cut it short to get the pruning done in time.

This one is also unusually compact in its manner of growth, a quality shared by a charming little variety called *Weigela florida variegata*. Not only does this bear its pink flowers in profusion, but its light green leaves are outlined with cream, which gives it a trim, freshly-laundered appearance well suited to the formality of a small, neatly-kept garden. We have it growing close to a thuja hedge whose roots must make severe demands on the soil. But the weigela does not seem to mind either that or the shade cast, which emphasises the slender demands these shrubs make, and the dark green of the thuja enhances their distinction of leaf.

One variety now gaining currency is specially suitable to light up a dull, sombre corner while it is in leaf, for it has golden foliage. It has the uncomfortable name of *looymansii aurea*. I can imagine the ample leaves giving a welcome impression of catching a shaft of sunlight even on dull, sunless summer days.

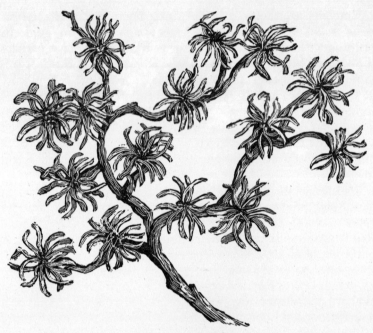

Witch Hazels

*Winter-flowering bushes: background of dark evergreen: bronze
flowers: planting in April: a host for morning glory*

By what strange alchemy does the witch hazel contrive to
defy the winter weather and push forth its flowers in the face
of harsh discouragement? Even on the coldest days of January
some bushes can be seen showing colour.

Frail and wispy, the flowers seem ill-adapted to withstand the
rigours they wilfully endure. Yet they are driven on by some
masochistic force. Unlike the winter-flowering cherry, whose
cloud of white blossom can be shattered in a night, the witch
hazel flowers are endowed with something that enables them to
go on to last their full term, whatever weather the first two, the
worst two, months of the year may bring.

These determined bushes are the Chinese forms of the witch
hazel, a plant given its common name by early settlers in North
America, who tried using the branches of the species they found
growing wild there for water divining.

Correctly we should call the winter flowering species *Hama-melis mollis*, whose curious flowers are wrought in gold. Its primrose yellow form *pallida* is now gaining prominence, perhaps showing up better in the garden; and after all you mostly see this in flower at a distance from the windows.

This means that the best place for it is against a background of some dark evergreen, perhaps a laurel hedge, to throw out its flowers in relief. If you can surround it with one of the deep red varieties of the winter-flowering heather *Erica carnea,* such as *praecox rubra* or Ruby Glow, the effect will be enhanced still further.

Recent seasons have seen the rise to general currency of witch hazels with flowers of bronze tones. Jelena is an apricot-coloured variety, and there is even one self-descriptively called Carmine Red which lives up to its name, though the flowers tend to be lost in the winter scene.

Sometimes you see a witch hazel bush fifteen feet tall, but more often four or five feet, always with an attractive winter silhouette like an open-shaped vase with a short stem. Hard-wooded and therefore almost impossible to grow from cuttings — the bushes sold have usually been grafted — it is therefore slow-growing, slow enough not to outgrow its welcome in small gardens.

Accordingly, a plant which can be put in any time before the middle of April needs a bit of encouraging in its early days in the form of peat worked plentifully into the soil around it, and a mulch of peat before the soil has a chance to dry in early summer. Otherwise this is a bush which will grow on any ground.

Winter-flowering plants are often indifferent to shade, but I have noticed that this is one which flowers best in full sun. Here, too, it develops its richest leaf colouring in autumn. For a show of fragile-looking flowers in the worst of the winter is not all a witch hazel gives you. Just before the fall of the leaf the colour can be some of the brightest of the season.

If this is not enough, one might still use the elegant little bush as a host for a morning glory planted to entwine it gracefully and flower in summer.

Yew

*The long-lived yew: mistaken emblem of mourning: the golden-
leaved Irish yew: the weeping yew: part of our heritage*

Symbol of longevity rather than of mortality, the yew tree
has a reputation which on several counts it ill-deserves. In an
age when there was time for such byways of endeavour, people
used to go round the country measuring ancient yews in the spirit
that others took rubbings of memorial brasses. Usually the trees
stood in churchyards, an association from which the plant deserves
to be released.

Gradually the mistaken idea has built up that the yew is an
emblem of mourning and so slow to develop that one would have
departed oneself before the yew one planted had reached a size to
justify itself. The great age of many celebrated yews eloquently
proclaims enduring life, while anyone who has planted a yew
hedge knows how wrong is the popular notion of its growth rate.

Of course it is slower than many cypresses, but that is just what
we want in our little gardens. It is dense yet malleable to the

shears. Its colour is lively, not sombre, with multitudes of tiny highly polished leaves to reflect the light.

Bitterly, I now regret having planted a hedge of thuja round the inner sanctum of our garden. Yew would have been far preferable. After all, I have the example of the Irish yews I put in at the same time standing there in reproach. They have extended by about eight inches a year, which is ample on a small canvas.

Now, whenever I have an idea that a bit of garden would be better for having some pillar-like evergreens — to flank an opening or to line an alley — I choose Irish yews, the golden-leaved form in some instances. Both kinds retain the column-like outline.

As you would expect from the name, the Irish yew has a touch of romance in its history. All those we know, every one sold by nurseries in the past, present and future, have sprung from a single tree. This was one of two found on an Irish hillside by one Willis (Christian name unrecorded), the tenant of a farm with the hardly credible name of Aghenteroak, in Co. Fermanagh, towards the end of the eighteenth century.

In complete contrast, another variant of the solid, dome-shaped yew has a slender weeping form. The branchlets droop like catkins; 'visibly obedient to the feeblest breath of air', is how the mid-Victorian horticulturist, John Loudon, who knew the original tree, described them.

Somewhere about the same time, a John Dovaston, of West-felton, near Shrewsbury, 'a man without education but of un-measured industry', dug a well for himself. But the soil was sandy and soon fell in. Knowing the binding power of the roots of a yew he decided to plant one beside his well and bought one for sixpence from a local cobbler, so the records say.

It is unrecorded whether the ultimate form this seedling assumed meant anything to him, but it does to us — it is a weeping evergreen. It is a permanent memorial to him inscribed in the most learned aboricultural treatises under the botanical name of *Taxus baccata dovastoniana*. Since his day it has thrown a golden-leaved form, which appears in catalogues as *Taxus baccata dovastoniana aureovariegata*.

In common with spaniels and retrievers and sheepdogs, these yews are never out of key with our environment. They belong here; while the cypresses, like poodles and corgis, much as we adore them, can sometimes set up a disturbing discord.

Flower Stall

'But where can you buy them?' This is the question one is
assailed with whenever one attempts to commend plants
to others to grow. In fact, a long association with the magazine
'Popular Gardening' has taught me that this is the problem that
worries more than anything else those whom we try to instruct
and stimulate horticulturally week by week. So it would be
infuriating to the reader who has come this far with me not to
offer a brief directory of plant suppliers.

Two things must be understood in buying garden plants. The
first is that they are so diverse that no one firm can stock everything gardeners want, and that you therefore have to send away
for them, since plant raising takes a lot of ground and nurseries
lie where both land and labour are available. The other is simply
that quality is roughly equated with price.

Perhaps the most resourceful nurseries in Britain — they claim
to have a bigger collection of trees and shrubs than any other
firm in the world — are Hillier and Son, of Winchester, Hants.

If you buy trees and shrubs from L. R. Russell Ltd., Richmond Nurseries, Windlesham, Surrey, you will find a very agreeable family atmosphere down at their place on the A30. At John Waterer, Sons and Crisp's nurseries at Twyford, Berkshire, you will find a good collection of trees and shrubs and herbaceous plants ready potted for taking away at any time of the year. Mr. Christopher Lloyd, Greater Dixter, Northiam, Sussex, has a huge collection of clematis — and other plants.

For ground cover plants, and shrub roses, you can safely go to Sunningdale Nurseries, Windlesham, Surrey. Mrs. Marjorie Fish, East Lambrook Manor, South Petherton, Somerset, keeps a most interesting collection of plants, including many ground-coverers. You can buy rare shade-loving plants from Perry's Hardy Plant Farm, Enfield, Middlesex. Every kind of bulb you are ever likely to want to plant can be bought from Walter Blom and Sons, Leavesden, Watford, Hertfordshire, or from P. de Jager and Sons Ltd., Marden, Kent. Sandhurst Nurseries, Camberley, Surrey, grow all the eucalyptus I have mentioned, and many more too.

As for garden equipment, fertilisers and plant medicines, E. J. Woodman and Sons (Pinner) Ltd., High Street, Pinner, Middlesex, make the justified boast that they can supply everything on the market.

INDEX

[240]

INDEX